Routledg

M000194241

Kant on *Religion within the Boundaries of Mere Reason: An Interpretation and Defense*

Throughout his career Kant engaged with many of the fundamental questions in philosophy of religion: arguments for the existence of God, the soul, the problem of evil, and the relationship between moral belief and practice. *Religion within the Boundaries of Mere Reason* is his major work on the subject. This *Guidebook* is an excellent starting point for anyone coming to Kant's important but complex work for the first time. Lawrence R. Pasternack presents and assesses:

- the philosophical background to *Religion within the Boundaries of Mere Reason*
- the ideas and arguments of the text
- the continuing importance of Kant's work to philosophy of religion today.

Lawrence R. Pasternack is Associate Professor of Philosophy at Oklahoma State University, USA.

ROUTLEDGE PHILOSOPHY GUIDEBOOKS

Edited by Tim Crane and Jonathan Wolff

University of Cambridge and University College London

Routledge Philosophy Guidebook to

Kant on *Religion within the Boundaries of Mere Reason*

Lawrence R.
Pasternack

Routledge
Taylor & Francis Group

LONDON AND NEW YORK

First published 2014
by Routledge
2 Park Square, Milton Park, Abingdon, Oxon OX14 4RN

and by Routledge
711 Third Avenue, New York, NY 10017

Routledge is an imprint of the Taylor & Francis Group, an informa business

British Library Cataloguing in Publication Data
A catalogue record for this book is available from the British Library

Library of Congress Cataloging in Publication Data
Pasternack, Lawrence, 1967–
Routledge philosophy guidebook to Kant on Religion within the boundaries of mere
reason / by Lawrence R. Pasternack. – 1 [edition].
   pages cm. – (Routledge philosophy guidebooks)
Includes bibliographical references and index.
1. Kant, Immanuel, 1724-1804. Religion innerhalb der Grenzen der blossen Vernunft.
2. Religion–Philosophy. I. Title.
B2792.P37 2013
210.92–dc23
2013018379

ISBN: 978-0-415-50784-4 (hbk)
ISBN: 978-0-415-50786-8 (pbk)
ISBN: 978-1-315-87430-2 (ebk)

Typeset in Garamond
by Taylor & Francis Books

CONTENTS

LIST OF ABBREVIATIONS

Unless otherwise indicated, translations will follow the *Cambridge Edition of the Works of Immanuel Kant*, Allen Wood and Paul Guyer, eds. (1992–). With two exceptions, works will be cited using the abbreviations below along with the volume and page number following the German Academy edition. The first exception is the *Critique of Pure Reason*, where citations will use the standard A/B edition format. The second exception is *Religion within the Boundaries of Mere Reason* (6:3–202), where no identifying abbreviation will precede the volume and page number.

AN	*Anthropology from a Pragmatic Point of View*
BL	Blomberg Logic
CF	*The Conflict of the Faculties*
CJ	*Critique of Judgment*
CPrR	*Critique of Practical Reason*
DL	Dohna-Wundlacken Logic
ET	"The End of All Things"
GR	*Groundwork of the Metaphysics of Morals*
ID	"Idea for a Universal History with a Cosmopolitan Aim"
JL	Jäsche Logic (aka, *Immanuel Kants Logik ein Handbuch zu Vorlesungen*)

LR   *Lectures on the Philosophical Doctrine of Religion*
MM   *Metaphysics of Morals*
MT   "On the Miscarriage of All Philosophical Trials in Theodicy"
PP   *Towards Perpetual Peace*
PT   "On a Recently Prominent Tone of Superiority in Philosophy"
Refl   *Reflexionen*
RP   "What Real Progress Has Metaphysics Made in Germany since the Time of Leibniz and Wolff?"
TP   "On the Common Saying: That May Be Correct in Theory but Is of No Use in Practice"
VL   Vienna Logic
WE   "An Answer to the Question: What Is Enlightenment?"
WO   "What Does It Mean to Orient Oneself in Thinking?"

LIST OF FIGURES

PREFACE AND ACKNOWLEDGMENTS

I began work on this book in the summer of 2011, after receiving an invitation from Tony Bruce to write a volume on Kant's *Religion* for Routledge's Guidebook series. Both the philosophy of religion and systematic theology have been important parts of my intellectual life as far back as my undergraduate education. Through my time at Yale and Boston University, my interests turned to German Philosophy, and eventually to Kant in particular. My professional scholarship on Kant ranges from his epistemology to his ethics; and, in recent years, my interests have moved full circle, or perhaps it would be more appropriate to say, have achieved a sublation through an increasing focus on his philosophy of religion. I am thus very grateful that such a fitting project was offered to me – and at a particularly apt point in my career.

After nearly a year of preparatory study, ranging from core Lutheran texts to current scholarship on *Religion*, I began drafting the manuscript in the spring of 2012, during which I received a reduced course load. I would like to thank my department head, Doren Recker, for granting this and other accommodations. From my department as well, I would like to thank Eric Reitan, Scott Gelfand, and our administrative assistant, Sarah Mutschelknaus, who helped me with formatting, with the bibliography, and with various other final tasks before submitting the manuscript. Let me also here express my gratitude to everyone at Routledge who helped shepherd the manuscript through its final stages.

My brother, Howard, created the five figures in this book. I hand drew what I wanted for each, faxed them to him, and he then created far more refined graphics than I could have on my own – including the use of a parabola to represent the asymptotic approach of our eternal striving to moral perfection. He also directed me to Pirkei Avot, quotations from which appear in Chapter 5.

Of course, I also have many Kant specialists to thank, many of whom I spent time with at APA or NAKS events, had long discussions with over the phone, or via email. On many occasions, these exchanges helped me refine the arguments and positions contained in this work. They include: Henry Allison, Sharon Anderson-Gold, Aaron Bunch, Andrew Chignell, Sam Duncan, Patrick Frierson, Courtney Fugate, Nathan Jacobs, Patricia Kitcher, Colin McLear, Kate Moran, Chris Surprenant, Kristi Sweet, and Oliver Thorndike.

I would like to make special mention of those who were the most generous with their time and most influenced the views presented herein. On numerous occasions, Pablo Muchnik and I spoke for hours over the phone, and had extended discussions at five different conferences during the past two years. He also came to Oklahoma twice during this period, the first funded by an OSU Arts and Humanities External Researcher Grant and the second by a NAKS travel grant. Although we interpret Kant's doctrine of the Highest Good differently, he most definitely drew my attention to the importance of its corporate aspects. Second, I would like to thank Steve Palmquist, who suffered through a very very rough early draft of the manuscript, and had the patience to see through that roughness to the philosophical positions buried beneath. His extensive comments on that draft are greatly appreciated, as is also his willingness to travel from Hong Kong to Oklahoma, staying here for nearly two weeks. As with Pablo's visit, Steve received funding from OSU's Arts and Humanities External Researcher Grant and, in addition to our time together, he also offered his time to a number of our graduate students. Third, I would like to thank Rob Gressis, who drew my attention to the relevance of Kant's "Theodicy" and persuaded me that it marks a key transition point in Kant's theory of evil.

Lastly, I would like to express my deep gratitude to my wife, Robyn. Hardly do I have the space to list all that she has so lovingly offered. From her endless emotional support during my years of surgery and physical therapy following a major car accident, to her faith in me as I struggled to regain my physical and scholarly footing as I recovered, to her Sisyphean efforts in trying to keep the house as quiet as possible during my seemingly endless hours of work at home, her willingness to adapt to my long nights at my desk, and her munificent delivery of morning coffee to my bedside. I want her to know that none of it has gone unnoticed or unappreciated.

INTRODUCTION

Kant's *Religion within the Boundaries of Mere Reason* is rarely read cover to cover or studied as a whole. Readers tend to focus on just Part One, sometimes Parts One and Two, but usually stop there, paying little to no attention to Parts Three or Four. The secondary literature on *Religion* accordingly reflects this imbalance, resulting in not only a reductive reading, where the text is treated as primarily an extension of Kant's moral anthropology, but also, given the subject matter of Part One, it is usually taken to be an overall gloomy and pessimistic text, one that casts humanity in a very grim light.[1]

However, just as there has been a broad reassessment of Kant's practical philosophy in recent decades, one that has revealed a far richer ethical theory than the formalist deontology that is especially pronounced in the *Groundwork*, so we are now at the cusp of a similar shift in how his philosophy of religion is understood. Some of the most recent secondary literature has sought to overturn the old biases against *Religion*, finding within it not just an addendum to his practical philosophy, but also a rich examination of the Christian religion crafted with the subtlety and sophistication that should be expected from one of history's greatest philosophers.

A central goal of this book is to participate in this reappraisal, battling against such well-entrenched claims as that *Religion* offers an essentially pessimistic account of human nature, that it offers merely a litany of "wobbles," fumbling between traditional Christianity and Enlightenment values, that it reduces religion to morality, and that it is a text ultimately hostile to faith. Most of these views arise from a piecemeal approach to *Religion*, one that reads the text too selectively, pays far too little attention to Parts Three and Four, and generally fails to understand the overall unity of its four parts. It is thus the purpose of this book to interpret *Religion* more holistically: presenting a vision of the whole shaped by a unifying interpretative scheme, and showing how that scheme is played out in each of its four parts.

The interpretation that I will here develop will be guided by Kant's doctrine of the Highest Good. That there is some connection between this doctrine and his positive philosophy of religion is commonly recognized. But, as I will show, each of *Religion*'s four parts concerns different components of this doctrine; and the shift from Parts One and Two to Parts Three and Four parallels the well-known dual structure of the Highest Good, a structure roughly akin to what has been variously characterized as its "immanent and transcendent conceptions," its "ectypical and archetypical forms," and its two elements, "one a demand and the other a promise."[2] As I will later discuss, the first of each paired set refers to a duty to promote the Highest Good, and the second of each paired set refers to an ideal state of affairs in which happiness is distributed according to moral worth.

Through his doctrine of the Highest Good, Kant develops a "pure rational system of religion" (6:12), and as we shall see, he makes use of this system to engage in an "experiment" that compares the contents of "alleged revelation" (6:12) to his Pure Rational System of Religion. More precisely, the experiment that runs through the whole of *Religion* (what in the Second Preface Kant enumerates as the "second experiment") tests a particular hypothesis.[3] From the doctrine of the Highest Good, Kant generates his Pure Rational System of Religion. From its alleged revelations, Christianity has produced a system of doctrines,

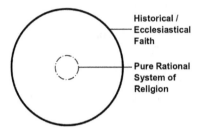

Figure 1 Inner and outer spheres of religion

rituals, and ecclesiastical traditions. The experiment then compares these two spheres, inquiring in particular as to whether all that is contained in the latter *that is essential to our salvation* can also be found in the former. Thus, the formula tested by the experiment of *Religion* is whether Pure Rational Faith (*Reiner Vernunftglaube*) = Saving Faith (*seligmachender Glaube*).

As I hope to show, this experiment has been well thought out by Kant. It is not, as Gordon Michalson has claimed, merely a series of "wobbles" between incompatible Enlightenment and Christian commitments (Michalson 1990: 8–10). Nor is it a "Failure," as John Hare has claimed, unable to offer an adequate bridge across the "moral gap" between our duties and our natural capacities (Hare 1996: 60–68). Throughout this book, I will defend *Religion* against these criticisms as well as offer an interpretation that neither distorts Kant into an Agnostic or Deist, on the one hand, nor a traditional Christian on the other.[4] As I will argue, the fundamental aim of *Religion* is to determine whether all that is essential and necessary to salvation appears not only in alleged revelation but can also be found in the Pure Rational System of Religion.[5] Implicit within this aim is Kant's own religious orientation, what in Part Four he describes as "Pure Rationalism" (6:155). But this could easily mislead. Kant is not here using "Rationalism" in the sense we associate with Spinoza or Leibniz. Nor is he endorsing the reduction of religion to reason.

Rather, the Pure Rationalist is one who allows for revelation, miracles, and other claims that are not amenable to universal agreement, but considers them *inessential* to Saving Faith.[6] As we shall see, Kant's Pure Rationalism is guided by the commitment that Saving Faith must be available to all. This puts revelation at a disadvantage as it "can extend its influence no further than the tidings relevant to a judgment on its credibility can reach" (6:103). Revelation may still carry the requisite content, but in order for salvation to be available to all, and, further, in order for there to be a "Universal Church" for all humanity, its doctrines must be discoverable through reason alone and "be convincingly communicated to everyone" (6:103).

We shall return to the parameters of Kant's Pure Rationalism and *Religion*'s experiment in due course. But first, let us consider the issues surrounding its publication and how these issues may challenge the view that *Religion* should be read as a unified treatise rather than just an assemblage of separate pieces (*Stücke*) that only through historical accident were brought together into a single volume.

RELIGION'S PUBLICATION

Kant originally intended to have each of *Religion*'s four parts published as separate articles in the *Berlinische Monatsschrift*. This is why each is called a "part" or, what might have been a better translation, a "piece" (*Stück*) (as we say in English, "That's a nice piece of writing" or "He has a piece in that collection"). However, political circumstances forced Kant to pursue a different course.[7]

The first essay, "On Radical Evil in Human Nature," was published in the *Berlinische Monatsschrift* in April 1792. But the second was denied an official imprimatur by the Prussian Censorship Commission. Although the *Berlinische Monatsschrift* had relocated to Jena after the tightening of censorship policies in Prussia, Kant asked its editor to continue to secure Prussian approval for each piece. The first was granted, on the grounds that "like other Kantian works, [it] is intended for, and can be enjoyed only by thinkers, researchers and scholars capable of fine distinctions."[8] But the second was denied the imprimatur by what had recently become a very conservative commission.

J. E. Beister, the journal's editor, appealed the decision first to the commission and then to the court of Frederick William II. But his attempts failed. Though Kant still could have had the *Berlinische Monatsschrift* publish the essays since the journal's relocation removed it from the reach of the Prussian censors, he did not want to so blatantly circumvent the commission's authority, and so instead chose a path that kept him within the letter of the law.

The king's predecessor, Frederick the Great, was far more sympathetic to Enlightenment ideals, and under his reign nearly all works produced within universities were allowed to forgo official review by the Censorship Commission. With the exception of treatises directly relevant to political policy, they merely needed to be assessed by the academic faculty appropriate to their subject matter. This still remained technically a legal option for Kant, and so he assembled all four parts into a single volume and sent it first to a member of the theology faculty at Königsberg, seeking to confirm that it was, indeed, *not* a work of theology but rather of philosophy. With that established, he then submitted it for examination to the dean of philosophy at Jena.[9] Then, with their approval of the manuscript granted, Kant chose to have it published by Friedrich Nicolovius, who recently established his publishing business in Königsberg after having apprenticed in Riga under Johann Friedrich Hartknoch (who published Kant's major writings of the 1780s).

The four essays thus became the single text, *Religion within the Boundaries of Mere Reason*, Kant's first book-length work since the *Critique of Judgment*. It was published in the spring of 1793, with a second edition appearing less than one year later, in early 1794. However, Kant's publication strategy (along with the contents of *Religion*) did not sit well with the commission, and he received a royal rescript in October 1794, prohibiting him from publishing further on matters of religion.

Kant responded with a letter that swore to "refrain altogether from discoursing publicly, in lectures or in writing, on religion, whether natural or revealed" (CF: 7:10). From late 1794 until the death of Frederick William II in 1797, he abided by the royal order and his promise. But with the succession of Frederick William III, who redressed the numerous abuses of his predecessor's conservative reign, including its more stringent censorship edicts, Kant considered himself again free to publicly examine religious topics. Thus, in 1798, he published *The Conflict of the Faculties*. The text addresses various questions about the proper scope of each academic discipline, including the relationship between philosophy and theology. It also includes within its preface, the remonstratory letter of 1794 signed by Johann Christoph Wöllner, the king's notoriously conservative Minister of Justice and Religious Affairs, as well as Kant's formal response to it, where he asserts that *Religion* makes "no *appraisal* of Christianity" and so "cannot be guilty of *disparaging* it" (CF: 7:8).

RELIGION'S AIM AND CONTENT

Despite their final form as four parts of a single work, we know from correspondence that Kant originally intended four separate essays on religion to appear serially in the *Berlinische Monatsschrift*.[10] We cannot know for certain the extent to which Parts Three and Four carry out his original intentions for his planned third and fourth essays, but the first two parts were written before Kant had to revise his original plans for publication. We may, nevertheless, consider ourselves fortunate that the project unfolded as it did, since the publication of the unified text of *Religion* also prompted Kant to add a first, and then a second preface, both of which contain extremely helpful remarks about *Religion's* overall expository structure and philosophical agenda. As briefly mentioned above, the Second Preface describes *Religion's* ongoing "experiment"[11] to compare traditional Christian doctrine with the Pure Rational System of Religion; and the First Preface not only discusses the relationship between philosophical and biblical theology, but also offers a new and important argument for the Highest Good. We shall return to the two prefaces in Chapter 2. But first, let me offer here a very brief overview of *Religion's* four parts, to begin to show how they each stand in relation to the Highest Good, and how through that relation, they contribute to an overall unified project.

The experiment of *Religion* moves through four central issues in Christianity. Part One examines the nature of sin or, more precisely, the doctrine of Original Sin. Part Two turns to the counterpart to sin: the question of how redemption is possible. Together, these parts follow an arc of inquiry at the level of the individual, and as we shall discuss more fully in subsequent chapters, this arc corresponds to the first layer of the doctrine of the Highest Good: our duty to promote it insofar as it is within our power. Part One's examination of sin articulates our common moral starting point: that we as a species are morally corrupt, have chosen to prioritize self-interest over morality, are riddled with self-deception, and harbor a Propensity to Evil. Part Two then carefully works through the Christian doctrine of Atonement through Christ, the nature of God's judgment, how we may become "well-pleasing" to Him, and how our "debt of sin" may be lifted.

The Highest Good, when taken as a duty, commands that we promote it insofar as it is within our power to do so. This conception of the Highest Good is first articulated in the Second *Critique*, and the scope of this duty, as we shall discuss in more detail, concerns what in that text in particular is characterized as our pursuit of moral perfection. However, we shall see that this duty is reformulated in *Religion*, in accordance with some of Kant's other revisions to his moral anthropology. Though this more radical duty for perfection still remains within *Religion*, the standard for moral worthiness is replaced by the "Change of Heart," a change in the order of priority that we give to the incentives of morality and self-interest.

Parts Three and Four move on to the second layer of the Highest Good, which may be understood as an ideal state of affairs wherein happiness is distributed in accordance with moral worth. Part Three begins with an important discussion of how even one who has undergone a Change of Heart is still vulnerable to recidivism due to the corrupting influence that human beings have on one another. This is an extension of our unsocial sociability, the *locus classicus* for which is Kant's 1784 "Idea for a Universal History with a Cosmopolitan Aim."

In the essay, Kant primarily describes our unsocial sociability in terms of a healthy competitive drive and believes that it can be adequately regulated by a constitutional civil regime (ID: 8:22). But in *Religion*, with its deepening grasp of the nature of immorality, Kant admits that no human juridical solution is sufficient (6:99). Secular social structures can govern our outward conduct (6:98). But our unsocial sociability is a manifestation of our inner moral nature and will infect our dealings with one another in too many subtle ways. He thus claims that our unsocial sociability must be dealt with through a change to our society that emanates from an inward change within its citizens. This change Kant presents in religious terms, describing an "Ethical Community" which is "conceivable only as a people under divine commands" (6:99). Unlike more secular ideals that at best keep our unsocial sociability at bay, the Ethical Community involves our liberation from this pathology and so offers us an "escape from the dominion of evil ... [and the] incessant danger of relapsing into it" (6:94).

Although the Ethical Community has often been taken out of context and treated as a secular social ideal,[12] *Religion* is unequivocal that this community is "a work whose execution cannot be hoped for from human beings but only from God himself" (6:100). It requires God as its founder, lawgiver, and agent of the distribution of happiness in accordance with moral worth (6:99). It is, thus, a way of representing the ideal of the Highest Good; and Part Three, after introducing this ideal and explaining its relationship to the scope of our moral duties and capacities, then makes use of it in its discussions of the Universal Church of the Pure Rational System of Religion, the history of Christianity, Providence, and eschatology.

Part Four continues with the ecclesiastical topics introduced towards the end of Part Three. When Kant introduces the Universal Church, he presents it as a prefiguration of the Ethical Community as well as a vital instrument for the collective human duty to replace our unsocial sociability with the shared goal of spreading the Good News of Pure Rational Faith to the whole of humanity. Unfortunately, though, our Propensity to Evil can just as much corrupt religious institutions as it can corrupt our agency. Thus, a key theme of Part Four is what attitude we should take towards the instruments of church ritual and doctrine, and how to guard against their being degraded into "counterfeit service" and "servile faith."

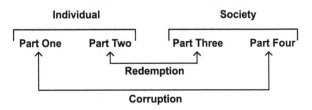

Figure 2 Religion's chiasmic structure

In short, Parts One and Two focus on that layer of the Highest Good germane to the individual, and Parts Three and Four concern its second layer in relation to history, society, and ecclesiology. *Religion* as a whole is thus balanced at mid-point, shifting its focus from the individual to society. Furthermore, as Parts Two and Three both concern moral transformation (at the level of the individual, then at the level of society) and Parts One and Four concern the sources and mechanisms of corruption (again, first for the individual, then for society), *Religion* as a whole has also a chiastic structure.

A chiasmus is a literary form found in classical literature, in the works of many great authors such as Milton and Shakespeare, and in many books of the Bible. It can occur at the level of a sentence, a paragraph, or the plot of a story, employing symmetries of language or narrative so that in a four-part chiasmus, the first part would have a parallel structure to the last, and the second part would parallel the second-to-last. We find precisely this in *Religion* as Parts One and Four focus on corruption and Parts Two and Three focus on redemption. This may, of course, be just a coincidence, but it does offer additional evidence that we should see *Religion* as composed by Kant with the intention that its four parts be taken as a unity.

PURE RATIONAL FAITH: AN INTERPRETATION AND DEFENSE

As expressed above, this book will offer an interpretation of *Religion* that presents each of its parts as stages in an experiment comparing Christian doctrine to the Pure Rational System of Religion. Of course, not all the doctrines of Christianity will overlap with this system. Various contents of alleged revelations, various traditional rituals and practices will fall outside of it. Kant is not troubled by this result, nor should the believer necessarily be, depending upon what remains within reason's sphere, what is outside it, and how Kant evaluates the importance of the latter.

The general issue taken up by his experiment is far from original to Kant. Many others have also addressed the scope of overlap between Natural and Revealed Religion. It is directly discussed in Aquinas's *Summa Theologica*.[13] It is also considered in Lutheran discussions of "pure" versus "mixed" articles of faith.[14] Further, the relationship between Natural and Revealed Religion is not merely a prevalent concern in the eighteenth century, but it may be seen as *the* central issue for the philosophical theology of that period.[15] What, however, is original to Kant is how he deals with the relationship between Natural and Revealed Religion. First, he rejects how Natural Religion is ordinarily approached, i.e., as an issue for theoretical reason. In the *Critique of Pure Reason*, he attacks the traditional arguments for God's existence, and even contends that we cannot form a determinate conception of God through theoretical reason. Accordingly, anyone who gains their impression of Kant's religious views from the First *Critique*'s Transcendental Dialectic will likely see him as an Atheist or Agnostic. Nevertheless, as he famously declares in the Second Preface to the *Critique of Pure Reason*, he wants to establish the limits to knowledge in order to make room for faith (Bxxx).

This is not, however, a concession to some sort of non-rational Fideism. Rather, Kant's conception of faith is one that is rational, but distinct from such epistemic forms of assent as knowledge and opinion. Faith, for Kant, is grounded in the needs of practical reason and thus the room for faith to which he alludes is the room for a practical activity of reason that is distinct from the theoretical.

Our understanding of salvation is, likewise, a matter of practical reason. It flows from the Highest Good's synthesis of morality and happiness; and for Kant, salvation is understood in terms of what we must do to become worthy of happiness. Hence, when Kant considers the relationship between Natural and Revealed

Religion, his central focus is on the practical, on the doctrines of Christianity *that are essential to our salvation* and whether or not they are coextensive with the religious needs of (practical) reason.

Kant accepts that there is more to religion than what is essential to our salvation, but for him, the remaining doctrines, rituals, and other ecclesiastical vestiges should be regarded as accidental and arbitrary products of history (6:158).[16] They may be "beneficial to the vitality of [one's] pure religious disposition" (6:182). They may offer symbols and rituals so that those struggling to grasp "the highest concepts and grounds of reason [have] something that *the senses can hold on to*" (6:109). Perhaps there is even an abiding need for some symbols and rituals given the difficulties that people face when trying to manage these "highest concepts." However, insofar as they fall outside the scope of Pure Rational Faith, they are each "internally contingent" (6:105) and none should be, in themselves, considered essential to our salvation.

Symbols may be valued as instruments that help us by way of their more "vivid mode of representing things" (6:83). Rituals may help build fellowship within a church. But the necessary articles of religion must either be derived directly from reason or, if subjectively arising out of an alleged revelation, must nevertheless be objectively derivable from reason (6:156). In other words, Kant accepts that revelation can be the source of religious tenets, but with the important qualification that whatever is essential to our salvation, even if offered in a revelation, must also be derivable from reason alone.[17] This is one of the core principles of *Religion*, and according to Kant, its violation is the common cause of "servile" and "delusory" faith, counterfeit service to God, and ecclesiastical despotism.

Contrary to the accusations made against *Religion*, those who claim it to be a litany of "wobbles" or an ultimate "Failure," this book will develop a defense of *Religion* as a frank and internally consistent treatise on philosophical theology, one that is thoroughly consistent with the main principles of Transcendental Idealism, and one that is eminently defensible by way of those principles. It will not paint Kant as an Agnostic or as a Deist.[18] Nor will it exaggerate his Christian credentials. There is no secret piety in *Religion* hidden behind an Enlightenment veneer. Kant was well-enough aware of the religious agenda of Frederick William II and his ministers so that any interpretation built upon the belief that he had to mask his true Christian commitments, commitments with which his censors would have sympathized, is untenable.[19] On my reading, there is (almost) no guile or prevarication in *Religion*.[20]

NOTES

1 For a survey of interpreters who offer reductive readings of *Religion*, see Firestone and Jacobs 2008. I would include as well James DiCenso's reading, such as is found in his recent work on Kant's *Religion* (DiCenso 2011 and 2012). Some examples from recent literature that attribute to *Religion* a gloomy picture of human nature include Muchnik 2009: xxiii and Frierson 2010: 48–55. Pessimism is also implied by those who interpret Kant such that we are so morally corrupt that we *must* depend upon a divine supplement to overcome sin. See my discussion of Gordon Michalson, Philip Quinn, and Nicholas Wolterstorff on this issue in Pasternack 2012. We will discuss many of these works throughout this book, especially in Chapters 4 and 7.

2 These refer respectively to Silber 1959, Wike and Showler 2010, and Insole 2008. In Chapter 1, I will move from these characterizations of the Highest Good to one that I think best reflects the two layers of the doctrine.

3 The Second Preface mentions two experiments. The first I understand to be the construction of the Pure Rational System of Religion, while the second compares this System to the doctrines of traditional Christianity. Given that the second experiment employs the first, the first, or more precisely, its outcome, is articulated through each of *Religion*'s four parts. However, it is the second experiment, the comparison between traditional Christianity and the Pure Rational System of Religion, that sets *Religion*'s purpose and agenda. Accordingly, unless otherwise indicated, phrases such as "*Religion*'s experiment" and "the experiment of *Religion*" refer specifically to the second experiment.

4 What I mean by "traditional Christianity" may be clear to some readers, but not so to others. While there are, of course, ample differences

that span across Christian denominations, theologians, and periods, I take the Christian tradition to (almost) uniformly hold that: (a) there is one God; (b) He is active in human history (i.e., I see Deism as not a form of Christianity); (c) the Doctrine of Hypostatic Union is true; (d) God chose the historical event of the Crucifixion as a necessary though not sufficient condition for our salvation; (e) its necessity stems from an Augustinian view about the depth of our sin; (f) its non-sufficiency stems from some commitment on our part through which we may "partake of a righteousness that is not our own" (this is a Pauline phrase that Luther is fond of and appears as well at 6:66 – see also: 1 Corinthians 1:30, Philippians 3:9). Hopefully, the above captures the most essential Christian doctrines in a way that accommodates denominational variants. The above also, I believe, captures not only the core tenets of traditional Christian theology, but also expresses the core tenets of such prominent Christian Philosophers as Philip Quinn, Nicholas Wolterstorff, and Eleonore Stump. On how I phrased (d) see Stump 1988 and Chapter 15 of Stump 2003.

5 From this point forward, I am going to use the definite article rather than "Kant's pure rational system of religion" or "a pure rational system of religion." *If* there truly is such a system, then "the" would be more appropriate to its universal and necessary status.

6 In "Kant's Deism," Allen Wood writes that "'pure rationalism' seems scarcely deserving of its name, and it is hard to imagine anyone who would hold to it. For it apparently takes the position that God has given us certain commands supernaturally while denying that we are morally bound to carry them out. This surely cannot be a position Kant intends to embrace" (Wood 1991: 11). Nevertheless, Kant writes that while we have "no reason" to assert that an ecclesiastical statute is divine in origin, it would be "arrogant peremptorily to deny that the way a church is organized may perhaps also be a special divine dispensation" (6:105). Kant also accepts as possible that "the historical introduction of the latter [a new religion] be accompanied as it were adorned by miracles" (6:84). Hence, quite in conformity with Pure Rationalism, these miracles could serve as the basis for celebratory festivals and other practices which are "intrinsically contingent" in that their observance is without moral value in itself, but nevertheless can be of instrumental value as means that help worshipers with "the highest concepts and grounds of reason" (6:109) or in other ways are

conducive to the visible church. In short, Wood dismisses Pure Rationalism even though Kant quite clearly accepts the possibility of "divine dispensations" that pertain just to religion's outer form. I will return to this issue in greater detail in Chapter 6.

7 A much more detailed account of the events can be found in Dilthey 1890: 418–50, also available in volume four of his *Gesammelte Schriften*. In English, see di Giovanni 1996: 41–48, Lestition 1993, and Hunter 2005.

8 See 11:329, dated March 6, 1792.

9 There is some disagreement as to which university Kant sent the manuscript. It was previously thought that he merely had his colleagues at Königsberg review it. However, the extant manuscript is signed by J. C. Hennings, the dean of philosophy at Jena. See Arnoldt 1909: 32–37.

10 11:429–30, dated May 4, 1793

11 As mentioned in an earlier footnote, and as we shall discuss more fully in Chapter 2, I take the second experiment to be the central project of *Religion*, i.e., the investigation of the scope of overlap between traditional Christian doctrine and the Pure Rational System of Religion. The first, unstated experiment, I take to be the construction of the Pure Rational System, originating with the Highest Good and its Postulates, and derived from these, the further principles that reason can identify as essential to our salvation.

12 See Reath 1988, Rossi 2005: 53–65, Guyer 2005: 289, and Moran 2009.

13 I.I.Q1.a1 (Whether, besides philosophy any further doctrine is required?), II.II. Q1.a5 (Whether those things that are of faith can be an object of science?), II.II.Q2.a3 (Whether it is necessary for salvation to believe anything above natural reason?), etc.

14 See Schmid 1889: 55, 115. Schmid's *Doctrinal Theology of the Evangelical Lutheran Church* presents the views of many of the key Lutheran theologians from the Augsburg Confession of 1530 through to the seventeenth century. In addition to Luther's own writings and Paul Althaus's *The Theology of Martin Luther*, it serves as the basis for much of this book's presentation of Lutheran theology. Unfortunately, there is no systematic study of the Lutheran Pietists comparable to Schmid's study of the Lutheran Scholastics. Nevertheless, Pietism was an important part of Kant's childhood and I have drawn from various collections of their works. Franz Albert Schulz, a Pietist, was both his

family's pastor and the director of the *Collegium Fridericianum*; and as we shall see as we move forward through this book, *Religion* considers not only some distinctly Lutheran doctrines, but also some that are even more particular to the Pietist movement. On the Pietism in Kant's youth, see Kuehn 2001: 35–55.

15 See for example Gerrish 2006.

16 This is, Kant claims, how they should be regarded *even if* they are genuine products of divine revelation or celebrations of actual miracles. Hence, as discussed in Note 6, above, and as we will discuss more fully in subsequent chapters, Kant accepts the possibility that God is active through history, offering us various forms of aid, some more directly related to our individual salvation, others on a larger scale, helping shape the institutions that take on that charge in the world. Of course, Kant also maintains that we cannot ever know whether or not some alleged revelation or miracle is genuine. We cannot distinguish between a natural and supernatural cause (cf. 6:191 and CF: 7:63), and to build a church around beliefs in supernatural interventions is a "dangerous religious delusion" (6:171), one that leads to the violation of our conscience (6:188).

17 To help reinforce an important but neglected point, let me reiterate that Kant further recognizes that revelation may not only convey tenets that are essential to our pursuit of salvation (i.e., those that must also be derivable from reason alone). Revelation may also offer ones that are "intrinsically contingent" but help shape the outer form of religion – giving us rituals that may help promote and sustain church membership or principles for how a church is to be organized. See 6:84, 6:105–6, and 6:155.

18 There are many who downplay religious commitment in Kant, turning it either into an Error Theory, or in other ways recommending that we do not take seriously faith in God and/or immortality. See for example: Reath 1988, Davidovich 1993 and 1994, Guyer 2000 and 2005, DiCenso 2011 and 2012. With the exception of Guyer, who has other grounds, the above build their views primarily from certain passages in the Third *Critique*. In the next chapter, we will discuss the salient Third *Critique* passages and will also return to the topic in the Conclusion.

19 Interpreters who want to bolster Kant's Christian credentials, pressing for even more than *Religion* explicitly suggests, include: Mariña 1997,

and Firestone and Jacobs 2008. This approach strikes me as neither textually supported nor one that fits the circumstances of Kant's life, especially during the conservative reign of Frederick William II. While the far more secular environment of contemporary academia may be less welcoming to such commitments, that was not the case during Kant's day. Hence, an interpretation of *Religion* shaped by the view that behind its Enlightenment veneer there are traditional Christian commitments that Kant chose to mask strikes me as built upon a misunderstanding of his historical and political circumstances.

20 The one place where I think Kant is not being forthright, and perhaps not honest with himself either, is in the First Preface's defense of his work as outside the purview of the theological faculty. This issue will be discussed in Chapter 2. See also my forthcoming Pasternack 2015.

1

FAITH, KNOWLEDGE AND THE HIGHEST GOOD

In the *Critique of Pure Reason*, Kant attacks the ontological, cosmological, and physico-theological (design) arguments, challenges the grounds used for the existence and immortality of the soul, and even contends that we cannot, through theoretical reason alone, formulate an adequate conception of anything within the realm of the supernatural, including God. On the basis of these and related objections, many have come to see Kant as no friend to religion, having created, so it seems, substantial barriers to any credible positive theology.[1] This, however, was not his intention. Although his writings contain numerous arguments against many religious tenets, they are not actually against these tenets as such, but against how they have been appropriated by the metaphysical tradition.

According to Kant, metaphysics is inherently flawed, a product of theoretical reason's illicit extension of concepts that should be limited to experience alone. Hence, when religion is approached as if it were a form of metaphysics, building argument through the powers of theoretical reason, it too must be dismissed as an illegitimate intellectual enterprise. Just as Kant argues that theoretical reason has failed, and by necessity will continue to fail in its various metaphysical endeavors, it will likewise fail to prove that God exists, that there is a soul, and so forth. Many have taken this to mean that Kant is, in the end, an Atheist or Agnostic, or perhaps at best, an Error Theorist, who sanctions self-imposed religious illusions for practical purposes.[2] But these misread Kant's intentions. His criticisms of religion were not meant to deny its tenets, but rather to liberate them from theoretical reason so that they could be given a more legitimate footing. This agenda has, in fact, considerable similarities to Martin Luther's own views on reason and religion – a point that should hardly be taken as coincidence since Kant was brought up in a Lutheran Pietist household and his childhood education was at the *Collegium Fridericianum*, a Lutheran Pietist institution (Kuehn 2001: 24–60).

Just as Luther himself asserts that reason is limited to our experience and "not able to apply itself to invisible things" (Luther 1883: 1.40III.51),[3] so likewise, a cornerstone of Transcendental Idealism is that knowledge is confined to the scope of possible experience. When we employ theoretical reason in our attempt to grasp a reality beyond experience, we fall into error and illusion. This holds for both metaphysics in general as well as for theology. So, just as Luther claims that "Reason is the greatest enemy that faith has" (Luther 1883: 2.3.68), Kant too regards religious belief as requiring a basis outside of theoretical reason.

Their similarities can be pressed even farther, for they not only see theoretical reason as incapable of warranting our assent to religious doctrines, but that such an approach occludes their true significance. Both the Lutheran understanding of Original Sin and Kant's rendering of it as an innate Propensity to Evil represent human beings as fallen creatures, fractured within, as our relationship with God is also fractured. This is not something that can be solved by reason, at least not in its theoretical mode. It is, rather, through faith that we must confront our state of sin and find our way to redemption. Religion is not, for either Luther or Kant, an intellectual enterprise, but a matter for the heart, a practical problem that demands a practical rather than theoretical solution.

The title, *Religion within the Boundaries of Mere Reason*, hardly suggests this Lutheran passion, but this is precisely what the text is about, as is Kant's overall philosophy of religion. He stands with Luther in a shared belief that there is a tension between faith and reason, though for Kant, this tension is specifically with reason in its theoretical employment. Practical reason, by contrast, is an ally of faith, and unlike its theoretical counterpart, it recognizes our fallen nature. In fact, in the *Critique of Practical Reason*, Kant acknowledges that even if we had all of eternity to improve ourselves, we would still, through our own powers, fall short (CPrR: 5:123n). If we were morally perfect, were unencumbered by sensuous inclinations, and had a "holy will," our actions would necessarily accord with moral laws. But this is not what we humans are. Our self-interested pursuit of happiness will always agitate against the moral incentive; and, as Kant declares on numerous occasions, this conflict can only be resolved through a turn to religion. He advocates for such a turn in all three *Critique*s, such as can be seen in the *Critique of Pure Reason*'s famous statement that we must find the limits to knowledge in order to "make room for faith" (Bxxx). It underlies his commitment to the Highest Good, and is manifest in the declaration of *Religion*'s First Preface that morality "inevitably leads to religion" (6:6).

We will begin our commentary on *Religion* in the next chapter, but before we move on to the text itself, it is important to understand the place of religion within Kant's overall Critical Philosophy, as well as what tenets of the latter are most important to his positive philosophy of religion. Hence, in this chapter, we will explore some of the key philosophical issues that underlie Kant's *Religion* and why he believes that practical reason must turn to religion. More advanced readers may find themselves tempted to skip over some of these discussions, but I want to emphasize that my commentary on *Religion* is guided by various stances on these underlying issues and familiarity with them will prove helpful as we progress through the many analyses to come. We will begin with a brief overview of Transcendental Idealism in order to set the stage for Kant's distinction between faith and other modes of assent. We will then turn to his understanding of faith as a propositional attitude. Lastly, we will begin our examination of Kant's doctrine of the Highest Good, a doctrine that in my view resides at the heart of his positive philosophy of religion.

TRANSCENDENTAL IDEALISM AND THE CRITIQUE OF METAPHYSICS

Kant interpretation has long suffered under the yoke of the so-called "two-worlds" interpretation. This interpretation dates back to some of the earliest reviews of the *Critique of Pure Reason* (see Feder and Garve 1782, as well as Garve 1783); and through the writings of H. A. Prichard and Peter Strawson, it came to dominate the Anglophone reading of Kant. According to this view, Kant proposes two metaphysical domains: things as they appear to us in experience versus things as they are in themselves, independent of us. The former's objects have such characteristics as being in time and in space, having unity and limit, and existing within a nexus of causal connections. The latter, by contrast, lack all the properties of the former, are unknowable as they are in themselves, and yet only become available to us once "filtered" or shaped by the a priori structures of our consciousness.

Many "two-worlds" interpreters see Kant's project as little more than a version of Subjective Idealism, of the sort we most commonly associate with George Berkeley.[4] They take Kant's position to be a sort of phenomenalism – that is, the world for us is nothing but a series of inner states, with the addition of an unknowable metaphysical ground behind phenomenal experience. Under this interpretation, Kant's philosophy languished through much of the nineteenth and early twentieth centuries. Like so many others, Strawson too thought that despite Kant's intentions, the *Critique of Pure Reason* presents just a more ornate version of this familiar philosophical model. However, unlike other Anglophone readers, he saw in Kant's writings resources that could be separated from their metaphysical encumbrances and be brought into the service of analytic philosophy.

The real value of Kant's philosophy, according to Strawson, comes from what he calls "the Principle of Significance." Strawson defines this as "the principle that there can be no legitimate, or even meaningful, employment of ideas or concepts which does not relate them to empirical or experiential conditions of their application" (Strawson 1966: 16). The conceptual aspects of experience (i.e., the determination of objects as unities, as bounded by limits, etc.), as well as time and space, are contributions provided by our faculties, whereas things-in-themselves are to be understood as the way things are once we abstract away from all that our faculties have contributed. Thus, as the latter is defined by its independence from our cognition, it is also defined by its independence from the concepts provided by our faculties. Hence, things-in-themselves would not be temporal or spatial, unities, bounded by limits, causally related, or, perhaps, even countable.

So, even though Transcendental Idealism holds that there can be no knowledge of things-in-themselves, it is still (putatively) committed to there being a reality of unknowable things-in-themselves as well as to the mysterious "transcendental affection" through which things-in-themselves transmit data to us. Thus, according to Strawson, Transcendental Idealism remains a form of metaphysics, and so is in violation of the Principle of Significance (Strawson 1966: 41), even though we can still extract this principle from "analytic argument" of the *Critique* and then use it to both bar any further metaphysical indulgences as well as the Cartesian-type skepticism that is predicated upon the distinction between experience and a reality beyond it.

Since Strawson, various alternative interpretations have arisen, the most prominent of which appears in Henry Allison's *Kant's Transcendental Idealism: An Interpretation and Defense* (2004). Unlike most other interpretations of Kant, Allison's "methodological" or "two-aspects" interpretation rejects the notion that things-in-themselves have any positive metaphysical standing. It rejects the view that there are two distinct sets of objects (one phenomenal, one noumenal) and, instead, maintains that Kant only discusses things-in-themselves in order to clarify that the epistemic conditions for possible experience presented in the *Critique* should not be mistaken for metaphysical claims.

The notion of things-in-themselves has only a negative function: to clarify to the reader what is *not* being examined. When

Kant discusses our forms of intuition and pure concepts, he wants us to understand that they are constitutive conditions for how we experience objects (and are determinative of objecthood as such). They pertain to how we experience the world and are not to be taken as about the world independent of how we experience it. Hence, references to things-in-themselves serve to distinguish between what these conditions do and do not concern. This is most clear in the section of the First *Critique* explicitly devoted to the phenomena/noumena distinction.

In "On the Ground of the Distinction of All Objects in General into Phenomena and Noumena," Kant states that the "noumenon must be understood to be such only in the *negative* sense" (A252/B309); "this concept is necessary in order not to extend sensible intuition to things in themselves" (A254/B310); and, "The concept of a noumenon is therefore merely a *boundary concept*, in order to limit the pretension of sensibility, and therefore only of negative use. ... The division of objects into *phenomena* and *noumena*, and of the world into a world of sense and a world of understanding, can therefore not be permitted at all in a positive sense" (A255/B311). These passages help to illustrate that the *Critique* does not carry the metaphysical commitments proffered by the two-world interpretation. Rather than a metaphysical treatise about two domains of objects, the text should be read as an inquiry into and demonstration of the a priori conditions that govern our experience, how we sense, think, and judge.

These conditions set out what is built into experience for beings such as ourselves. They provide, on the one hand, what may be considered subjective conditions (since they pertain only to finite beings), while on the other hand, should still be understood as objective in that they determine what objects are like for us, for all of us. That is, unlike the phenomenalist reduction found in the two-worlds interpretation, the methodological interpretation presents the objects of experience as there for one and all – as intersubjective and as part of a shared empirical reality of matter dwelling within time and space.

To concretely illustrate the intersubjective character of this reading of Transcendental Idealism, imagine a group of individuals who (per their experience) are sitting around a table with a sculpture at its center. Some will see the sculpture's face in profile, while others will see it from a frontal view. Each spectator will, therefore, have a different experience. For a Subjective Idealist, the object of experience is merely phenomenal, existing just in the minds of each perceiver. Their objects will be qualitatively different, but more significantly here, they will also be numerically distinct since there is no shared physical object, presented to each relative to their viewing angles. Each observer rather just has his own mental contents, a bundle of colors and shapes. These contents may be qualitatively similar (similar shades of color for example), perhaps even qualitatively identical (in ideal lighting), but there is no quantitatively identical thing that is common to the observers.

By contrast, the Transcendental Idealist who takes time, space, limit, unity, etc. as the epistemic conditions through which experience is constituted, will take the object as one that is shared, just as these conditions for experience are shared; and rather than foundering upon the fact that the numerically identical sculpture will take on qualitatively distinct appearances for each observer, the Transcendental Idealist will rather regard the latter as simply illustrative of the Euclidean nature of shared space. In other words, the conditions upon which each experience is made possible likewise set out how the object will be experienced by others, including how the singular object in a shared space and time will appear differently to each observer, depending upon the present angles, lighting, etc.

It may be hard for some readers to get away from the psychological and phenomenalist reductions of Kant's forms of intuition and pure concepts, but they are not like filters we each apply to an undetermined noumenal object affecting us. Rather, they are features of a shared space and shared objects determined not by the discrete psychological processes of each observer; they are features of the world for beings such as ourselves. It is, thus, best to read each step of transcendental analysis found in the *Critique of Pure Reason*, not as stages along a psychological assembly process, but rather as an analysis that penetrates into how the world is given to us: what *Empirical Reality* is like.[5]

Returning to the metaphysical question, where does this leave things-in-themselves? It is tempting to answer this question by reference to Kant's caution that we should not mistake the conditions for possible experience as metaphysical claims about a transcendent reality. This is, at least, the dominant point made in his comments about things-in-themselves in the *Critique*'s Transcendental Analytic.

As for its Transcendental Dialectic, Kant likewise continues to oppose any positive use of things-in-themselves by showing the folly of trying to gain knowledge of them through the application of the epistemic conditions presented in the Analytic. It is not that we cannot think about things-in-themselves by way of our pure concepts, but rather, as illustrated in the Dialectic's Antinomies, we cannot adjudicate between the plurality of speculative metaphysical projects that have been developed over the centuries. Concepts alone may be able to generate internally consistent metaphysical models, but once untethered from experience, there is no way to determine which model is correct.

The Antinomies thus serve to illustrate why we cannot have knowledge of things-in-themselves. Although our conceptual apparatus makes empirical knowledge possible, when we try to use it to generate metaphysical systems, we certainly can accomplish the task, but we can do it too well, so to speak: reason can demonstrate that the world must have had a beginning in time, and it can demonstrate that it never had a beginning; it can demonstrate that all things are composites and so there is no ultimate simple, and it can demonstrate that there must be an ultimate simple.[6] A moment's reflection on the history of philosophy, with its multitude of metaphysical systems, illustrates Kant's point. Theoretical reason can forever continue spinning its wheels, developing and defending different answers to questions about ultimate reality.

This point of reflection, he notes, may lead to skepticism and despair, or to obstinance and dogmatism favoring one answer despite the equal credentials of the alternative. Either way, metaphysics, Kant claims, is the "death of a healthy philosophy" and the "euthanasia of pure reason" (A407/B434). The Transcendental Dialectic thus shows us the damage that metaphysics can do to "healthy philosophy." It also serves as a form of therapy by trying to bring us to terms with reason's pathological drive to know what ultimate reality is truly like.

Nevertheless, in the Transcendental Dialectic, Kant seems to deviate from the Analytic's more ardently negative, methodological use of things-in-themselves. The Third and Fourth Antinomies, in particular, intimate a more positive use than anywhere else in the *Critique* so far. The Third Antinomy presents us with the conflict between freedom and determinism, while the Fourth Antinomy deals with the affirmation and denial of the existence of a necessary being. In response to these two "Dynamical" Antinomies, Kant suggests that both thesis and antithesis may be affirmed, so long as one of them is attributed to the phenomenal realm and the other to the noumenal. Accordingly, in the case of the Third Antinomy, freedom and determinism may both be affirmed by having the phenomenal realm determined by causal laws, while allowing for at least the possibility that freedom reigns in the noumenal.

This is no proof of freedom, but it does show "that nature at least *does not conflict with* causality through freedom" (A558/B586). Moreover, in his Solution to the Third Antinomy, Kant explores the idea of a "causality" of reason, distinguishing it from deterministic physical laws, and linking it to normative laws. The noumenal realm is thus no longer simply a limit-concept introduced for methodological purposes. Rather, in the last two Antinomies, as well as in his ethical theory and philosophy of religion, we find Kant exploring the noumenal – and though he always holds on to the claim that through theoretical reason, we can never *know* anything of its nature, he nevertheless permits assent in the form of *faith*.

This is the upshot of our brief venture into Transcendental Idealism. Kant's claim in the *Critique of Pure Reason*'s Second Preface that he sought out the limits to knowledge in order to make room for faith should not be discounted as just an empty bromide. Quite to the contrary: we see both in the Transcendental Dialectic and then later in the Canon, how the *Critique* champions the Lutheran aspiration discussed at the beginning of this chapter.

Although this book will still generally follow the methodological interpretation of the noumenal where theoretical reason is concerned, as we advance into Kant's practical philosophy and philosophy of religion, a new affirmative stance must be added. This move is essential to Kant's entire positive theology – and to understand how such positive noumenal intimations can be reconciled with the dominant anti-metaphysical thrust of the Transcendental Dialectic, let us turn to how Kant distinguishes faith from knowledge.

FAITH AS A PROPOSITIONAL ATTITUDE

The *Critique of Pure Reason* has many more pages that at least appear to be antagonistic to religion than offer it any support. As mentioned at the beginning of this chapter, it attacks the traditional arguments for God's existence, challenges the existence of the soul, and argues that through theoretical reason alone, we cannot generate a sufficiently determinate conception of God. Yet, as also mentioned in brief, these objections should not be misinterpreted as anti-religious. Kant's aim is not to do away with religion, but rather to save it.

As long as religious doctrines are thought to be within the purview of theoretical reason, theology can be treated as a science, requiring a class of specialists whose life is devoted to the technical analysis of doctrines, and expecting the laity to put their faith in the hands of these presumed experts. But this can lead (and has led) to religious despotism, for it expects us to accept the professional theologian's word on doctrinal disputes over subtle distinctions and obscure details that only they presumably can understand.

The alternative that Kant recommends has its roots in Luther's doctrine of universal priesthood (i.e., that we are all our own priests). Like Luther, Kant wants to remove religion from the "monopoly of the schools" and set it on a footing suitable to "the common human understanding" (Bxxxii). Yet, at the same time, he does not want it to fall into the blind fervor of Enthusiasm, wishful thinking or superstition. Although Kant distinguishes faith from both opinion and knowledge, this is far from a license to irrational assent. Just as there are a priori principles governing experience, so likewise there are universal grounds pertinent to faith, grounds shaped by the common needs of our practical lives. They pertain to our fallen nature, a nature that all of humanity shares, and thus for Kant, faith is grounded in such a way that it (like other legitimate forms of assent) is intersubjectively valid (see Pasternack 2011).

However, this validity, unlike that of opinion and knowledge, is not grounded epistemically. These other propositional attitudes gain their justification through evidence, argument, or other common theoretical warrants that, Kant claims, if communicated to others, should lead them to assent as well (assuming no biases stand in the way). He refers to the modes of assent that command universal assent as "conviction" (*Überzeugung*), against which he contrasts "persuasion" (*Überredung*). The latter he describes as having its "ground only in the particular constitution of the subject" (A820/B848), and as such has "only private validity" (A820/B848). We may think of such instances of assent as having their roots in personal bias or emotional needs such as is present in wishful thinking, bandwagonism, and what Kant calls the delusion of "logical egoism" (JL: 9:80; VL: 24:874–75).

By contrast, conviction has grounds that are "universally valid" (BL: 24:202), "valid for everyone merely as long as he has reason" (A820/B848), "necessarily valid for everyone" (A821/B849), or objectively valid (CJ: 5:461).[7] Knowledge (*Wissen*) is an obvious instance of conviction. In its case, it carries sufficiently forceful objective grounds that we can hold the proposition to be true with certainty. Similarly opinion (*Meinung*), though it falls short of certainty, is also based upon objective grounds that if communicated should lead others to a similar (though measured) assent. Unlike persuasion, where our assent is driven by a particular psychological interest that does not hold common to all, opinion is based upon some evidence and/or some argument, enough still to justify assent, but in a weaker form that corresponds to the level of probability that the grounds have established. We can, for example, find in lecture notes from the Blomberg Logic: "One can opine something without believing, namely if one has more grounds for the cognition than against it. Here I hold something to be true without its having an influence on our actions. To know something, however, is nothing other than to cognize it with certainty" (BL: 24:241–42). Similarly, we have "*to opine*, or holding-to-be-true based on any insufficient ground, which nevertheless has more importance than the ground of the opposite" (BL: 24:227).[8]

Kant does not, however, limit our legitimate modes of assent to just knowledge and opinion. Although these modes gain their legitimacy from epistemic grounds, he further claims that faith (*Glaube*) is also a mode of conviction, and thus is likewise "necessarily valid for everyone" (A821/B849). Nevertheless, its legitimacy cannot be epistemic, as its objects are outside of possible experience. It cannot be based upon evidence, nor by way of theoretical reason, since valid use of the latter must still rest upon the conditions for possible experience. Instead, faith gains its legitimacy through the needs of practical reason, needs that are in their own way still "necessarily valid for everyone."

Although in earlier texts, Kant more closely followed the looser account of faith found in George Friedrich Meier's *Auszug aus der Vernunftlehre* (1752), the textbook from which Kant lectured on logic for forty years, as the Critical Period advanced, he came to narrow the proper objects of faith to those that are "based on a practical principle of reason (which is universally and necessarily valid) … [and so] can make a sufficient claim of conviction from a purely practical point of view" (CJ: 5:463). These objects include the Highest Good (as a state of affairs that will ultimately come to be) and the two Practical Postulates that he considers to be necessary for its realization: God's existence and the immortality of the soul. However, as we will discuss at length through much of this book, while the above should be understood as the foundational objects of faith, many further principles (Divine justice, the Propensity to Evil, the Change of Heart, etc.) flow from them, perhaps in a manner similar to the relationship between the First *Critique*'s pure concepts and the further "predicables" that are "derivative and subalternate" from the former (A82/B108). Collectively these principles of faith, which command universal conviction, are called by Kant the Pure Rational System of Religion, or the doctrines of Pure Rational Faith.

Still, the question remains as to how Kant draws upon the needs of pure practical reason to ground faith – how, that is, he is able to distinguish faith from persuasion. After all, one might assent to God, immortality, and so forth, on grounds that are idiosyncratic or irrational. One might, for example, claim a special private dispensation, some revelation or insight for oneself alone. Or, one might merely desire so ardently that the tenets of faith are true that one comes to affirm them out of wishful thinking.

The latter, in fact, was an accusation made by Thomas Wizenmann, one of Kant's contemporaries. Wizenmann argued that just as love leads to delusions about the beloved, so this may as well be the case with regard to the Highest Good and its Postulates. That is, the needs which lead to religious assent are simply driven by emotional desire rather than practical reason. Kant directly responds to this accusation, acknowledging that if one's assent has to do with a need "based on inclination," then it falls to persuasion. However, he asserts that legitimate faith has its roots in "a *need of reason* arising from an *objective* determining ground of the will, namely the moral law, which necessarily binds every rational being" (CPrR: 5:143n). Thus, as we are all bound by the moral law, if it in some way depends upon or draws us to the Highest Good, and in turn, to its Postulates, then, unlike the variable and subjective character of persuasion, faith has an objective and universal basis.[9]

But to repeat, this basis does not come out of theoretical reason. Its source, rather, is in the practical. Precisely what this source is will be a topic for later in this chapter, but put very roughly, Kant argues that our commitment to morality is intertwined with a commitment to the Highest Good and the conditions that make its realization possible.[10] This is, moreover, a conviction for Kant, and, like knowledge, it is supposed to be certain for us. Yet, the nature of this certainty is different than what applies to knowledge. The difference is not only in the grounds for assent, but in some further way that Kant expresses cryptically as follows: "I must not even say 'It is morally certain that there is a God,' etc., but rather 'I am morally certain' etc." (A829/B857). Accordingly, faith has in some sense a personal or subjective character to it; yet it still has grounds that distinguish it from persuasion in that the grounds of faith, as rooted in the needs of practical reason, are grounds that hold for everyone.

An analogy may here be drawn to Descartes' *Cogito*, for the certainty one has in one's own existence seems more aptly expressed as Kant did above with "I am certain" rather than "It is certain." The latter formulation is less indicative of the first-person privileged character of the *Cogito*. So faith, we might say, has a similarly privileged first-person status. Despite the fact that we all have a need for faith arising from our inward moral struggles, this assent develops out of a personal path through these struggles and should be understood, in a certain sense, as subjective. Although there is a universal need for faith, it is not characterized by Kant as objective, for it is not rooted in a process of logical inference. It is, rather, "subjectively necessary" in that it is a need we each encounter in our practical lives.[11]

One might worry that if its certainty has a first-person character, perhaps no account of why faith is needed is possible. But its putative ineffability does not follow from the first-person character of its certainty. Just as Descartes describes a first-person process through which we each can come to certainty with regards to our own existence, Kant explains why faith is needed in terms that allow each of us to reflect, become aware of the compelling force of the moral law within, and come to see how it further calls for the Highest Good and the Postulates. However, beyond such generalities, Kant has great difficulty formulating the nature of our practical needs and how they are supposed to lead to the Highest Good. All three *Critiques* as well as the First Preface to *Religion* contain arguments whose aim is to establish this connection, but they all differ from one another – not just in minor details, but in philosophically substantive ways. Through the remainder of this chapter, we will examine the accounts he offers in the *Critiques*, and as part of the next chapter's discussion of *Religion*'s prefaces, we will examine its presentation of the practical grounds upon which our hope and faith depend.

KANT'S DOCTRINE OF THE HIGHEST GOOD

It is generally accepted that Kant's doctrine of the Highest Good contains two layers or aspects. They have respectively been called its immanent vs. transcendent aspects, its ectypical vs. archetypical layers, or its form as a demand vs. as a promise.[12] The first (immanent, ectypical, demand) aspect of the doctrine presents the Highest Good as a duty to which we are bound. It is, as we will discuss below, more specifically an imperfect duty, one that we are obligated to positively promote, rather than a perfect and negative sort of duty, such as the prohibitions against lying, stealing, or killing. It is, rather, more like our duties to be charitable or to further our talents, in that it commands that we conscientiously pursue an end insofar as it is within our power to do so. The second (transcendent, archetypical, promise) aspect of the doctrine pertains, by contrast, to an ideal whose realization is beyond our power. It is usually rendered as an ideal state of affairs wherein there is a distribution of happiness in proportion to moral worth. For the sake of convenience, let me refer to the first aspect of the doctrine as HG_d (the Highest Good as *duty*) and the second as HG_i (the Highest Good as *ideal*).

In the next section, we will explore Kant's actual arguments for the Highest Good. But first, let us look more closely at the doctrine itself, the respective roles of HG_i and HG_d, and the view, found in recent literature, that Kant substantially revised HG_i during the Critical Period, removing all or some of its religious elements. As we shall see, this view, despite its current popularity, cannot be sustained once one looks carefully at its presumed textual basis. Later in this section, we will look more closely at HG_d. But we shall begin with HG_i, and the controversy regarding whether or not it refers to a state of affairs that takes place in a "future life" or is merely a social and secular ideal pursued for the sake of future generations.

HG_i AS A SECULAR VS. RELIGIOUS IDEAL

It is generally agreed that at least in the *Critique of Pure Reason*, Kant did see HG_i as taking place in the afterlife, where through

Divine justice, we receive happiness in proportion to our moral worth (A814/B842).[13] He there argues that this principle of distribution cannot be realized in this life, either through the causality of nature or through our common moral efforts: "how their consequences will be related to happiness is determined neither by the nature of the things in the world, nor by the causality of actions themselves and their relation to morality" (A810/B838); and a few pages later, he also states that: "the sensible world does not promise us that sort of systematic unity of ends" (A814/B842).[14] Thus, in order for HG$_i$'s distributive principle to be realized, Kant posits God as its agent along with an extra-mundane "*realm of grace*" (A812/B840) separate from the causal order of nature and governed by Divine justice. As he states, it is only through the positing of this alternate realm that "our conduct in the sensible world" (A811/B839) can receive its just deserts, for in this world, nature "does not offer such a connection" (A811/B839) to what we each morally deserve.

In my opinion, Kant continues to hold to an extramundane model of HG$_i$ throughout the Critical Period, and does so for the same reasons we find stated in the First *Critique*. Although, as we shall see, he moves through numerous different arguments for the Highest Good, and makes various other changes to the religious principles tied to it (such as to the conditions upon which our moral worth is judged as well as whether or not punishments can be eternal), his commitment to the core Postulates of God and Immortality remain unchanged.

Not all interpreters, however, agree. Andrews Reath, for example, in his "Two Conceptions of the Highest Good," argues that by the Third *Critique*, Kant abandoned his earlier "theological conception" of the Highest Good in favor of a secular one, one that refers simply to a social agenda, without any need for either God or immortality (Reath 1988). A similar view has also been expressed by Paul Guyer, who claims that even in the Second *Critique*, Kant began to show some reservations about his former portrayal of HG$_i$ and "dramatically separates the postulation of immortality from the postulation of God" (Guyer 2005: 289). Guyer even asserts that "the highest good is not any part of a doctrine of punishment or retribution: It does not imply that the virtuous should be rewarded with happiness and the vicious punished with unhappiness"(Guyer 2005: 289n).

Nevertheless, there is a surfeit of textual evidence that runs against these views. Despite Guyer's assertion that "the highest good is not any part of a doctrine of punishment or retribution," there are dozens of passages, found as much in Kant's writings of the 1780s as the 1790s, that very clearly assert that HG$_i$ does involve the distribution of happiness in accordance with moral worth. A few relevant passages from the First *Critique* have already been quoted. In the Second *Critique*, we have, for example: "happiness distributed in exact proportion to morality (as the worth of a person and his worthiness to be happy) constitutes the *highest good* of a possible world" (CPrR: 5:110).[15] We can also find similar formulations of HG$_i$ in *Religion* (6:5, 6:99, 6:161) and in various essays of the 1790s, including the Theory/Practice essay (TP: 8:279), "The End of All Things"(ET: 8:328–30), and the "Real Progress" (RP: 20:298). In all of these, reward and punishment are unambiguously linked with the Highest Good. This is a position that appears from the start of the Critical Period and is a view that is never retracted.

As for the view that Kant eliminated the Postulate of Immortality from HG$_i$, I suspect that it is rooted in a preference on the part of some contemporary Kantians to alter his views so that they better suit the secular tendencies of contemporary academia. Of course, there is nothing intrinsically wrong with such alterations. There may be good philosophical reasons for rejecting this Postulate or in other ways adapting Kant's doctrine.[16] But the trend, unfortunately, has been to present HG$_i$ as if the texts themselves advance this secular position.

The most frequently cited passage used to support the secularization of the Highest Good is 5:450 in the *Critique of Judgement*. It contains the phrase "the highest good in the world," and since Reath's "Two Conceptions of the Highest Good" it has been the primary basis for the view that by 1790 Kant migrated from an other-worldly to a this-worldly rendering of HG$_i$. The Highest Good, so it has been argued, is no longer viewed by Kant as taking place in a "future life," but in this one. It will obtain "in the world" and so it is humanity rather than God who is to be held responsible for its realization.

Of course, it is granted that Kant does use "in the world" when discussing the Highest Good. In fact, the phrase appears in various texts of the Critical Period – a point that might prompt one to see the secular interpretation as all the stronger. However, these passages cannot offer such a benefit. This is because "in the world" appears well before the putative shift to a secular model of the Highest Good. It occurs in both the First *Critique* (e.g. A814/B842) and quite abundantly in the Second *Critique*, (CPrR: 5:122, 5:125, 5:126, 5:134, 5:141, etc.). Moreover, it is used in contexts where one could not plausibly take it to have a secular meaning. The most glaring example of this is at 5:122 in the *Critique of Practical Reason*, right in the opening line of the section "The Immortality of the Soul as a Postulate of Pure Practical Reason" – that is, right where Kant argues for the Postulate of Immortality! Similarly, it can be found in the Second *Critique*'s section that discusses how we are justified through the "extension of pure reason for practical purposes" (CPrR: 5:134) to affirm freedom, immortality, and God. Kant there reminds us that by "the theoretical path," they cannot be established; yet "by the practical law that commands the existence of the highest good possible in a world, the possibility of those objects of pure speculative reason ... is postulated" (CPrR: 5:134).

Thus, it hardly seems reasonable to assume that "in the world" should be read as referring to just the natural causal order of this life. Instead, there are many passages where Kant uses the phrase to indicate something more broad, akin to "in all that is" or "in all of creation." In fact, he explicitly discusses the meaning of *Welt* in the *Critique of Pure Reason*, noting that "We have two expressions, *world* and *nature*, which are sometimes run together" (A418/B446). But, he continues, they can also differ in meaning. When dealing with cosmology, for instance, Kant assigns to "world" a "transcendental sense," namely, "the absolute totality of the sum total of existing things" (A419/B447). Therefore, given that he does use "in the world" in contexts that clearly include the afterlife, it is appropriate to understand it in this sense.

The above textual argument may be sufficient to rebut the secular reading of HG_i. But we may also challenge it by looking closely at the passage most often used to support it. Although the phrase "in the world" is gleaned from 5:450, the context in which it appears is simply ignored. This is a passage drawn from section 87 of the *Critique of Judgment*, where Kant discusses moral teleology and in relation to it "the moral proof of the existence of God" (5:447). This proof is built upon the Highest Good as the final end or purpose of creation. It calls upon us to "strive after" the Highest Good, i.e., the imperfect duty identified by HG_d. But then Kant continues on to a discussion of HG_i. Just as he argued in the First and Second *Critiques*, so in the Third, he writes, "it is impossible for us to represent these two requirements of the final end [i.e., happiness and morality] ... as both *connected* by mere natural causes" (CJ: 5:450), and thus God is again posited as "a moral cause of the world (an author of the world)" (CJ: 5:450).

Immortality is not explicitly mentioned in the passage but it appears not long after, still within the same section of the *Critique of Judgment*, in what I would like to call the Parable of the Righteous Atheist. In this parable, Kant discusses "a righteous man (like Spinoza) who takes himself to be firmly persuaded [*überredete*] that there is no God and ... there is also no future life" (CJ: 5:452).[17] Kant then argues that the Righteous Atheist will succumb to despair and lose his motivation to follow morality. Kant by no means dwells on the issue of immortality here, but it is mentioned, for it is only through the faith that HG_i will obtain in the "future life" that one can face down the "purposeless chaos of matter" (CJ: 5:452) and sustain one's commitment to morality.[18]

We can also find similar comments through the rest of the 1790s. They appear in the "Theodicy" essay of 1791, throughout *Religion*, in 1794's "The End of All Things," and in the "Conflict of the Faculties," published in 1798. In fact, it turns out that there are more texts containing affirmations of the immortality of the soul in the 1790s than in the 1780s. Of course, that is not to say that Kant migrated *to* a belief in the afterlife as the Critical Period advanced, but it does seem more on his mind in later years, as religious topics in general also were. Moreover, while Kant's argument for the Highest Good evolved through the years, the phases of which we will discuss shortly, throughout all these changes, we find the same core argument for the Postulate of Immortality. As discussed briefly above, and as we will return to shortly, Kant holds that HG$_i$'s distributive principle cannot be secured within the order of nature, and thus some other order of existence, one that takes place in a "future life," is postulated (cf. A811/B839; CJ: 5:452; TP: 8:279; RP: 20:298).

Once we come to *Religion*'s discussion of the Ethical Community in Chapter 5, we will also consider its secular interpretation, but for now let us bring this discussion to a close with one more passage that reinforces my contention that Kant did not abandon the Postulate of Immortality in the 1790s and continued to treat HG$_i$ as a religious principle rather than, as some would have it, a secular social ideal. The following comes from the "articles of confession of pure practical reason," presented in his 1793 "Real Progress" essay (note once again Kant's use of "the highest good in the world"):

I believe in one God, as the original source of all good in the world, that being its final end; – I believe in the possibility of conforming to this final end, to the highest good in the world, so far as it is in man's power; – I believe in a future eternal life, as the condition for an everlasting approximation of the world to the highest good possible therein.

(RP: 20:298)

WHAT DOES HG$_d$ COMMAND?

The second layer of Kant's doctrine of the Highest Good, HG$_d$, is first articulated in the *Critique of Practical Reason*. It is there rendered as a duty to "further," "promote," or "strive after" the Highest Good. This may seem simple enough, but if HG$_d$ is interpreted as a duty to promote the realization of HG$_i$, then we appear to be charged with a duty that is beyond our power. Kant makes this quite clear at CPrR 5:113: "no necessary connection of happiness with virtue in the world, adequate to the highest good, can be expected from the most meticulous observance of the moral laws." Likewise, in the *Critique of Pure Reason*, he claims that even if *"everyone* do[es] what he should," "how their consequences will be related to happiness is determined neither by the nature of the things in the world, nor the causality of actions themselves and their relation to morality" (A810/B838).

We thus have (so it seems), a duty that violates Kant's commitment to the logic of *ought implies can*. We might with luck be able on some occasions to reward or punish someone as they deserve, but neither can we secure such justice in the face of all exigencies of nature, nor can we regard ourselves as cognitively capable of judging anyone's moral worth correctly. On the first point, it should be obvious that the "purposeless chaos of matter" (CJ: 5:452) often intrudes upon our best laid plans, wreaking havoc upon the lives of the virtuous and vicious alike. Of course, there certainly are instances where our intended outcomes do come to pass. But these are minor victories, ultimately swamped by nature: "One wide grave engulfs" us all and our hopes for moral justice cannot be sustained before the litany of "all the evils of poverty, illness, and untimely death" (CJ: 5:452).

To the above, one might want to rebut that if some success is possible, however slight, it is still enough to satisfy the *can* of *ought implies can*. There are times where we are fortunate enough to have nature not interfere with our attempts to exercise justice in the world. However, if HG_d is interpreted in this way, where it is our duty to distribute justice, success needs to be more than the product of occasional luck. Of course, improved social policies could aid in this distribution, but far more is still needed: control over disease, the weather, and the routine accidents of daily life. Moreover, an interpretation of HG_d that places justice in our hands faces an even more profound difficulty: as Kant consistently maintains, we cannot know anyone's true moral worth, not even our own (GR: 4:407, 6:99; MM: 6:447). We therefore lack a capacity that is necessary for our serving as agents of distributive justice. God, of course, may know what we each deserve, and perhaps we may be His instruments at times. However, as we lack (as a matter of the constitution of human beings) the epistemic means to determine who deserves what, we are not in a position to take on a duty that is supposed to execute such judgments. That is, if the *ought* of HG$_d$ concerns our being agents of distributive justice, and a necessary condition for being such an agent is that one has the epistemic means to determine moral worth, then such a duty is not one in which we can engage.

So let me instead offer a different way to understand HG$_d$. As Kant consistently maintains, what is to be realized in HG$_i$ is the distribution of happiness in accordance with moral worth. But this ideal should be understood as more than its core equation of just deserts. If we took it as only this, it would still be realized even if no one deserved anything other than punishment. Justice would be served if we all remained wicked and we all received due punishment. Hence, if HG$_i$ were understood as merely the distribution of just deserts, it could still obtain – even where its realization took the form of the eternal suffering of all humanity. However, I presume that that is not the *Highest* Good. It surely is not the whole or complete good (see CPrR: 5:111), for it is without any actualization of the two goods of moral worthiness and happiness.

Kant offers passing remarks on this issue in various texts, often in relation to the doctrine of Universalism (that *everyone* will ultimately gain moral worthiness and receive happiness). Sometimes he seems to endorse the doctrine (TP: 8:279), while in other texts, he rather supports the bifurcation of rational beings into those that gain moral worthiness and those that do not (ET: 8:328–30). But, either way, he nevertheless envisions HG$_i$ as having at least some morally worthy beings to populate it. So, when we consider what it is within HG$_i$ that is within our power, and thus what serves as the basis for HG$_d$, attention should be shifted away from the demand that happiness be distributed in accordance with moral worth to our striving to become worthy of happiness. It is that, rather than the distribution of happiness, that is within our power.

As put in the Second *Critique*, "the first and principal part of the highest good" is the "practical task" of morality (CPrR: 5:124) while the "second element of the highest good, namely happiness proportioned to that morality ... lead[s] to the supposition of the existence of a cause adequate to this effect, that is, it must postulate the *existence of God*" (CPrR: 5:124). HG_d is, therefore, most appropriately rendered in terms of our duty to become morally worthy beings. This is the "practical task" within Kant's doctrine of the Highest Good that is within our power. In the Second *Critique*, it is even presented as something we continue to pursue after death (CPrR: 5:122), though in later texts, he shifts to the position that it is only in this life that we have the opportunity to become morally worthy of happiness in the next, or at least that it is "wise to act *as if* another life – and the moral state in which we end this one, along with its consequences in entering on that other life – is unalterable" (ET: 8:330). Likewise, in *Religion*, Kant states that "at the end of life our account must be completely closed, and nobody may hope somehow to make up there for what was neglected here" (6:71n).[19]

Before we move on, let me add one further point regarding the constitution of HG_d. As just indicated, Kant shifts his view after the Second *Critique* from one where we in the afterlife continue to strive to gain moral worth to the position that we should consider our afterlife fates as decided in this life. This shift does not preclude some supplementary moral development in the afterlife, as is described in his Lectures on the Philosophical Doctrine of Religion (see 28:1085), but the shift does point to something decisive taking place in this life.

This shift also comes about as a result of another important change in Kant's soteriology. We see in the Second *Critique* as well as in the Lectures on the Philosophical Doctrine of Religion that our moral worthiness is to be measured in terms of the pursuit of moral perfection. As stated in the *Metaphysics of Morals* as well, we have a duty "to *strive* for this perfection" (MM: 6:446), a perfection that involves the development of virtue. Yet, in *Religion*, Kant uses "virtue" polemically, and repeatedly declares that it is *not* through virtue that we become Justified before God.

For example, in Part One, Kant describes virtue in terms of one's "habits" and "firm resolve" to comply with one's duties. But this, he continues, involves "only a change in *mores*" (6:47).[20] That is, virtue is here represented as the observance of one's duties and control over inclinations, such as when "an immoderate human being converts to moderation for the sake of health; a liar to truth for the sake of reputation." But all such changes remain "in conformity with the prized principle of happiness" (6:47). Likewise, the opening pages of Part Two focus specifically on the continence fundamental to virtue theory and emphasized by the Stoics. Yet, Kant writes, "those valiant men [the Stoics] mistook their enemy" (6:57). They erroneously located our moral battle in relation to our inclinations, and so have failed to adequately address the existence of an "active and opposing cause of evil" (6:57) within us. So, while in other texts (and even in some later passages of *Religion*), Kant presents virtue as *both* a psychological adjustment to the demands of morality and also a commitment to morality for its own sake (e.g. CPrR: 5:110 and MM: 6:407), the polemical use of "virtue" in Parts One and Two helps Kant show that his understanding of moral worthiness has moved away from the perfectionism that is bound up with virtue to what in *Religion* he calls the "Change of Heart."

We will return to the above treatment of virtue in subsequent chapters, but here I would like to just take note of the fact that insofar as HG_d is understood as a duty to populate HG_i, at least in *Religion*, Kant maintains that we become Justified before God and so worthy of happiness through, specifically, the Change of Heart. This is a spontaneous "revolution" that overcomes our state of sin and restores the moral incentive to its rightful priority over self-interest. By contrast, the acquisition of virtue is realized "little by little" gradually over time (6:47). We may begin our pursuit of virtue prior to the Change of Heart, perhaps merely to gain greater self-control for non-moral reasons, a scenario that Kant discusses in his *Anthropology* (see AN: 7:292–95); or we may only move on to seek such control after we have undergone the more fundamental moral revolution.

One may also choose to read HG_d with greater latitude as involving both demands, i.e., the Change of Heart and the acquisition of virtue. However, at least in *Religion*, Kant claims that it is the former that is decisive for the determination of the fate that befalls us in the afterlife. It is presented as a necessary condition for our becoming Justified before God and no longer deserving of punishment (6:73). The latter, by contrast, although it remains a command, is not on its own sufficient to make us worthy of happiness. Nevertheless, it could be added to *Religion*'s focus on the Change of Heart. If one wants to retain the idea of a proportionate distribution within HG_i, then there must be a standard of moral worth that admits of degrees. Virtue offers the basis for this proportionality since the Change of Heart is just binary: one either has given priority to morality over self-interest or one has not. With virtue, by contrast, there are degrees. Hence, it may be that a necessary condition for any Divine reward is the Change of Heart, and the character of that reward may then be modulated by one's level of virtue. This, I grant, is quite speculative, but it does reconcile a tension in the text.

As we will discuss in Chapter 3, central to Kant's argument for Rigorism is that the moral status of our *Gesinnung* does not come in degrees. It is either good or evil. So, one should either adjust HG_i to reflect this binary principle, eliminating the proportionality of happiness with moral worth (i.e., one is either deserving of happiness or one is not), or one must look to some other standard through which moral worth can have degrees. Of course, a contradiction would result if one understood moral worthiness to, in the same respect, both have degrees and not have degrees. But we have a basis for separating it into two different standards of evaluation. One is binary: whether or not one has undergone a Change of Heart. The other takes on degrees: the extent of one's development of self-control, the cultivation of various morally conducive traits, and the other elements associated with Kantian virtue. Both are duties for us, and both, in their respective ways, can have a role within the doctrine of the Highest Good.

KANT'S ARGUMENTS FOR THE HIGHEST GOOD

In the preceding section, we examined the two aspects or layers of Kant's doctrine of the Highest Good: HG_i (the Highest Good as an ideal state of affairs) and HG_d (the Highest Good as a duty). The former first appears in the *Critique of Pure Reason* and the latter is added in the *Critique of Practical Reason*. Through the remainder of the Critical Period, much of the doctrine remains stable, including the need for both the Postulate of God and

Immortality. There are some changes in detail, including what is required of us to be worthy of happiness, and how immortality is envisioned. But the most drastic change is in how Kant argues for the doctrine. In fact, his arguments change from one *Critique* to the next, each assigning a different role to the Highest Good within his practical philosophy.

These changes are, unfortunately, commonly overlooked, with interpreters either attempting to merge the various arguments into one, as if Kant never substantively revised his views, or deferring to one single argument, most commonly the one found in the Second *Critique*. We will, by contrast, take a very different approach, one that acknowledges that Kant changed his mind, more than once in fact, and so presents quite different arguments for the Highest Good through the 1780s and 1790s. It is my view that Kant was not randomly groping for an argument with which he could finally be satisfied. Rather, there is a developmental story that can be told here, one that shows his own awareness of the weaknesses of the preceding argument(s) and the need for further refinements that track with other changes that took place through the Critical Period. Through the remainder of this chapter, we will examine the arguments for the Highest Good from each of the three *Critiques*. There is also a fourth argument for the Highest Good, one that appears in the First Preface of *Religion*. But we shall reserve that argument for the next chapter.

THE HIGHEST GOOD IN THE *CRITIQUE OF PURE REASON*

As we briefly discussed earlier, towards the end of the *Critique of Pure Reason*, Kant presents the framework for what he calls the "Canon of Pure Reason." The aim of such a canon is to catalogue "the sum-total of the *a priori* principles of the correct use of certain cognitive faculties in general" (A796/B824). He then separates the principles that are to compose the Canon into three groups, corresponding to the questions: "What can I know?" "What should I do?" and "What may I hope?" (A805/B833). We can bypass the issues surrounding the first two questions for it is through his answer to the third that Kant finds his way to the Highest Good.

He asserts that all hoping is directed towards happiness (A805/B833), but happiness *simpliciter* is inadequate as a response to the question as framed by the Canon. The question is not "What do I hope?" but rather "What may I hope?" "May" (*dürfen*) calls for a normative element to justify the hope, and it is through its justification that happiness can gain membership within the canon of a priori principles. Kant finds this justification by way of what hope offers to our moral motivation. He puts forward the thesis that "everyone has cause to hope for happiness in the same measure as he has made himself worthy of it in his conduct, and that the system of morality is therefore inseparably combined with the system of happiness, though only in the idea of pure reason" (A809/B837). In other words, we *may* hope for happiness (i.e., are rationally justified in holding to this hope) insofar as we have become worthy of receiving it. Let us refer to this thesis as the principle of proportionate distribution (or PPD). If he can successfully demonstrate PPD, then the hope for happiness is not simply a psychological phenomenon or a matter of wishful thinking. Rather, he will have shown that there is a necessary relation between morality and happiness (A809/B837).

This relation, he claims, is based upon the motivational force that the desire for happiness provides. Although this may seem shocking to many readers, the view we find presented in the First *Critique* is that all our actions, including those that heed a principle of morality, are motivated by the desire for happiness. Kant's better known account of moral motivation, where it is both possible and obligatory to not merely act on moral maxims but also to act on them *because* they are moral, does not appear until the *Groundwork*. According to it, and throughout all subsequent ethical writings, Kant distinguishes between acting merely in conformity with duty and acting *from* duty, and so regards our recognition that something is our duty as the proper motivational basis for our actions.

However, this vision of moral agency lagged behind the other innovations of the Critical Period. Even though 1781 is usually taken to demarcate the point of transition from Kant's early to his more mature philosophical period, it still takes a few more years before he fully develops, or at least fully articulates, the conception of moral motivation that has us capable of acting from pure practical reason. Thus, the vision of moral agency in the First *Critique*, the vision that first draws him to the Highest Good, is not that of the *Groundwork*.

Through his pre-Critical years, and lingering still in the First *Critique*, Kant's conception of morality was split between Rationalist and Sentimentalist theses. He subscribed to the former's claim that morality must be law-like, its "principle of appraisal of obligation" needs to be universal and necessary. But he followed the latter's view that "the principle of performance or execution" is driven by affective desire. We find this schism in his "Inquiry Concerning the Distinctness of the Principles of Natural Theology and Morality" (the so-called Prize essay of 1764) as well as through many of his lectures and *Reflexionen* of the 1760s and 1770s. For instance, we find in Collins 2 lectures: "the supreme principle of all moral judgment lies in the understanding; the supreme principle of the moral impulse to do this thing lies in the heart" (27:274); and in the so-called Mrongovius notes, Kant discusses what he sees as a fundamental disconnect between the understanding and feeling: "When a man has learned to appraise all actions, he still lacks the motive to perform them. ... [T]he understanding has no *elateres animi* ... man has no such secret organization, that he can be moved by objective grounds" (27:1429).[21]

Similarly, in the Canon of the First *Critique*, Kant writes that "the majestic ideas of morality are, to be sure, objects of approbation and admiration but not incentives for resolve and realization" (A813/B841). Thus, in order for us to move from our awareness of a moral principle to an action that (at least) conforms to it, we still need something that can bring us to act on "the majestic ideas of morality," to turn them into "incentives for resolve and realization." By the time of the *Groundwork*, Kant comes, of course, to see pure practical reason as itself able to motivate us. But in the First *Critique*, while still at the cusp of the Critical Period, he continues to follow Sentimentalism's view that reason is motivationally impotent: "man has no such secret organization, that he can be moved by objective grounds" (27:1429).

Accordingly, the Canon proposes that we "connect appropriate consequences with their rule *a priori*, and thus carry with them *promises* and *threats*" (A811/B839). Without these incentives, the "majestic ideas" of morality would have no connection with our practical lives. They could be "objects of approbation and admiration" (A813/B841) but would be impotent and "empty figments of the brain" (A811/B839). This is where the hope for happiness gains its justification. The stature of morality depends upon its having some way to connect with our wills, and the connection is here established by the hope to be rewarded if one obeys and the fear of punishment if one does not. Through this connection "the system of morality is therefore inseparably combined with the system of happiness" (A809/B837).

It is in relation to the connection between happiness and morality that Kant first introduces the doctrine of the Highest Good: "I call the idea of such an intelligence, in which the morally most perfect will, combined with the highest blessedness, is the cause of all happiness in the world, insofar as it stands in exact relation with morality (as the worthiness to be happy), the ideal of the highest good" (A810/B839). HG_i is here introduced as the object of hope, one that is rationally justified in order that morality's "majestic ideas" can be accepted as commands for us, which they "could not be if they did not connect appropriate consequences with their rule *a priori*, and thus carry with them *promises* and *threats*" (A811/B840).[22]

Before moving on to the Second *Critique*'s argument for the Highest Good, let us briefly revisit the Canon's justification for the Postulates of God and Immortality. As was discussed above, Kant argues that HG_i cannot be realized either through the laws of nature or through our human efforts: "how their consequences will be related to happiness is determined neither by the nature of the things in the world, nor by the causality of actions themselves and their relation to morality" (A810/B838). A few pages later, he also writes that "the sensible world does not promise us that sort of systematic unity of ends" (A814/B842). Even if "*everyone* do[es] what he should" (A810/B838), there is far too much outside of our control. We cannot fully safeguard the morally worthy from accidents, disease, natural disasters, etc. Hence, some further agency beyond our capabilities must be postulated, as well as a life beyond this one within which rewards and punishments are meted out.[23] The Postulates of God and Immortality thus become the two fundamental articles of faith in Kant's philosophical theology.[24]

THE HIGHEST GOOD IN THE *CRITIQUE OF PRACTICAL REASON*

Once Kant altered his conception of agency to allow for the motivational potential of pure practical reason, the hope for happiness was no longer needed to bring the "majestic ideas of morality" into "incentives for resolve and realization." From the *Groundwork* on, Kant saw these "majestic ideas" as themselves able to motivate us to action. Thus, the First *Critique*'s argument for the Highest Good becomes nugatory and so too might the doctrine, unless, of course, Kant can find for it a new role within his practical philosophy.

That new role is announced in the *Critique of Practical Reason*'s "Dialectic of Pure Practical Reason." Just as the First *Critique* contains a Transcendental Dialectic devoted to the faculty of reason in its theoretical employment, so we have in the Second *Critique* an inquiry into practical reason's quest for "the absolute totality of conditions for a given conditioned" (CPrR: 5:107). But there is a profound difference between the two dialectics, one that Kant briefly acknowledges, but does not give as much attention as it deserves.

In the First *Critique*, Kant takes great pains to expose the errors that may arise from theoretical reason's quest for the unconditioned condition. It generates various illusions, *focii imaginarii* (A644/B672), that on the one hand can help direct our intellectual practices, but on the other hand lead us into error. The latter can be avoided so long as these *focii imaginarii* are used merely regulatively, such as by facilitating scientific inquiry through their setting out various desiderata. However, Kant claims that reason's quest for the unconditioned condition leads us to latch on to what should be merely regulative principles and treat them instead as transcendentally real principles or entities.

Hence, the primary aim of the First *Critique*'s Dialectic is to prevent our slide from illusion into error. It begins by identifying the cause of this slide, illustrates what philosophy has become as a result, and thereby seeks to disabuse us of such enduring errors. From its opening paragraphs, it seems at first as if the Second *Critique*'s Dialectic is going to offer us a similar exposé of reason in its practical employment. It begins by comparing its mission with its predecessor, stating that "reason in its practical use is no better off. That is, as pure practical reason, it likewise seeks the unconditioned for the practically conditioned (which rests on inclinations and natural needs)" (CPrR: 5:108). Yet as we move forward, we discover that the fate of practical reason's quest for the unconditioned condition is quite different from what Kant presents in the Dialectic of the First *Critique*. Shortly after the above quote, Kant identifies the Highest Good as the object that fulfils pure practical reason's quest; but rather than declaring it to be an illusion and cautioning us against affirming it, he instead launches into a defense of it and of the Postulates necessary for its realization.

As discussed in the previous section, Kant had a reason for affirming the Highest Good in the Canon of the First *Critique*. At the cusp of the Critical Period, he still needed some affective principle through which "the majestic ideas of morality" could become "incentives for resolve and realization" (A813/B841). He thus turned to the hope for happiness offered by the Highest Good as the motivational ground for moral action. But after the developments first seen in the *Groundwork*, this strategy could no longer be used. We are now past Kant's introduction of the possibility of acting from duty, and thus the Highest Good cannot be justified as it was in the First *Critique*. This is something that Kant does seem to recognize, as he states that "though the highest good may be the whole *object* of pure practical reason, that is, of a pure will, it is not on that account to be taken as its *determining ground*" (CPrR:5:109).

This quote further illustrates the shift in how he employs the Highest Good, rejecting its earlier motivational role and repositioning it as, rather, an architectonic principle for practical reason. It is now cast as the "whole object" or "unconditioned totality of the object of pure practical reason" (CPrR: 5:108). Put succinctly, this object functions as the unconditioned condition for pure practical reason. It is the object that the faculty seeks to bring its principles into systematic unity. But this should be an arresting claim for astute readers, for in it we see a very different attitude towards the quest for the unconditioned in theoretical versus practical reason. We are taught in the Dialectic of the First *Critique* that we should guard against such objects and regard them as illusions cast by the pathologies of reason. Yet in the Second *Critique*'s Dialectic, Kant celebrates practical reason's quest for an object that can serve as its unconditioned condition.

It would be outright bromidic to explain this difference simply as a result of the former's Dialectic having to do with theoretical reason, while the latter concerns practical reason. Merely appealing to these two modalities or applications of reason does not explain why the latter is justified in its pursuit and adoption of what is taken as illusion and error in the former. Hence, we need to ask why we are justified in affirming the unconditioned condition of practical but not theoretical reason. I take this to be a pivotal demand for the Second *Critique*'s Dialectic: why are we here justified in affirming the (practical) unconditioned condition rather than merely relegating it to an illusory ideal?

There must be some warrant that permits our assent, though one that has its basis in the needs of practical reason, since the assent is a matter of faith rather than knowledge or opinion. Of course, it would be just as bromidic to settle the issue by stating that as faith, rather than knowledge or opinion, it is perfectly fine to just affirm it. If faith were so open, so blind, then presumably we could also affirm the various illusions of theoretical reason as well. So, although the distinction between theoretical and practical reason is germane to the question of what warrants our assent to the Highest Good, a more precise account of how it is germane is still needed. The Second *Critique* must therefore provide some argument, rooted in the needs of practical reason, in order to explain why in its Dialectic, as opposed to that of the First *Critique*, we may accept its pursuit of the unconditioned condition and the object it identifies with this condition as meriting legitimate, intersubjectively valid assent.

As we have discussed, the First *Critique*'s argument for the Highest Good is rooted in our need to find some motivation to act morally. But this is not how Kant argues for the Highest Good in the Second *Critique*. It is not about our human motivational needs. It is rather, so Kant at least for the moment argues, that the authority of the moral law itself depends upon the Highest Good:

> Now, since the promotion of the highest good, which contains this connection [between morality and happiness] in its concept, is an a priori necessary object of our will and inseparably bound up with the moral law, the impossibility of the first must also prove the falsity of the second. If, therefore, the highest good is impossible in accordance with practical rules, then the moral law, which commands us to promote it, must be fantastic and directed to empty imaginary ends and must therefore in itself be false.
>
> (CPrR: 5:114)

The above quotation captures the core argument for the Highest Good in the Second *Critique*. It presents the elusive warrant that justifies our assent to the doctrine and, thereby, also what justifies the Dialectic of Pure Practical Reason's having a more positive outcome than its theoretical counterpart. Regrettably, however, the argument, I believe, contains a significant flaw as it only achieves its goal(s) by way of conflating HG_i and HG_d.

The secondary literature has helped to clarify the two aspects of Kant's doctrine of the Highest Good, and there are passages where Kant as well provides relatively clear characterizations of the two. But in other passages he also conflates them. We can see two such examples in the following: "Now it was a duty for us to promote the highest good; hence there is in us not merely the warrant but also the necessity, as a need connected with duty, to presuppose the possibility of this highest good" (CPrR: 5:125); "a need *of pure practical* reason is based on a *duty*, that of making something (the highest good) the object of my will ... thus I must suppose its possibility and so too the conditions for this, namely God, freedom, and immortality" (CPrR: 5:142).

The problem here is that time and again Kant claims that because we have a duty to promote the Highest Good, we must affirm that the ideal of the Highest Good can (or will) obtain. His reasoning for this seems to be based upon the logic of *ought implies can*, but, unfortunately, he misuses the axiom here, as his argument slides from the *ought* of HG_d to the *can* of HG_i. To fully see how this mistake unfolds, let us briefly revisit some issues related to HG_d. We have seen that since the distributive justice required by HG_i is outside of our power (and thus God is posited), HG_d makes us responsible for populating HG_i by becoming worthy of the happiness that it offers. Although our pursuit of HG_d is thereby linked to the realization of HG_i, the link is to its becoming populated by worthy agents rather than the implementation of PPD. As such, the *can* of HG_d pertains specifically to our becoming worthy of happiness rather than the full achievement of HG_i. The *ought* of HG_d therefore does not require the *can* of HG_i. If what HG_d requires of us is an imperfect duty to pursue moral improvement, then its *can* merely requires that we can make some progress in its pursuit.

In fact, we would be subject to the same moral expectations built into HG_d even if it were not denominated as such. We would still be obligated to improve ourselves morally, even if there were no reward for doing so. Yet when Kant turns to the *ought* of HG_d, he makes it a condition of the *ought* that HG_i *can* obtain. This simply does not follow. If it did, and HG_i were not otherwise possible, then Kant would be right that the logic of *ought implies can* would be in jeopardy as would the normative character of pure practical reason. Thus, although the Second *Critique* argues for HG_i and its Postulates through an appeal to what HG_d requires of us, neither our promotion of moral improvement nor even our becoming fully worthy of happiness entails the possibility or realization of HG_i. As expressed above, the *ought* of HG_d does not imply the *can* of HG_i. The former, let us grant, is commanded by the moral law. However, as its possibility does not rest on HG_i, so likewise the authority of the moral law is also severable from the question of whether or not HG_i can or will obtain.

So, even though the Second *Critique*'s Dialectic has become the *locus classicus* for discussions of the Highest Good, this is an epithet that, in my view, is more an artifact of the attention it has received than either its intrinsic merits or its status in relation to Kant's considered view. Once we disentangle HG_d and HG_i, we are left with HG_i as a *focus imaginarius*. It is an ideal that captures the harmonious and lawful connection between morality and happiness, but its actuality, or our need to have faith that it is so, has not been established. Kant has thus failed to provide an argument that moves us beyond the corresponding situation in the Dialectic of the First *Critique*. Of course, we need not claim that HG_i or its Postulates are matters of *knowledge*, but Kant has not even been able to show us that it is a justified object of faith or hope. That justification is supposed to have its foundation in a need of practical reason, but as we have seen, Kant has not been able to show that this need actually exists. The *ought* of HG_d does not depend on the *can* of HG_i.

THE HIGHEST GOOD IN THE *CRITIQUE OF JUDGMENT*

The Second *Critique* goes so far as to assert that the moral law would be "directed to imaginary ends," "fantastic," and "false" if HG_i turns out not to be possible. It thus treats the doctrine of the Highest Good as built into the justificatory structure of pure practical reason. We do not, however, find such claims in the Third *Critique*. In fact, in at least two passages, Kant explicitly renounces the Second *Critique*'s contention that the authority of the moral law depends upon the Highest Good. The first of these passages is as follows:

> This proof ... is not meant to say that it is just as necessary to assume the existence of God as it is to acknowledge the validity of the moral law, hence that whoever cannot convince himself of the former can judge himself to be free from the obligation of the latter. No! ... Every rational being would still have to recognize himself as forever strictly

> bound to the precepts of morals; for its laws are formal and com-
> mand unconditionally without regard to ends.
>
> (CJ: 5:451)

Then, a few paragraphs later, he adds that even if one were to become persuaded that there is no God and that there will not be an ultimate distribution of rewards and punishments, it would be a mistake "on that account ... to hold the laws of duty to be merely imaginary, invalid, and nonobligatory" (CJ: 5:451).

The Third *Critique* does perpetuate the distinction between the Highest Good as an ideal state of affairs and as a duty "to strive after" (CJ: 5:450). It also continues to endorse the Postulates of God and Immortality as necessary for the realization of the former. But in the place of the Second *Critique*'s convoluted and (in my view) flawed argument, Kant returns in this text to an argument more akin to the *Critique of Pure Reason*'s far simpler appeal to our motivational needs. As in the First *Critique*, so in the Third as well, he argues that our motivation to follow the moral law depends upon the happiness that it promises to those who are worthy of it. But in its revised form, the motivation that the Highest Good offers is merely a buttress that helps maintain our commitment to morality.

Kant certainly does not give up on the motivating power of the moral law in the *Critique of Judgment*. His new argument for the Highest Good does not retreat back to his earlier model of moral agency. We are still able to act from duty, but with the qualification that our commitment to do so is vulnerable to impeding psychological states. To illustrate this point, Kant offers his Parable of the Righteous Atheist.

This Parable describes someone who "actively honors" the moral law and pursues "the good to which that holy law directs all his powers," who as an Atheist is also "firmly convinced that there is no God ... [and] there is also no future life" (CJ: 5:452). So long as he is sheltered from "all the evils of poverty, illness, and untimely death" (CJ: 5:452), the Righteous Atheist will have the fortitude to remain committed to morality. But exposure to them, Kant contends, will chip away at his moral resolve. He will look at his best moral efforts and see them swamped by the "purposeless chaos of matter." Life will come to seem futile as all living beings, both animal and human, both virtuous and vicious, will ultimately suffer the same fate with "one wide grave" engulfing all (CJ: 5:452). As a result, the Atheist will, so Kant contends, ultimately succumb to despair and lose his commitment to morality.

The Theist, however, will, according to Kant, have greater resilience. Armed with the hope of an afterlife through which justice will finally be meted out, the believer can see moral effort as ultimately rewarded rather than swamped by the "purposeless chaos of matter." This will, accordingly, offer sufficient motivational support so that the Theist can sustain his moral resolve in the face of all the suffering and injustice in this life. Thus, we find Kant returning in the Third *Critique* to a motivational justification for the Highest Good. No longer is the hope for happiness necessary to transform "the majestic ideas of morality" into "incentives for resolve and realization," but it nevertheless offers an invaluable "motivational supplement."[25]

This is most definitely a far less recondite argument for the Highest Good in comparison to what is presented in the Second *Critique*. One might further speculate that in the Parable, Kant was retreating not only from some of the bolder elements of his prior argument but also from its convolutions. Unlike its failed attempt to justify our belief in the Highest Good on the basis of its relationship to the moral law, the argument here retreats to the simplicity of the First *Critique*'s appeal to our moral motivation, adapting it to the theory of motivation held from the *Groundwork* onwards. This retreat, however, comes at some cost.

Although Kant does not withdraw his view that pure practical reason can itself move us to action, he does qualify its motivational force and presents us as morally frail, lacking adequate fortitude to rebuff the psychological threats arising from the "purposeless chaos of matter." Despite his claim that we (generally) have sufficient self-control to not give in to our desires, it does appear that fear and despair seem now able to condition our autonomy; and when they take hold, they must be fought back with a different affective motivation, namely hope. Interestingly, this gives the Highest Good a role that some will consider quite appropriate. The *Groundwork* and Second *Critique*'s account of our agency may ascribe to us greater continence, but in the Third *Critique*'s turn to hope as the response to despair, we see here a moment where Kant intimates a need for religion, one that is drawn from an inward, subjective struggle over the meaningfulness of our existence.

Yet this need still does not go deep enough. If the hope for the Highest Good only becomes important when the injustices of life threaten to psychologically overwhelm us, it relegates the doctrine to the margins of his moral theory. We can, for the most part, get along well enough without it, and, further, as there are those who are either more resilient in temperament or sheltered from all the injustices of the world, fortunate enough to slide through life without having encountered all "the evils of poverty, illness, and untimely death," the significance of the Highest Good becomes all too contingent upon individual circumstances.

Ironically, then, the First *Critique*'s claim that moral motivation in general requires the Highest Good gives to this doctrine a far more central role than what we have just seen. If it is, instead, just a supplement, something to buttress our moral resolve if and when it is needed, it is set farther out, at the margins of his practical philosophy. However, as we shall soon see, the pendulum will swing back again, for in *Religion* Kant once again characterizes the Highest Good as a deeply rooted need of practical reason, one that is neither marginal nor contingent. He there presents yet another argument for the doctrine, one that neither returns to the motivational account of the First *Critique* nor to the architectonic argument of the Second. He instead strikes a remarkable compromise between the positions of the Second and Third *Critique*s, drawing from the former a commitment to the Highest Good having a fundamental importance, while drawing from the latter an appeal to the particular needs of our all-too-human agency.

NOTES

1 See Wolterstorff 1998. I will return to his reading of the history of philosophical theology since Kant in Chapter 7.

2 I take this to be an increasingly popular view among Anglophone Kantians. See Introduction, n. 18. I will also return to it in Chapter 7.

3 Citations to Luther will be to the *Weimer Ausgabe*. Its volumes are divided into four sections and so citations will follow the format: section. volume. page.

4 In addition to this view being expressed by Kant's early critics, see Rescher 1999.

5 Helpful texts that develop the methodological interpretation include, of course, the works of Henry Allison. See also Abela 2002 as well as another Guidebook in this series: Gardner 1999.

6 That we can think about things-in-themselves, including religious matters, is a vitally important issue for anyone dealing with Kant's philosophy of religion. Too often this point has been lost or muddied. See Wolterstorff 1998 and Byrne 2007. This will be discussed more fully in Chapter 7, as the first of three concluding questions related to Kant's overall philosophy of religion.

7 The conviction/persuasion distinction also applies to aesthetic judgment. But in its case, we would not have objective validity, but subjective-universal validity. See Kant's discussion of the young poet at CJ: 5:282. Note that Guyer/Matthews mistranslates *Überredung* as "conviction" in a crucial sentence within this discussion. That the poet is erroneously holding his work to be beautiful due to his personal bias should make it evident that the German *Überredung* is what Kant did intend and so it should have been translated as "persuasion."

8 Also in the Blomberg Logic: we can "have a grounded opinion for something, when the data that one now has for the thing outweigh the grounds for the opposite" (BL: 24:219). See also, Refl: 16:263, 24:638; VL: 24:825, 24:881, etc. Kant frequently characterizes probability in terms of the weighing of grounds and commonly equates opinion and probability. For example: "someone who adheres to an opinion holds the opinion to be something probable" (VL: 24:825; DL: 24:742, etc.). In the published corpus, see A770/B798, A775/B803, CJ: 5:463, 5:465ff – all of which associate opinion with degrees of probability. For a more detailed discussion of the topic, see my forthcoming Pasternack 2014.

9 Note that Kant sometimes refers to faith (or its objects) as having an objective character, including in the footnote to the *Critique of Practical Reason* that was just cited (CPrR: 5:143n). He there characterizes the

objects of faith as having objective reality. By contrast, in the *Critique of Judgment*, he seems to shy away from this (CJ: 5:450n). In Chapter 4, I discuss how to understand "objective reality" in the context of faith.

10 A separate but related issue is that Kant's appeal to morality is not merely relevant to the proper nature of religious belief; he further argues that it is only through morality that we can form a fully determinate conception of God. See A628/B656 and A817/B845.

11 Although faith is a form of conviction and Kant generally associates conviction with communicability, in Refl: 2489 (16:390), Kant writes, "Glauben giebt eine Überzeugung, die nicht communicabel ist. (wegen der subiectiven Gründe)." (Faith yields a conviction that is not communicable (because of its subjective ground).) This passage also is redacted by Jäsche at 9:70, but Refl: 2489 is presumably the original form. This leads me to view faith as an exception to Kant's typical correlation between conviction and communicability. (That faith is identified as a form of conviction: A829/B857; CJ: 5:463, 5:472, 5:475, 6:103; WO: 8:142; Refl: 2450, 2454, 2489; JL: 9:72, 24:148–49, 28:1082, etc.) However, as we shall discuss, in *Religion*, Kant emphasizes that Pure Rational Faith, as the basis for a universal church, is communicable. We shall return to this tension in Chapter 5. See also my discussion of the relationship between faith and communication in Pasternack 2011.

12 See Silber 1959, Insole 2008, Wike and Showler 2010.

13 Similar characterizations appear throughout this section of the Canon: "happiness proportionally combined with morality" (A809/B837), " ... insofar as it [happiness] stands in exact relation with morality" (A810/B838), etc.

14 As an empirical thesis, we see that the laws of nature do not follow the laws of justice. In addition, Kant's earlier analysis of causality on a priori grounds excludes norms from nature: "In nature the understanding can cognize only *what exists*, or has been, or will be. It is impossible that something in it *ought to be* other than what, in all these time-relations, it in fact is ... . We cannot ask at all what ought to happen in nature, any more than we can ask what properties a circle ought to have" (A547/B575). Of course, the *Critique of Judgment* turns to the question of a final end of nature, but even there the judgment, as reflective, is a projection on our part onto nature. Moreover, there too we do not expect justice to be realized in nature and thus turn to a future life (CJ: 5:460, 5:469, 5:471n, etc.).

15 See also, CPrR: 5:113, 5:124, 5:129, etc. Although the Highest Good continues to involve reward and punishment in the Third *Critique*, there is no passage sufficiently short to quote on this point. However, the association between the Highest Good and reward/punishment is present. This can be seen for instance as the alternative to the "righteous atheist," for it is only through the expectation that happiness will align with moral worth that, so Kant argues at CJ: 5:452, we can remain committed to morality. This alignment is not something we can achieve on our own – it "is not congruent with the theoretical concept of the physical possibility" (CJ: 5:450) and so we posit God and immortality for its sake. In addition to the discussion from 5:450–55:453, see 5:469–5:470, 5:473–75:474 and the Third *Critique*'s closing "General Remark on Teleology" (5:475–84).

16 Lara Denis, for example, argues that Kant's conception of happiness is so tied to the body that the Highest Good must be understood as this-worldly. But there are various alternatives. One is to focus on the non-physical happiness or contentment that Kant periodically discusses and especially associates with one who has committed himself to morality (see 6:75n as well as CPrR: 5:117 and MM: 6:406). Alternately, a corporeal afterlife may be posited. While this might seem odd to some, the idea of the resurrection of the dead and a "glorified" form of the body has a long tradition in Christianity. Moreover, it was part of the Pietism of Kant's day and held by Franz Albert Schulz, the family pastor of Kant's youth and the director of the *Collegium Fridericianum*. On this alternative view, see Surprenant 2008 and Bunch 2010.

17 The English text incorrectly translates *überredete* as "convinced." As briefly discussed above (n. 7), Kant distinguishes between *Überredung* and *Überzeugung*. However, this technical distinction is overlooked in some of the Cambridge translations, particularly in its translation of the Third *Critique*.

18 This is not, by the way, the only reference to immortality in the *Critique of Judgment*. Sections 89, 90, and 91 contain dozens of affirmative comments about it. For example, at CJ: 5:460, Kant refers to the "hope for a future life," and at 5:469, during an important discussion of the Highest Good, he writes that "the existence of God and the immortality of the soul, are matters of faith, and are indeed the only ones among all objects that can be so designated."

19 I am here emphasizing our duty as individuals to morally improve ourselves. As we will discuss in Chapters 5 and 7, there is also a related corporate duty, a duty "not of human beings toward human beings but of the human race toward itself" (6:97).

20 In contrast to this more polemical discussion of virtue, other texts present virtue as more than just continence (or other psychological modifications). We see in both the Second *Critique* and (sometimes) in the *Metaphysics of Morals* uses of "virtue" that include moral motivation (cf. 5:110 and 6:407, respectively). Hence, labels aside, *Religion*'s polemic against virtue is a polemic against various deficient models of moral worthiness including: (a) the perfectionism of self-control and an idealized alignment of one's inclinations with the moral law; and (b) the mere observance of duty through habits and other psychological traits whereby correct action is performed, but ultimately still for the sake of one's happiness. We may interpret Kant's use of "virtue" to be part of *Religion*'s broader polemic against the institutions that advance the mere outer form of religion while rejecting or ignoring its inner value. We will return to this issue in Chapter 4.

21 This quote comes from a set of lecture notes whose author is unknown. They carry a date of February 11th, 1782, which is presumed to refer to the date that the copying of the notes from a prior source was completed, rather than the date of their original composition.

22 Though Paul Guyer has claimed "the highest good is not any part of a doctrine of punishment or retribution" and rejects "the supposition frequently made that Kant's doctrine of the highest good rests on a principle of proportionality" (Guyer 2005: 289n), we can see from the above quotations that at least in the Canon of the First *Critique*, the Highest Good is identified with PPD. Whatever else it is, it includes a doctrine of punishment and retribution and rests upon the hope for happiness.

David Sussman suggests that we may see the Canon's argument for the Highest Good in two different ways. One, as we have discussed, pertains to the gap between the purity of the moral law and a Humean account of our will. There are various beliefs that must be added in order to direct our desire for happiness to morality. His other suggestion follows a more Hobbesian picture where moral laws must have a lawgiver and be promulgated in relation to promises and threats. See Sussman 2001: 120–27. On such an appeal to a lawgiver, see also Kain 2005.

23 That the world cannot secure PPD may be interpreted as either an empirical claim built upon what we regard as the unjust suffering of the morally good and the perverse successes of the wicked or something more, perhaps a transcendental claim tied to the status of natural causation as morally indifferent. The former is presumably too weak as empirical claims are evaluated probabilistically and are subject to error. The Practical Postulates, by contrast, are matters of faith, and faith is supposed to be certain (see A829/B857). So it seems more appropriate to take Kant's rejection of PPD in this world as a transcendental claim. This appears to be the position expressed in the Solution to the Third Antinomy:

> The *ought* expresses a species of necessity and a connection with grounds which does not occur anywhere else in the whole of nature. In nature the understanding can cognize only *what exists*, or has been, or will be. It is impossible that something in it *ought to be* other than what, in all these time-relations, it in fact is; indeed, the *ought*, if one has merely the course of nature before one's eyes, has no significance whatever.
>
> (A547/B575)

It is not merely that we lack empirical warrants to attribute to the mechanisms of nature some process which could allocate happiness and suffering according to morality. Rather, physical laws are not adapted to the requirements of PPD. Moreover, not even under the teleological principles advanced in the *Critique of Judgment* could we make such claims: "it is impossible for us to represent these two requirements [morality and happiness] of the final end that is set for us by the moral law as both connected by merely natural causes" (CJ: 5:450).

24 Some wish to distinguish between the status of the Postulate of Freedom versus the Postulates of God and Immortality. We can see here one reason why. Freedom *is* a necessary condition for the bindingness of morality. We may only believe in it by virtue of our belief in the bindingness of morality, but if bindingness is a fact, so must freedom be. Whereas the other Postulates have a more subjective role, at least insofar as the Highest Good is understood as an object of hope for us rather than as a condition for morality itself (as Kant claims in the

Second *Critique*). Whether or not those who deserve happiness are actually rewarded, and whether or not there is a God and an afterlife, what matters here in the Canon is that such beliefs motivate us to follow morality. At least in the Canon, the principles of morality would still be "majestic" whether or not there actually is a God and immortality – what is of greatest importance is that we believe in the Postulates so that we are motivated to be moral. See Kain 2005.

A separate issue worthy of examination concerns Kant's appeal to God and immortality as the sole means through which HG_i is possible. Some have argued that PPD could just as well be satisfied through Eastern doctrines that involve karma and reincarnation. See for example Shade 1995.

25 See Denis 2005. A similar position can be found in Insole 2008.

2

RELIGION'S TWO PREFACES AND
THE MORAL FOUNDATIONS OF
PURE RATIONAL FAITH

The prefaces to books are often skipped or, if read, are often done so out of politeness to the author. They typically contain the author's acknowledgments, sometimes a few brief auto-biographical notes, or anecdotes related to the book's development. The contents of Kant's prefaces, however, are of a completely different order. They are not to be skipped, not to be skimmed, for they will often contain claims or arguments that are of eminent value to their ensuing project.

We can find numerous instances of such prefaces throughout the Kantian corpus. For example, it is in the Second Preface to the *Critique of Pure Reason* that we find Kant's infamous allusion to the Copernican Revolution (Bxvi), as well as his statement: "I had to deny knowledge [*Wissen*] in order to make room for faith [*Glaube*]" (Bxxx). Similarly, in the *Groundwork*'s Preface, Kant articulates some important presuppositions to his deontology as well as the telling statement that he wants to work out once and for all "a pure moral philosophy, completely cleansed of everything that may be only empirical and that belongs to anthropology" (GR: 4:389). In the Preface to the *Critique of Practical Reason*, Kant explains at length how the Postulate of Freedom differs from the Postulates of God and Immortality: the former is a condition of the moral law itself, whereas the latter two "are not conditions of the moral law but only conditions of the necessary object [i.e., the highest good] of a will determined by this law" (CPrR: 5:4). And in the Preface to his *Anthropology*, Kant enumerates various impediments to the development of any empirical science of human nature: 1) we tend to dissemble when we are aware of being studied; 2) since it is difficult to observe one's own emotional states while engulfed in them, self-reflection tends to lack the sort of clinical or detached perspective that should be maintained in the human sciences; and 3) it is difficult to separate the "second natures" of habit and custom from the more raw features of human nature that lie behind them (AN: 7:121).

Religion's two prefaces also fall within this category, as they both contain much of great importance to the main body of the text. We find in the First Preface, for example, a new argument for the Highest Good as well as a general defense of the philosopher's right to explore theological issues. And in the Second Preface, which is not even three pages long, Kant presents two illuminating metaphors. The first is meant to elucidate *Religion*'s title, using the image of two spheres, one set within the boundaries of the other. The second describes the project of *Religion* as an "experiment," one that seeks to determine the scope of overlap between the Pure Rational System of Religion and the doctrines of Historical Faith.[1]

Hence, rather than moving directly into the main body of *Religion*, we will begin with a chapter devoted to its two prefaces, starting with the First Preface's argument for the Highest Good; and so we will be returning to where we left the preceding chapter, completing its study of how the argument for the Highest Good develops through the Critical Period. We will then turn to the other main issue of the First Preface, namely, where the boundary lies between philosophical and biblical theology. Lastly, we will move on to the Second Preface, and will discuss its characterization of the two spheres of religion as well as its depiction of *Religion* as an experiment whose purpose is to determine the relationship between these spheres.

RELIGION'S FIRST PREFACE

THEOLOGICAL ETHICS VERSUS MORAL THEOLOGY (6:3–4)

The First Preface to *Religion* develops by way of an intriguing dialectic between two seemingly contradictory claims. In the opening paragraph, Kant states that "morality in no way needs religion" (6:3); yet the third paragraph begins with "[m]orality thus inevitably leads to religion" (6:6). The tension between these two claims is obvious and what lies between them is yet one more argument for the Highest Good. We shall examine this argument shortly, but before we do, let us first consider the meaning of Kant's initial claim that "morality in no way needs religion."

In other texts, Kant distinguishes between "theological ethics" and "moral theology." The former pertains to the view that there cannot be laws without a lawgiver, and so the authority of morality depends upon its having its source in God. The latter, by contrast, reflects "a conviction of the existence of a highest being which grounds itself on moral laws" (A632/B660). The former position is one that Kant repeatedly rejects, as he holds that the authority of morality arises from pure practical reason itself. Our duties are derived rationally and our moral autonomy depends upon their originating in one's own will rather than Divine authority. We are bound to morality because we bind ourselves to it, as opposed to being subject to a commanding authority outside of ourselves.

This does not, however, preclude our representing morality as also willed by God, for He too, as a rational being, carries the law within Himself. But God's moral authority should not be separated from the authority that morality has as a matter of rationality itself. That is, morality neither needs God to justify its principles nor to impose them upon us. With the possible caveat of the Third *Critique*'s turn to the "motivational supplement" offered by the Highest Good, Kant presents morality as having no need "of the idea of another being above" or "of an incentive other than the law itself" (6:3).[2] Nevertheless, Kantian theology is deeply intertwined with morality, for as previously discussed, it is through morality that we are able to form a determinate conception of God. As stated in the *Critique of Pure Reason*, "only pure reason, although only in its practical use, always has the merit of connecting with our highest interest a cognition that mere speculation can only imagine but never make valid" (A818/B846). Likewise, in the Third *Critique*, Kant writes: "the cognition of our duty and the final end which is therein imposed upon us by reason is what could first produce the determinate concept of God" (CJ: 5:481).

So, in the above way, we gain a moral theology, not as a Divine command theory, but rather in the sense that morality guides our theological, and more broadly, our religious conceptions.[3] It is only through morality that we can justify or produce (depending upon which passage one heeds) the particular conception of God "that we now hold to be correct" (A818/B846). We may further add that since:

> it was these laws alone whose inner practical necessity led us to the presupposition of a self-sufficient cause or a wise world-regent ... we cannot in turn regard these as contingent and derived from a mere will, especially from a will of which we would have had no concept at all had we not formed it in accordance with those laws.
>
> (A818/B846–A819/B847)

In other words, there is a priority to morality over religion such that the former not only provides us with the conceptual resources for the latter,[4] but also, as we discussed in the preceding chapter, it is only through moral faith that we can legitimately affirm God's existence.

The legitimacy of this advance from morality to religion rests upon the Highest Good – or put differently, the whole of Kant's moral theology is motivated by this doctrine. Although he continually revises his argument for the Highest Good, it remains, nevertheless, the fulcrum by which we pivot from morality to religion. Yet so long as Kant lacks a persuasive argument for the Highest Good, the legitimacy of this shift, and thus all that falls within the scope of his Pure Rational System of Religion, remains in question. Fortunately, though, Kant obliges, offering yet one more, a fourth, argument for the doctrine.

THE HIGHEST GOOD IN *RELIGION'S* PREFACE (6:4–6)

Religion contains Kant's most comprehensive presentation of his positive philosophy of religion. It is thus appropriate that it begins with a defense of the Highest Good, the doctrine that lies at its foundation. Although the argument for the Highest Good here bears some resemblance to those found in earlier texts, it is still quite distinct from them. For example, it reaffirms the First and Third *Critiques'* focus on our human limitations and needs, but it does not justify our commitment to the Highest Good by way of our need for either a primary or supplementary moral motivator. It also follows the Second *Critique's* claim that the Highest Good is centrally important to our practical lives, rather than the Third *Critique's* more contingent and marginal place-ment of it. However, unlike the Second *Critique*, it does not conceive of its centrality in terms of the faculty of pure practical reason's architectonic, abstracted from our human limitations. Thus, we may see this argument as something of a hybrid, one that came about through Kant's having reflected upon the various strengths and weaknesses of his previous arguments.

The First Preface transitions to this new argument for the Highest Good after reiterating the claim that morality does not need religion. But this time, Kant expresses the claim more spe-cifically in relation to HG_i: "on its own behalf, morality does not need the representation of an end" (6:4). Unlike the argument of the Second *Critique*, where he did claim that the authority of the moral law depends upon the Highest Good, he here rather states that "the law that contains the formal condition of the use of freedom in general suffices to it" (6:5). Yet, he continues, although the authority of the moral law does not demand the representation of an end, it does not follow that *we* are indifferent to the *consequences* of our actions. Although it is well established that, for Kant, consequences cannot serve as the basis for whether or not an action is morally right or wrong, this does not mean that human beings are disinterested in them, that consequences have no practical relevance to us.

For example, a conscientious moral agent who wills to be charitable will take an interest in whether or not his donated time or money actually results in the betterment of people's lives. He may choose to do something charitable as it is his duty to do so. But he will also want to pick his charity based upon the likelihood that his contributions will make a difference. Thus, despite how it is often represented, Kantian morality is not limited to the testing of maxims and the observance of duty. Since our duties pertain to states of affairs in the world, there are still further practical rational considerations relevant to the causal relationship between the actions we take and the ends that are intended by those actions.

These considerations, Kant claims, are not just addenda for our moral lives. Rather, they are crucial for human rationality. Although practical success does not determine moral worth, we are nevertheless still rationally committed to some consequentialist considerations. They flow out of our moral interest, such as we can see in the case of charitable action. They also, as we will see once we hit the core of *Religion*'s argument for the Highest Good, concern as well the formal conditions for determining the will to action. That is, insofar as actions are means towards some end, in willing the action, we also will it in relation to some end. In the case of charity, when we will the duty to be charitable, we are willing an end having to do with the improvement of people's lives. Absent such an association between the means of action and its ends, we would, Kant suggests, not will at all. As he puts the point: "in the absence of all reference to an end no determination of the will can take place in human beings at all" (6:4). This is a crucial step in his new argument for the Highest Good, and so let us take a moment to consider it more fully.

The hypothetical imperative involves the general principle of rational willing that to will an end, one ought to will the means towards that end. So, if I choose as an end that I will become more physically fit, there is a rational constraint to which I have subjected myself having to do with the adoption of appropriate means. The general form of the imperative would be violated if I were to will to become more fit yet not also commit to some appropriate means (jogging, cycling, etc.). This is a well-known and generally accepted principle of rational willing: one who wills an end is rationally required to will means towards that end (see Hill 1973). But to be clear, this is a constraint having to do with our beliefs or judgments rather than with the physical world. The means that what one wills may actually have no causal connection with the end, for the agent may have false beliefs about the salient causal laws. But the rationality of his commitment to some end demands a commitment to means that at least are thought to be causally efficacious.

I would like to suggest that this principle of practical judgment is actually bi-directional: just as to commit to an end demands that one commits to actions that are at least believed to be genuine means towards that end, so likewise, for one's will to be determined to some action, one's actions must at least be believed to be means towards some end that one has chosen. So, to will an action – which is a means – requires that one has also committed to some end. The former is highlighted in the hypothetical imperative, but the latter is also a fundamental principle of willing. The latter may also be taken as analytic, if actions are construed in the way I have presented them.

Consider, for example, the maxim *whenever I run out of food at home, I will go to the grocery store to acquire more food*. If I take the action of going to the grocery store (the means), I do so because of my belief that they will have food for me to purchase, that I am able to purchase it, and that I can get the food home and so will ultimately be able to eat it. If I thought that my heading to the store would not bring this about more or less in the way described above, I could not rationally adopt the maxim. In other words, the determination of the will through which the action is taken depends in part upon that action being understood as causally relevant to an end that I have adopted. We may see this as the point underlying Kant's claim that "in the absence of all reference to an end no determination of the will can take place in human beings at all" (6:4), and it may be taken as the first major step in *Religion*'s new argument for the Highest Good.

All actions that we take, be they matters of duty or just for the sake of more mundane self-interested ends, depend upon the will being determined through reference to one or another end; and so presumably if we thought some action to be causally unrelated to any end, it would not be one that we would ever will. Accordingly, actions related to going to the grocery store depend upon our conceiving of them as efficacious towards the end of acquiring and ultimately eating some food. Analogously, actions having to do with the furthering of one's talents would not be taken without the belief that they are genuinely conducive towards one's self-development. So, akin to the concerns that Kant raised in the Third *Critique*'s Parable of the Righteous Atheist, if one saw one's other-regarding moral actions as swamped by the "purposeless chaos of matter" such that they no longer could stand up as believable means towards the betterment of people's lives, then a condition would not be met for the determination of the will.

This last point is not intended to return us to a thesis about our affective motivational needs. Kant's argument here is not, as it was in the Third *Critique*, to justify our hope for the Highest Good in order that it may help to shore up our commitment to morality. Although that may remain a motivational consequence of having such a hope, the point made here is that we must understand what we do, even in morality, as being efficacious, else a condition through which the will is determined to action would be lacking. Charitable action, for example, would be pointless if what is contributed never improves anyone's lives. Thus, if we were to see the world such that our moral efforts carried with them no benefits, we would lack not merely a motivational commitment (as depicted in the Third *Critique*), but more fundamentally a rational condition for action. We might even still intensely want to help realize the moral end of charity, but if we thought our actions futile, it would be irrational for us to act in pursuit of it.

The above point is particularly relevant to positive and imperfect duties, as their ends are separated from their means. Negative and at least some perfect duties, by contrast, have their ends satisfied immediately. That is, moral prohibitions against lying, stealing, killing, etc., are simply achieved by one's not acting in such a way. However, duties to improve one's talents, to morally improve oneself, to be charitable, etc., will not be pursued if one views the world in such a way that one's efforts are futile. Without a belief in causal efficacy, one cannot rationally commit to an action as *means*. We thus have, as Kant argues, a rational interest in the "whither" (6:4), the what-for, of our actions. It is an interest that is readily met in the case of perfect duties, but such is not the case with our positive duties, be they to aid in the betterment of others' lives or the development of one's practical talents or moral virtue.

This does not mean that consequences creep in to the determination of an action's moral worth (as Kant reiterates at 6:5), but outcomes are, nevertheless, important to us. As expressed in an important footnote: it is "one of the inescapable limitations of human beings and of their practical faculty of reason ... to be concerned in every action with its results" (6:7n). This interest is not a formal requirement pertinent to the authority of the moral law, but it is a formal requirement of a different sort: one that has to do with how we human beings come to determine our wills. Just as rational agency entails that whatever is chosen is chosen based upon some criterion, so what is chosen must also be understood in relation to an end. We do not choose to act without purpose, but rather always for the sake of some end. It is, following what was stated earlier, the flip side of the hypothetical imperative: for just as the willing of an end commits us to the willing of appropriate means, so in order to will ourselves into action, we must understand that action as an appropriate means to an end. Or more succinctly put: just as to will an end requires that we will its means, so to will a means requires that we also will an end.

The next major step in this argument for the Highest Good is as follows: "It cannot be a matter of indifference to morality, therefore, whether it does or does not fashion for itself the concept of an ultimate end of all things" (6:5). In the previous step, we see that action, understood as a means, must be taken as efficacious towards some end. As a general claim about practical reason, it holds for both morality and our routine prudential choosing. But Kant then adds that our human desire to make sense of action in relation to a *whither* carries us as well to want to have an ultimate *whither*, a way of seeing our actions as part of something grander, something that unifies our ends, including the disparate ends of morality and happiness. Accordingly, he asserts that we need a "special point of reference for the unification of all ends" (6:5).

We may take the implicit reasoning here to be that just as we cannot be indifferent to whether or not our actions actually promote ends, we cannot be indifferent to the relationships between those ends. Thus, it may be argued that since we are interested in the realization of ends, and at least one end (morality) dictates how it should stand in relation to another end (happiness), our more formal interest in ends moves us to a substantive rule about how our ends are ordered. In other words, if our wills become determined to action only through reference to an end, and the end of morality calls for "happiness proportioned to its observance" (6:5), then insofar as we commit ourselves to a moral action, we commit ourselves to its end, which involves, as we have seen through Kant's earlier discussions of the Highest Good as well, the principle of proportionate distribution (PPD).

This point may be further bolstered by understanding this call for a "special point of reference for the unification of all ends" (6:5) as necessary to resolve the axiological conflict between morality and happiness. If willing an individual act involves a reference to an end, and ends can come into conflict, then the determination of our wills even with regards to an individual act calls for the unification of ends. We may also take the idea here to be similar to the Second *Critique*'s interest in the unconditioned total object of pure practical reason. However, it is now presented in far less grandiose terms as just a "natural need," "with reference to the characteristic, natural to the human being" (6:7n). *We* want to bring our ends into relation because they would otherwise stand at odds with each other and frustrate our wills. Morality directs us one way, but happiness another. Fortunately, though, as the former makes claim to what order of happiness is appropriate (just as Aristotle challenges the self-sufficiency of the value of pleasure), it produces a representation of how these two ends *ought* to stand in relation.

The third and final step of this argument explains why the Highest Good is not merely the axiological principle that morality overrides happiness, but rather involves the faith and hope that a state of affairs, what I have been calling HG$_i$, will obtain. The first step holds that in the willing of an action, we are not indifferent to whether or not it promotes an end. The second step expresses our practical need to bring order to our ends, to have them stand in some appropriate relation to one another. The third and final step adds (or perhaps just makes explicit) that the agent must harbor various beliefs about the relationship between his actions and their *whither*. So, insofar as we adopt the Highest Good as our supreme end, we must (to have such a commitment) maintain beliefs about its realization. In other words, out of our natural need to see our actions as promoting realizable ends, in our commitment to moral action, we commit ourselves to the realizability of the Highest Good.

It is in this way that "[m]orality thus inevitably leads to religion" (6:6). Insofar as the will cannot be brought to determination without regarding one's action as taking place in a world where its ends are realizable, one further doxically commits oneself to the conditions for its realizability. Thus, insofar as we align our wills with the moral law, we must doxically commit to the Highest Good and to its Postulates.[5]

PHILOSOPHICAL VERSUS THEOLOGICAL TREATISES (6:7–11)

The Preface to the First Edition is divided into two parts. Its first half concerns what we have just discussed: a fourth argument for the Highest Good. Then in the second half of this preface, Kant turns to the relationship between biblical and philosophical theology. As we briefly discussed in the Introduction to this book, the Prussian Censorship Commission blocked the publication of the essay that came to be Part Two of *Religion*. This prompted Kant to seek its publication through a different path, one that resulted in his combining what were initially intended to be four separate essays into a single volume of philosophical theology. Even though he technically followed the law, he nevertheless used part of the First Preface to defend the path that he chose and, more broadly, to defend the philosopher's right to examine the Bible and Christian doctrine.

Kant's defense begins with a brief account of the responsibilities that may be assigned to biblical theologians. Their first responsibility is to care "for the welfare of souls" (6:8), and if they are also part of a university faculty, they will have a second responsibility, for as members of an institution of higher learning, they are broadly entrusted with the "cultivation and protection" (6:8) of all the sciences. This requires that they guard against the encroachments of one field into another. They must keep a check on all theologians (university affiliated or not), that they do not "venture ... into astronomy or other sciences such as the ancient history of the earth" (6:9); and, of course, they are also charged with the duty to guard their own domain against transgressions from other fields.

Kant then moves on to distinguish between biblical and philosophical theology. It is not the responsibility of the latter to care for the welfare of souls, and in fact, they ought to avoid doing so. What they write should be for a philosophical audience and should not be used to influence public doctrine or otherwise encroach upon ministerial duties. Philosophers stand "on the side of the sciences" (6:9) and should be recognized as having a level of autonomy so long as they stay "within the boundaries of mere reason" (6:9). Kant further buttresses this point through an allusion to the Catholic Church's censorship of Galileo. Each discipline must respect the purview of the other, and thus recognize their rights to examine issues according to their own methodologies.

Beyond such generalities, however, we fall into some interpretative difficulties. In Kant's attempt to differentiate biblical from philosophical theology, he actually presents three distinct standards.

The first and most clearly articulated concerns *how* the philosopher presents his views. Although he has "complete freedom to expand as far as its science reaches" (6:9), he ought to take care that his audience is limited to those with the appropriate powers of discernment, and so neither seek to influence public doctrine nor out of negligence instigate reform. As noted in the Introduction to this book, the essay that became Part One of *Religion* was approved by the Prussian censors on the grounds that it "is intended for, and can be enjoyed only by thinkers, researchers and scholars capable of fine distinctions."[6] Similarly, in his official response to the royal rescript of 1794, Kant defends *Religion* on the grounds that it "is not at all suitable for the public: to them it is an unintelligible, closed book, only a debate among scholars of the faculty, of which the people take no notice" (7:8).

Let us refer to this division between biblical and philosophical theology as the Audience Distinction (AD). It pertains to intent and mode of communication rather than any matters of content, particular doctrine, or techniques of biblical interpretation. Given the statement that the philosophical theologian has "complete freedom to expand as far as its science reaches," we may even think that AD is about all there is to the boundary. That is, the only way in which the philosopher can trespass into the domain proper to biblical theology is by intentional or unintentional influence on public doctrine or on how the clergy ministers to the laity.

Of course, things are not so simple. Kant also states that biblical theologians hold privilege "with respect to certain doctrines" (6:9). This may be read merely in terms of AD, since in *The Conflict of the Faculties*, Kant writes that accepted doctrines should not be "attacked publicly in the churches or even passed over dryshod" (CF: 7:42). But there are indications that he intended something more. Turning once again to his response to the royal rescript, Kant protests that *Religion* "make[s] no *appraisal* of Christianity" (CF: 7:8). Although the philosophical theologian may explore the proofs for God's existence, consider Divine Command Theory, and evaluate whatever falls within Natural Religion, there should be no appraisal of Revealed Religion.[7] Let us refer to this standard as the Natural Religion standard (NR), i.e., that the philosophical theologian must limit himself to the realm of Natural Religion and should keep "a respectful distance from" (6:191) anything of the latter that does not overlap with the former.

As reinforcement to NR, we can find an even more stringent standard for the philosophical theologian. Kant recognizes that there is considerable "anxiety about a transgression of boundaries by philosophical theology" (6:9) and so offers a suggestion to avoid all "mischief." He realizes that philosophical theologians "borrow" from biblical theology, as well as directly from the Bible, and so employs an analogy to help characterize what he considers to be an appropriate way in which the Bible may be used. His analogy is to how a "teacher of natural right" might use the Roman Codex. The latter contains "many a classical expression and formula" (6:10) and may even use these "not quite in the same sense in which, according to the interpreters of the Codex, they are to be taken" (6:10). This, Kant finds permissible, so long as the philosopher "does not wish that the jurists proper, or perhaps the courts of law, should also use them that way" (6:10).

On the one hand, this may just seem to return us to AD, for in the analogy, the philosopher is allowed to borrow from the Codex, and even modify the meaning of what is borrowed, but must not seek to influence those outside his discipline. Yet, something further is expressed. As we learn in *Religion*'s Second Preface, Kant's aim is to conduct an "experiment" that seeks to determine the scope of overlap between traditional Christian doctrine and the Pure Rational System of Religion.[8] According to his response to the royal rescript, this is not an "*appraisal* of Christianity" but rather a turn to "biblical texts to corroborate certain purely rational teachings in religion" (CF: 7:8). Thus, we may say that insofar as the philosophical theologian is examining doctrines or Scriptural material that dwell in the overlap between Natural and Revealed Religion, he may only use the latter to "corroborate" the former, rather than using the former to "appraise" the latter. As expressed above, the biblical theologian has "privilege" with respect to certain doctrines and thus the direction of evaluation may only go one way. We will call this the Interpretative Privilege standard (IP): when the philosophical theologian is examining issues within the overlap between Natural and Revealed Religion, the latter may be used to corroborate (and so in that sense appraise) the former, but no appraisal of the latter via the former is permissible.

Thus, we have in the First Preface to *Religion* (as well as in Kant's official response to the royal rescript of 1794), three ways in which biblical and philosophical theology are distinguished. AD is not concerned with content or methodology, just with audience and potential impact. On its own, it does not prohibit the philosopher from interpreting the Bible or criticizing the doctrines that have been drawn from it. However, NR does impact what content the philosopher may concern himself with. Although he may explore biblical passages and doctrines that overlap with Natural Religion, a "respectful distance" must be kept from the Holy Mysteries, miracles, sacraments, and much else that falls solely within Revealed Religion.[9] Lastly, where there is overlap, the philosopher must only use the Bible or traditional doctrine to corroborate the finding of reason rather than allow reason to offer its appraisals.

These are, at least, how Kant chose to package both *Religion* and *The Conflict of the Faculties*. As part of their prefaces, they offer, quite literally, their *prima facie* hermeneutical views. But it may be argued that this is just a strategic feint on Kant's part. He was in the midst of battle with the Prussian censors and, more broadly, with the foes of the Enlightenment that came into power after the death of Frederick the Great. He thus clad his writing in armor meant to defend the text against these foes.[10] However, once we turn to the actual body of *Religion*, it is not clear that Kant holds firmly to any of the above standards.

As we shall soon discuss in more depth, the Second Preface claims that the purpose of *Religion* is to conduct an experiment to determine the scope of overlap between the doctrines of Christian tradition and the religious principles that can be drawn from reason alone. Put in this way, one might think that *Religion* merely compares the two, and so his protest that the text makes no appraisal of Christianity may be accepted as honest and accurate. Yet, as we shall see, the text does not bear this out: for throughout *Religion*, Kant does interpret biblical passages and appraises core Christian doctrines. In Part One, for instance, he recommends a symbolic interpretation of the story of the Fall, and dismisses the idea that Original Sin is inherited as "most inappropriate" (6:40). Then, in Part Two, we find Kant criticizing the doctrine of Vicarious Atonement, claiming that the debt of sin "cannot be erased by somebody else. For it is not a *transmissible* liability" (6:72). He also argues that for practical purposes we have cause to reject the divinity of Jesus, since "the elevation of such a Holy One above every frailty of human nature would ... stand in the way of the practical adoption of the idea of such a being for our imitation" (6:64).

Further, in Part Three, Kant discusses biblical hermeneutics quite directly and asserts: "There is, therefore, no norm of ecclesiastical faith except Scripture, and no other expositor of it except the *religion of reason* and *scholarship* (which deals with the historical element of Scripture). And, of these two, the first alone is *authentic* and valid for the whole world, whereas the second is merely *doctrinal*" (6:114). Part Three as well argues that "[t]he only faith that can found a universal church is *pure religious faith*" (6:103), that "[t]he distinguishing mark of the true church is its *universality*" (6:115), and that universality can only be achieved for doctrines whose foundation is reason as opposed to revelation. Only the former, he claims, can be "convincingly communicated to everyone" (6:103).

In fact, one might even see the whole of *Religion* as an appraisal of Christianity, as it does not merely compare its doctrines to the Pure Rational System of Religion, but divides Christian doctrine into two domains. Because salvation must be available to all, the doctrines that govern it must be available through reason alone. So, those Christian doctrines that do overlap with what reason determines to be essential to our salvation are treated as necessary and essential. By contrast, Christian doctrines that fall outside of the System must be soteriologically inessential and thus are "intrinsically contingent" (6:105), "arbitrary precepts" (6:106). They are not irrelevant as Kant recognizes some need for symbols, rituals, and so forth that help us grasp "the highest concepts and grounds of reason" (6:109). But they are potentially "dispensable" (6:121).

Hence, the experiment of *Religion*, despite Kant's protests to the contrary, does appraise the Bible and Christian doctrine. It does so through the principle that whatever is soteriologically necessary must be discoverable through reason alone, and so uses this principle to separate out two strata of doctrine: those that accord with reason and those that are outside of it. To be outside does not mean to be false. But Kant does recommend, depending upon specifics, that we either remain agnostic about them or if we do adopt them, treat them as of only instrumental worth, such as to give "something that *the senses can hold on to*" (6:109).[11]

THE SECOND PREFACE

THE SPHERES OF REASON AND REVELATION (6:12–14)

In early 1794, a second edition of *Religion* was published. Kant added to this edition a handful of new footnotes, a long paragraph at the end of Part One where he more fully explains the function of the General Remarks at the end of each part, and a brief but significant Second Preface. This preface includes a few comments about the reception of the first edition of *Religion*, but more importantly it offers two extremely valuable and illuminating characterizations of *Religion*'s overall project.

The first of these describes two concentric spheres/circles. The wider one contains all that has been derived from the record of alleged revelation. It includes the traditional doctrines of Christianity as well as "what is historical in revelation" (6:12) – that is, claims about events ranging from the story of Adam and Eve through to the miracles performed by Jesus, his death and resurrection. Then, within this wider sphere, there is another, a narrower sphere that contains the "pure *religion of reason*" (6:12). Its contents are those that can be derived through reason alone. This

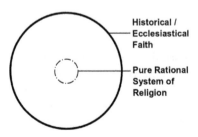

Historical /
Ecclesiastical
Faith

Pure Rational
System of
Religion

Figure 1 Inner and outer spheres of religion

does not mean that reason is their only possible source, but rather that reason on its own is capable of generating them. Circumstantially, at "a given place [it] might be wise and very advantageous to the human race" (6:155) for some principle of the inner sphere to have been disseminated through revelation. However, in such a case, this principle would still be "*objectively* a natural one, though *subjectively* one-revealed" (6:156).

As there is only a partial overlap between the two spheres, there are contents in the wider sphere that are not present in the one that it encloses. Hence, Christianity also contains doctrines that reason cannot on its own generate. In the inner sphere, we have the principles of faith that can be derived a priori, principles that Kant at least for the moment represents as also part of the religious tradition. But beyond their overlap, i.e., what is found only within the outer sphere and not the inner, are those doctrines of Historical Faith that cannot be derived from reason alone. They may have their source in actual (or alleged) revelation, may have arisen in celebration of a miracle, or may, more plainly, have just been products of the imagination.

Kant is willing to acknowledge that some elements of the outer sphere may have come from "a special divine dispensation" (6:105). However, he recommends that we keep "a respectful distance" from them (6:191). In this regard, he tends to accept NR, one of the boundary principles we discussed above. Yet there is an important qualification. Even though he recommends that we maintain a respectful distance from the veracity of miracles, revelation, as well as the natural historical reports of the Bible, this deference pertains specifically to their truth-value. Kant is not so impartial once we consider the practical role that any of the above may or may not have in our religious lives.

As noted above, he does accept the possibility of divinely ordained ecclesiastical statutes. Thus, it may be that God wants us to be baptized, observe sharia, or wear a yarmulke. However, one of the pivotal theses of *Religion* is that none of these practices should be understood as in themselves soteriologically necessary. Even if humanity needs some rituals, symbols, and so forth in order to help them grasp "the highest concepts and grounds of reason" (6:109) and to foster fellowship and devotion within the church, all such elements of Historical and Eccesiastical Faith are in themselves "arbitrary and contingent" (6:168), each substitutable for others that can have similar *instrumental* worth. To think otherwise, to regard any (even if they are divinely ordained) as in themselves essential to our religious lives (or, more precisely, to our salvation), is "a *delusion of religion*, and acting upon it constitutes counterfeit service [to God]" (6:168).

RELIGION'S EXPERIMENT(S) (6:12–14)

After describing the two spheres of religious principles, Kant writes: "From this standpoint I can also make this second experiment, namely, to start from some alleged revelation or other and, abstracting from the pure religion of reason ... hold fragments of this revelation, as a *historical system*, up to moral concepts, and see whether it does not lead back to the same pure *rational system* of religion" (6:12). The basic aim of this "second experiment" should be clear: to compare the scope of the "historical system" to the "pure rational system of religion."

Unfortunately, however, Kant does not tell us what the first experiment is, nor does he even use that enumeration explicitly. There are a few peculiar readings of what the experiment might be, but as the second experiment seeks to compare the elements of Historical Faith associated with "alleged revelation" to the Pure Rational System of Religion, whatever the first experiment is, it must be understood as conceptually or logically prior to the second.[12] Thus, as it is through the body of *Religion* that the second experiment is conducted, I think it is reasonable to understand the unstated first experiment as the construction of the Pure Rational System of Religion from an a priori procedure rooted in moral concepts.

It is, in other words, the first experiment that fills out Kant's claim that "morality ... inevitably leads to religion" (6:6). It generates first the doctrine of the Highest Good, then the Postulates, and then the additional derivative principles that follow from them and fills out the contents of the inner sphere. Its results are thus used in the second experiment as the first experiment is what produces the Pure Rational System of Religion.

This is not to say that *Religion* does not also reveal for the first time various principles within the Pure Rational System, but the agenda of the text is more fundamentally shaped by the enumerated "second experiment." It is for this purpose that, as above, I will continue through this book to refer to the "second experiment" simply as "*Religion*'s experiment." It is, really, *the* experiment of *Religion*, as each of its parts considers whether various revealed doctrines can be also derived from reason. Part One aims to show that through reason alone we can examine and defend the doctrine of Original Sin. Part Two considers the revealed doctrines related to our salvation and offers their rational corollaries. Part Three turns to issues of Providence, Eschatology, and the spread of the Pure Rational System through the Universal Church. Part Four then compares what reason versus (alleged) revelation claims about the sort of service that God requires of us for us to become "well-pleasing" to Him.

Implied throughout the experiment of *Religion* (i.e., the second experiment), is a division between what doctrines are necessary for our salvation and what doctrines are "intrinsically contingent" (6:105).[13] As we have discussed, the experiment of religion does not merely compare the Pure Rational System of Religion to the doctrines of traditional Christianity. It also applies an evaluative standard that divides Christian doctrine between what is essential and what is inessential to our salvation. Accordingly, we may think of the experiment as testing a hypothesis. Kant does not merely separate Christian doctrines into the essential and inessential. Nor does he merely distinguish between the inner sphere of rational principles and the outer sphere of the merely historical. More fully, the experiment of *Religion* seeks to prove that these two modes of division offer parallel results. That is, the inner sphere contains all that is necessary to salvation – which in turn means that all that is necessary to salvation can be derived from reason alone. *Religion*, thus, conducts an experiment that seeks to prove true the formula: Pure Rational Faith (*reiner Vernunftglaube*) = Saving Faith (*seligmachender Glaube*).

By way of the logic of *ought implies can*, Kant maintains that since we all *ought* to become well-pleasing to God, we must all be capable of doing so. In Part Three, he argues that this capability demands that the principles that govern our salvation are equally available to everyone (since salvation ought to be available to everyone). This leads him to stratify religious doctrine, distinguishing between those that are essential to our salvation and those that are intrinsically contingent to it. Doctrines whose sole basis is alleged revelation "can extend ... [their] influence no further than the tidings relevant to a judgment on ... [their] credibility can reach" (6:103). Thus, they cannot be taken as soteriologically necessary. On the other hand, the principles of reason are universally available, and so Kant maintains that whether or not over time some of those principles also were revealed, universal access to salvation requires that its governing principles are also available through reason alone.

Of course, it does not, however, follow from this that religious principles outside of reason are irrelevant. As we have discussed, and as Kant expresses in his response to the royal rescript: "what we have cause to believe on historical grounds ... that is, revelation, as contingent tenets of faith – it [reason] regards as nonessential. But this does not mean that reason considers it idle and superfluous" (CF: 7:9). Historical doctrines can still help "depending on the times and the person concerned – to satisfy a rational need" (CF: 7:9). The contents of the outer sphere can thus remain important and should be accepted as part of religious life. They can have a vital role even in the True Church. We have a need for symbols, for stories, images, rituals, and much else that helps people grasp "the highest concepts and grounds of reason" and are "beneficial to the vitality of ... [one's] pure religious disposition" (6:182). It may even be that "pure faith can never be relied on as much as it deserves, that is [enough] to found a Church on it alone" (6:103), and though Kant does at one point also express the hope that the "leading strings of holy tradition, with its appendages, its statutes and observances, which in its time did good service, [will] become bit by bit dispensable"(6:121), at least provisionally (and perhaps more than that) he considers the outer sphere to have contents that "must be cherished and cultivated [but] as a mere means, though a most precious one, for giving meaning, diffusion, and continuity to natural religion" (6:165).

NOTES

1 As noted in the Introduction, and as we will discuss later in this chapter, Kant enumerates two experiments. I regard the first as the construction of the Pure Rational System of Religion. The second, though, is what shapes the agenda of *Religion*. It is the experiment to determine the scope of overlap between this System and traditional Christian doctrine.

2 For a more detailed and quite interesting discussion of the relationship between the moral law and God, see Kain 2005.

3 We will return to this issue in the concluding chapter, exploring the common objection that Kant reduces religion to morality.

4 This might be considered something of an overstatement, since according to Kant we can independently of morality formulate both the idea of a necessary being as well as a conception of a demiurge. It is more particularly that morality serves as the source for the idea of God as benevolent and just. According to Kant, neither natural theology nor rationalist metaphysics can, on their own, provide these attributes. One might also wonder whether his claim about the conceptual origins of religion in morality is also an overstatement if one moves past the Postulates to the multitudes of religious doctrines found in the various historical faiths. In my view, some of the conceptual elements present in some such doctrines have their roots in morality, but hardly does it follow that all conceptual elements have this source. I will return to this issue in Chapter 7.

5 One might wonder whether the argument just presented reintroduces the Third *Critique*'s psychological foundation for our commitment to the Highest Good. While *Religion*'s argument is framed in terms of our human needs, these needs are not the same as those in the Parable of the Righteous Atheist. In that case, the Highest Good is meant to overcome feelings of despair that could compromise our commitment to the moral law. But in this, there is a relevant point of difference between the two arguments. As noted earlier, the Third *Critique* grounds the Highest Good on a marginal and contingent phenomenon (i.e., a despair that may arise in response to particular experiences of the exigencies of nature). Here, however, the Highest Good is given a ground that is central to our practical lives. Secondly, this ground reflects the general structure of our rational agency, and so

rather than arguing for the Highest Good as a defense against various feelings that may threaten our moral commitment, the argument of *Religion*'s First Preface is, as I have hopefully conveyed in my reconstruction of it, drawn from the needs of a rational agent to understand and justify his actions in relation to a *whither* as well as in relation to the axial order between conflicting *whithers*.

6 See 11:329, dated March 6, 1792.

7 See 6:154–55; CF: 7:44–45; LR: 28:998–1000.

8 See note 1 of this chapter and notes 3 and 11 in the Introduction.

9 One might see a parallel here to the "parerga" that constitute the four "General Remarks" appended to each of *Religion*'s parts. On this, see 6:52–53.

10 In a letter to Carl Friedrich Stäudlin, a liberal theologian at the University of Göttingen, Kant admits that the First Preface to *Religion* is "rather *geharnischte*" (11:430 – dated May 4, 1793). In the Cambridge translation of Kant's correspondence, the term is simply translated as "violent," but this misses its dual meaning as "armor-clad" as well as "sharp" or "strong."

11 Of the three standards mentioned above, the only one that Kant generally sustains is NR. He writes, for example, that we "leave the merits of ... miracles, one and all, undisturbed" (6:85). With regards to their veracity, "reason is as paralyzed" (6:87). Thus it is "salutary to keep ourselves at a respectful distance" (6:191) from them. Rather than, as one might otherwise expect, appealing to the Second Analogy of the *Critique of Pure Reason*, where Kant argues that all events in time and space must follow the laws of nature, he actually accepts the possibility of "supernatural intervention" (6:191). How this is possible, is "absolutely unknown to us and so must remain" (6:86); yet Kant concedes the possibility, supporting it by way of analogy to our free will: "freedom itself, though not containing anything supernatural in its concept, remains just as incomprehensible to us" (6:191). There are, however, two qualifications that must be made. First, the above agnosticism pertains to the outer sphere – the realm of Historical Faith that does not overlap with what also falls within the Pure Rational System of Religion. The second qualification to NR is that even though Kant recommends that we maintain a respectful distance from the veracity of miracles, revelation, as well as the natural historical reports of the Bible, this deference pertains specifically to their

truth-value. Kant is not so impartial once we consider the practical role that any of the above may or may not have in our religious lives.

12 For a contrasting view of how the two experiments are related to the text, see Firestone and Jacobs 2008. They equate the first three parts of *Religion* with the first experiment and link the last part with the second experiment. Since Parts One and Two provide so much exposition of the Pure Rational System, while Part Four in particular is more polemical, we may see why they thought that it is only towards the end of *Religion* that Kant "hold[s] fragments of this revelation … up to moral concepts" (6:12). Yet most others, including myself, see the body of *Religion* as conducting the second experiment, since throughout it evaluates the relationship between traditional doctrines and the Pure Rational System.

13 The differences between my interpretation of *Religion* and the interpretation presented in DiCenso 2012 are ample. Readers of both texts will likely recognize many. While I am generally sympathetic with DiCenso's treatment of Historical Faith, I regard his neglect of Pure Rational Faith to be at the heart of our differences of interpretation. For DiCenso, it seems that "faith" involves nothing more than a commitment to the moral law (see pp. 99, 127). While I agree that this commitment is part of Kant's positive use of the term, it is not all there is to it. The Highest Good and its Postulates, which are the foundational tenets of the Pure Rational System of Religion, are not just symbols of heuristic value to our moral vocation. Rather (as I discuss in Chapter 1 as well as in Pasternack 2011), each is an object of assent, an assent to their *truth* – and in fact, an assent with *certainty*. These points are made quite explicitly in all three *Critiques* (e.g. A829/B857; CPrR: 5:145; CJ: 5:469), in the Jäsche Logic (9:70), lecture notes (e.g. BL: 24:148, LR: 28:1082), *Reflexionen* (16:373, 16:375), and in many of the shorter works, especially of the 1790s (e.g. RP: 20:298). Although our grounds for the assent are moral rather than theoretical, Kant repeatedly asserts that we must genuinely believe in them. By contrast, heuristic and regulative principles call for no such commitment.

3

PART ONE OF *RELIGION*
GOOD, EVIL, AND HUMAN NATURE

Of all *Religion*'s parts, its first has received the most attention. It contains some of Kant's most important (and most cryptic) discussions of philosophical anthropology. It also contains one of the most infamous of his moral theses: that the whole of the human species "by nature is evil" (6:21). We may consider this claim to be the first datum of *Religion*'s experiment, the first point of overlap between the Pure Rational System of Religion and traditional Christian doctrine, as it is how Kant presents the doctrine of Original Sin.

As we will see, the core argument of Part One is quite complex. It is laden with new terminology and distinctions that are either not found elsewhere or not elsewhere used so technically. These include newly drawn distinctions between "predispositions" (*Anlagen*) and "propensities" (*Hänge*), between "incentives" (*Triebfederen*) and "inclinations" (*Neigungen*), as well as a deepening of his moral anthropology such as through his introduction of a fundamental moral disposition (*Gesinnung*), and a choice that I will refer to as the *"Gesinnung* choice," through which the agent commits himself to a supreme maxim.[1]

Because of the complexity of Part One, we will move very slowly through some of its passages, pausing at times in order to explore a few of the more significant interpretations found in the secondary literature. In particular, we will take a careful look at some of the reconstructions of Kant's argument for the moral status of the species, evaluate their strengths and weaknesses, and consider what desiderata a successful interpretation must satisfy. Kant's claim that the species as a whole is morally evil bears within it a serious tension, since our evil nature is supposed to be both innate and universal while also being freely chosen. Once the appropriate groundwork has been laid, I will then present an interpretation of my own, one that satisfies the core interpretative desiderata, including a resolution of the aforementioned tension.

THE SUBJECTIVE GROUND OF OUR POWER OF CHOICE (6:19–22)

Part One begins with a brief presentation of various origin myths. It starts out with a handful of myths that describe a fall from a Golden Age or an expulsion from a state of paradise. With both, there is a "decline into evil" (6:19) and, in some instances, a corruption of our moral potential for recovery. The text then turns to a second cluster of myths which follow a different trajectory. Instead of portraying humanity as falling away from a better condition, they rather depict a movement from "bad to better" (6:20). As Kant notes, the latter vision of history has gained in popularity during the Enlightenment, inspired by scientific advances, improved social circumstances, the birth of new democracies, etc. Proponents of this vision, rather than seeing humanity as fallen, propose instead that we are naturally driven to better ourselves and our society, acting on a "predisposition to move in this [positive] direction" (6:20).

Kant introduces these two sets of myths in order to raise the issue that governs Part One: is the human species corrupt and fallen, or does it have an untainted seed of goodness that defines our moral status and warrants optimism about our future?

However, he chooses to broach the issue through mythology because he sees myths as reflecting what experience suggests about the moral status of the species. More precisely, experience suggests different views depending upon what is observed. At times it suggests that we are corrupt, at times it suggests that we are not; and if one considers then the whole of what experience suggests, we end up with something in-between. This middle position is then divided by Kant in two: either we simply have no fundamental moral status (i.e., such evaluations simply do not apply), or we are partly good and partly evil (i.e., in some respects, each person is good, while in other respects, he is evil).

Kant will return to these options in his "Remark" on Rigorism, but at the moment, his goal is to generally discredit empirical approaches to the question of the moral status of the species. Although experience does provide us a basis for moral judgment when someone is performing an immoral action, beyond that it can do very little. We cannot experience anyone's maxims, not even our own. Experience cannot determine whether or not an agent is heeding morality out of self-interest or whether he is acting from duty. Experience only reveals behavior. However, since the moral status of both the individual and the species reside in our maxims, "the judgment that an agent is an evil [or good] human being cannot reliably be based upon experience" (6:21). Thus, we must turn away from experience if we hope to answer the question at hand. We need instead an a priori strategy, one that allows us to uncover not only the moral status of each individual, but of the species as a whole.

Kant follows his rejection of the empirical approach with a discussion of his use of "nature" as in "the human being is evil by nature" or "the radical evil of human nature."[2] He realizes that claims about a natural or innate moral status do not seem compatible with freedom and responsibility. What is innate within us is presumably beyond our choosing, and so we cannot be held responsible for its presence. As we shall see, some pages later he seeks to resolve this tension by distinguishing between two different ways of understanding claims of this sort so that we can make compatible our being both innately evil and responsible for being evil (6:29). Here, though, he focuses on how to understand "nature," stating that by the term he means "the subjective ground ... of the exercise of the human being's freedom in general" (6:21).

He equates this subjective ground with a maxim or, more precisely, a supreme maxim that serves to regulate all other maxims that are adopted. He claims that the supreme maxim, the ultimate subjective ground of all of our deeds, must be "a deed of freedom" (6:21). But this, of course, does not resolve the above tension, for we still need to understand how this "deed" is related to our innate evil. To help distinguish between the deed through which our moral status is set and the innate traits for which we cannot be held responsible, Kant considers and then eliminates one possible source of evil. As he will repeat many times throughout *Religion*, since our inclinations exist within us innately and not by choice, they cannot be the source of evil. No doubt, they are still relevant to why we violate morality, but the mere fact that we have them, a fact over which we have no control, must not be taken as the ultimate determining ground of our moral status.

This rejection of the moral standing of inclination is an issue of considerable importance to Kant. The view that our inclinations are responsible for moral evil is deeply entrenched in popular thought, and so Kant returns to the topic multiple times through Part One, as well as at the start of both Parts Two and Three. Throughout, he claims that neither are inclinations themselves evil nor is our accession to them. Evil must, rather, be understood in terms of a stance taken towards the moral law, one that does not simply say "yes" to desire, but also says "no" to morality. Further, Kant also reiterates on various occasions that the affective force of our desire is not on its own able to explain the choice. If it could, then our liability would be dissolved into an inner frailty: "for if this ground were ultimately no longer itself a maxim, but merely a natural impulse, the entire exercise of freedom could be traced back to a determination through natural causes – and this would contradict freedom" (6:21). Accordingly, our moral responsibility for evil requires that we are agents in this, active choosers of a principle that both endorses desire and denies morality. Evil must come not simply from weakness, but as "a consequence of a real and opposite determination of the power of choice, i.e. of a *resistance* on its part" (6:22n).

Before we move on to the next step in Kant's protracted argument regarding our moral status, we should briefly take note of three comments where he describes our supreme maxim or ultimate subjective ground as "antecedent to every deed that falls within the scope of freedom" (6:21), as "to us inscrutable" (6:21), and "as the ground antecedent to every use of freedom given in experience (from the earliest youth as far back as birth)" (6:22). Many interpreters take these and similar passages in Part One to indicate some timeless or noumenal agent who is responsible for the adoption of our supreme maxim. Thus, the self we are empirically aware of, the one that we think of as existing in time, with choices made earlier and later in life, is understood as in some way distinct from another agent that dwells outside of time. This certainly is a view that would comport well with the "two-worlds" interpretation of Transcendental Idealism, but obviously would not be easy to reconcile with the "methodological" or "two-aspects" view. We will return to this issue later in the chapter.

THE "REMARK" (6:22–26)

The section simply titled "Remark" returns us to the question of what experience teaches us regarding the moral status of human nature. Its goal is to defend Rigorism, the view that there is no mitigation or compromise with regards to moral standing. Human nature is either good or evil, with no middle ground. Kant sees this as the position that would come out of an a priori analysis, versus an empirical approach which would instead support one or another form of what he here calls Latitudinarianism. As discussed above, experience suggests that humanity either has no definitive moral standing or that we are each a "coalition" (6:22) of attributes with varying moral values. The former he calls Indifferentism and the latter, Syncretism. It is through his elimination of these alternatives that the case for Rigorism is developed.[3]

Kant's objection to Indifferentism comes from his presumption that "[a] morally indifferent action ... would be one that merely follows upon the laws of nature" (6:23n). It thus falls outside our freedom and so fails to hold us responsible. Once again, Kant is targeting a popular view about our inclinations, its contention that our desires can be so powerful as to determine our actions on their own. His alternative view is that we "cannot be determined to action through any incentive *except so far as the human being has incorporated it into his maxim*" (6:24). This has come to be known as the Incorporation Thesis, and is taken as a fundamental tenet of Kant's theory of human agency from the *Groundwork* on.[4] When we feel an urge to do something, we must affirm that urge, saying "yes" to it by framing it in a maxim such as "when I feel a very intense desire, I give myself permission to act on it." Principles, for Kant, must mediate between inclination and the will, and only by bringing inclination into a principle, "incorporating" it into a maxim, can our wills act on them. Thus, whatever we do, we must choose to do it and do so through a maxim, a subjective principle of volition (GR: 4:400n).[5]

As for Syncretism, we may assume that it can meet the above requirement regarding our inclinations, as it seems quite plausible that we operate through a plurality of maxims, some of which accord with morality and some that do not. Perhaps in some aspects of our lives, we follow moral maxims while in other aspects of our lives, we do not. For example, it may be that in our dealings with friends and family, we consistently abide by the moral law, while in our professional lives, we have fewer scruples. Alternately, it may be that we ebb and flow between good and bad maxims, either capriciously or as a result of certain inclinations that we have incorporated. We may, for example, hold fast to morality even when we feel the pressure from one type of inclination, but perhaps we have not acquired such control when it comes to other types. For example, we may lie to ourselves when we count calories, but we may be more honest with ourselves when we assess how well we are performing while practicing a talent. Syncretism, moreover, also seems to fit well with the depiction of our agency given by the *Groundwork*. This is not to say that the *Groundwork* clearly advances a Syncretistic account of our agency, but, as it describes us as sometimes acting from and sometimes merely in conformity with duty, one may wonder whether or not in the early 1780s Kant had not yet fully worked out the Rigorism we find in the following decade.

In *Religion*, however, Kant directly opposes Syncretism, arguing that behind our more particular maxims, there must be one ultimate subjective ground which governs the rest. To support this position, he presents us with a reductio argument, one which first appears in a footnote that precedes the Remark:

> The first subjective ground ... must not be sought in any incentive of nature [for that would undermine our freedom], but always again in a maxim; and, since any such maxim must have its ground as well, yet apart from a maxim no *determining ground* of the free power of choice ought to, or can, be adduced, we are endlessly referred back in the series of subjective determining grounds, without ever being able to come to the first ground.
>
> (6:21n)

Kant repeats the last point a few pages later, writing "there cannot be any further cognition of the subjective ground ... for otherwise we would have to adduce still another maxim into which the disposition would have to be incorporated, and this maxim must in turn have its ground" (6:25).

In both instances, he is arguing for a singular supreme maxim because if there were not one, we would end up with an infinite regress. The argument, however, is far from complete for what has been written so far does not explain why an infinite regress could not be stopped. Syncretism may claim that we have a plurality of fundamental maxims, but that does not mean its number is infinite. Instead, there may be just a handful, dividing our practical lives into a few different domains.

Rigorism holds to two theses: (a) there is a singular supreme maxim; and (b) that supreme maxim is either good or evil. Syncretism rejects both, with its stance on the second being a consequence of its rejection of the first. However, Rigorism can rebut Syncretism by directly arguing for (b) since it implies (a). This, I take it, is Kant's strategy for fending off the contention that at the most fundamental level of our hierarchy of maxims there could be more than one. So, rather than directly addressing the possibility of a plurality, he instead presents an argument whose aim is to demonstrate that the composition of the most funda-mental level of our hierarchy of maxims entails that we are either fundamentally good or evil. This then implies a commitment, and thus a maxim that sets our moral status.

His argument on this point is actually fairly straightforward and may be reconstructed as follows: 1) if we are bound by the moral law, it will either dominate our will or something else will; 2) because we are subject to this law, and so all our choices are subject to it, whatever maxims we will, they bear a normative relationship to it; 3) since the moral law demands complete obe-dience, either all our maxims will accord with it, or they will not; 4) thus, we are ultimately either comprehensively committed to the moral law or we are not – or in other words, we must either hold to a maxim that gives priority to morality over all other interests or we hold to a maxim that subordinates morality to them.

This is why Kant claims that we may infer "from a number of consciously evil actions ... the presence of a common ground, itself a maxim, of all particular morally evil maxims" (6:20). This inference is not a generalization, but is rather built upon what he regards as necessarily following from the moral law's absolute command. All specific violations of the moral law imply a shared stance, a shared valuing of the moral law. That shared stance is our supreme maxim and it can only take one of two forms: either the moral law will be given priority over self-interest, or that order will be reversed, with self-interest taking priority over morality. Since these are our two most fundamental incentives, and all other maxims are in one way or another invested with them, they all are therefore shaped by the choice we make regarding the priority of self-interest and morality.[6]

It should not be overlooked that there is an important parallel between Kant's argument for Rigorism and the argument for the Highest Good in the First Preface. As discussed in the preceding chapter, Kant argues that we need "a special point of reference for the unification of all ends" (6:5). As portrayed in the First Pre-face, this is a need built upon our all-too-human interest in the *whither* of our actions, but it is also, as we can see more vividly here, part of the logic of practical agency. As all actions are ends-directed, and ends may come into conflict, the determination of the will that precedes action logically requires that we subscribe to some principle of hierarchy or conflict resolution with regards to our end. Absent such a principle, then there would be no determination of the will as there would be no choice as to which of the conflicting maxims should be given priority over the other.

Hence, in both cases, we see arguments that endorse a systematic unity of practical principles. With the adoption of a supreme maxim, a choice is made as to whether to make morality the condition for happiness or vice versa. If it is the former, then the supreme maxim carries the same axial relation between these two incentives as is found in the Highest Good. Someone who chooses to prioritize morality over self-interest in his supreme maxim thus has brought his various ends into harmony with the Highest Good. The implications of this correlation with the Highest Good will be discussed more fully in Chapters 5 and 6. But for the moment, we can here see how Part One prepares the way for the second half of *Religion*, where Kant more overtly discusses the Highest Good.

THE PREDISPOSITIONS TO THE GOOD (6:26–28)

We have made our way through Kant's argument for Rigorism, an argument that has brought us to the claim that we are either fundamentally good or evil by virtue of our having a supreme maxim that either gives priority to morality over self-interest or the reverse. But this argument, on its own, does not itself disclose what our supreme maxim is, or whether all of humanity shares the same supreme maxim. Thus, on its own, it does not go so far as to demonstrate whether human nature is fundamentally good or fundamentally evil.

As we shall see, some qualifications will eventually be made, but Kant wants to show that there is a common moral quality shared by all of humanity such that we can say that human nature itself is evil. Rigorism might have established that we are ultimately good or evil, but considerably more argumentation is still needed to bring us to this dramatic conclusion. Not only does

Kant have to show that all of humanity shares the same moral status, but that this status is that we are evil. His ensuing argument will involve an exposition of three innate Predispositions (*Anlangen*) to the Good, an innate Propensity (*Hang*) to Evil, and then, finally, a choice that sets the moral status of our *Gesinnung*. Throughout, a delicate balance must be maintained such that Kant can have the whole species share a common moral status without undermining our individual responsibility. This balance, moreover, is one that must also manage both a priori and empirical propositions, for as we shall see not all of Kant's anthropological claims (nor all of his inferences from these claims) are a priori.[7]

Turning now to the first of our innate Predispositions, the Predisposition to Animality, Kant characterizes it as "merely mechanical self-love." It drives our self-preservation, the propagation of the species, and the pursuit of various non-moral ends that are closely connected with our physical appetites and biological necessities. It reflects the familiar array of desires and behaviors rooted in those natural instincts that we share with animals. Kant also intends here to mirror Rousseau's *amour de soi*, as the Predisposition to Animality has a kind of innocence where we, like animals, are simply moved, unreflectively, to satisfy our basic physical needs.

Likewise, Kant's second Predisposition also parallels an aspect of Rousseau's moral anthropology. According to both philosophers, human beings have not only biological needs, but psychosocial ones as well. Like the Predisposition to Animality, the Predisposition to Humanity also involves a form of self-interest. But in its case, its ends are contingent upon the values in one's society. Rousseau refers to this aspect of self-interest as *amour-propre* and, again like Rousseau, Kant describes this Predisposition as a desire for happiness shaped by our social relations. It is an "inclination *to gain worth in the opinion of others*" (6:27).

Because of this inclination, we aspire to various ends that otherwise would not interest us. We adjust our physical appearance to convey a certain image and are not only careful about what we say, but even feel social pressure to take on popular opinions so that we are accepted (or held in esteem) by our peers.

This propensity underlies most of our material desires, and for good or ill is also responsible for our competitive drives, a point conveyed more directly in Kant's 1784 "Idea for a Universal History with a Cosmopolitan Aim."

Perhaps the most famous thesis found in "Idea" is that there is a natural antagonism in society, an "unsocial sociability" that not only brings us together but also "constantly threatens to break up ... society" (ID: 8:20). On the one hand, out of a basic need for survival, we are drawn to one another. But in both "Idea" and *Religion*, Kant adds to this the further social drive related to our need to be acknowledged, accepted, and esteemed by others. To some extent, this has a positive effect as it prompts us to act in ways that promote communal well-being, but it also drives us to compete with one another, as victory brings with it a gain in social status. This moves us to further our talents, to invent new technologies, to master nature, and in so many other ways to exert our powers.

However, to some degree, in "Idea", but more robustly in *Religion*, Kant addresses the dark side of our social drive. In competition there is both a victor and a vanquished. The victor's sense of his own worth will be reinforced or heightened while the vanquished will suffer shame and abasement. Victory will often foster arrogance and schadenfreude, while defeat leads to jealousy and self-loathing. The reciprocality of our social needs leads, moreover, to a reciprocally corrupting process. Insecurity leads us not only to seek others' approval, but to dominate the other so that we can master them rather than give them the chance to master us.

It is through our Predisposition to Humanity that we seek "to acquire superiority for oneself over others" (6:27). And though Kant calls it a Predisposition to the Good, it really has quite a tenuous relationship with anything that is good (even in the non-moral sense). It seems far more the cause of angst and woe rather than happiness. Akin to Hegel's infamous master–slave dialectic, we at the same time desire the approval of others and resent the power that others have over us. Further, as will be discussed in the next section of this chapter, there is a deep connection between the Predisposition to Humanity and the Propensity to

Evil. In my view, the former is the psychological structure from which the latter emerges.

The third Predisposition is quite different from the preceding two. Unlike Animality and Humanity, the Predisposition to Personality is without a dark side. It can, of course, be ignored, but it cannot be corrupted. Also, unlike the other Predispositions which concern non-moral goods, it is a Predisposition to the good of morality. Kant defines it as "the susceptibility to respect for the moral law *as of itself a sufficient incentive to the power of choice*" (6:27). This susceptibility is also described in the *Groundwork* (e.g. GR: 4:400) as well as in the Second *Critique*'s important discussion of the moral feeling of humility and respect (CPrR: 5:71–89). Our Predisposition to Personality can, further, be linked with what Kant calls the "seed of goodness" whose development can be hindered (6:38) by the "active and opposing cause of evil" (6:57), but "cannot be extirpated or corrupted" (6:45).[8]

THE PROPENSITY TO EVIL (6:29–44)

PROPENSITY VERSUS PREDISPOSITION

Kant initially presents a propensity as "the subjective ground of the possibility of an inclination (habitual desire, *concupiscentia*), insofar as this possibility is contingent for humanity in general" (6:29). He then distinguishes this from a predisposition in that it is also innate but "*may* be represented as not being such: it can rather be thought of (if it is good) as *acquired*, or (if evil) as *brought* by the human being *upon* himself" (6:29).

Kant needs the Propensity to Evil to be innate in order for it to be a universal trait of the species. But if innate, then, as we have discussed, it seems that we cannot be held morally responsible for it. Just as we have three innate Predispositions to the Good that on their own do not warrant the claim that human beings are by nature morally good, so the innateness of the Propensity to Evil does not, and cannot, on its own justify the claim that we are by nature morally evil. Yet, unlike our inclinations, Kant does call this propensity *evil*. On their own, the inclinations do not oppose morality. They are just a different incentive towards action. The Propensity to Evil, however, is an "active and opposing" force (6:57) that both affirms our self-interest and actively opposes morality. That it may be, but the question remains as to how we can be held morally liable for the Propensity if it is innate?

Even if it is something that opposes morality, and so is evil, this is still not enough to warrant the claim that *we* are evil. Our moral status must be grounded in something for which we can be held responsible, and though Kant suggests that we may think of the Propensity as both in some sense innate and in some sense not (i.e., it can also be thought of as acquired), this does not clearly settle the question at hand. It seems as if he wants to resolve the tension by distinguishing between the phenomenal and noumenal, having the Propensity innate from one perspective, but not innate from the other. The difficulty here is that moral attributions, as Kant has already argued, are not empirical. They pertain to our will and thus there is no gain in construing the Propensity as phenomenal as well.

Let me then suggest an alternative way to distinguish between the innateness and acquired aspects of the Propensity to Evil. We can, on the one hand, think of it as a fact of human nature, something that is innate and shared by the whole species. But on the other hand, it is up to us how we allow it to affect us. As a fact of human nature, it is unchosen and thus we cannot be held responsible for its mere existence. But if we are free with regards to what role it is given in our practical lives, then we can be seen as morally responsible in that regard. Still, this suggestion is only the first step, and only part of a larger interpretative problem. We still need to more fully grasp the nature of this Propensity, how it arises within us, why it leads us to choose a supreme maxim that prioritizes self-interest over morality, and why, as Kant claims, the species not only universally carries it but also universally accedes to it when making the *Gesinnung* choice. Interpreting the Propensity to Evil is one of the core challenges for any interpretation of Kant's theory of evil, and through the subsequent subsections, we will work through various interpretative desiderata and explore how each can be satisfied.

INTERPRETATIVE DESIDERATA

To begin, let us turn to some of the better known works on the topic, beginning with Gordon Michalson's *Fallen Freedom: Kant on Radical Evil and Moral Regeneration*. Unlike this book, *Fallen Freedom* does not regard *Religion* as offering a philosophically unified and defensible vision. Rather it quite harshly maligns the text as "makeshift" and "haphazard," a litany of "wobbles" that reflect Kant's deep ambivalence between the two competing cultural forces of traditional Christianity and the Enlightenment. According to Michalson, among these putative wobbles is Kant's attempt to interpret Original Sin as both an innate and species-wide attribute and one that is both freely chosen and something for which we are responsible (Michalson 1990: 8). Although Kant claims that these conflicting properties can somehow be reconciled, Michalson is unmoved. He dismisses the suggestion and claims, instead, that Kant has created for himself a "conceptual logjam" (Michalson 1990: 67) from which there is no rescue.

Most other interpreters, however, read *Religion* with greater charity. Though there is some truth to Michalson's point about the intertwining of traditional Christianity and the Enlightenment, those who read Kant more generously see him as consciously aware of this duality; and so rather than fumbling time and again as he is pulled in different directions, they see him as having reconciled their competing world views. With respect to the issue at hand, it is quite common for interpreters to see the conflicts within the Propensity to Evil as resolved through the deflation of either Kant's claims about universality and innateness or freedom and responsibility. Which side is chosen often correlates with whether or not the interpreter wants to take Kant's moral anthropology to be the result of an a priori proof, or whether they consider it to be shaped by more empirical elements.

As we saw at the very opening of Part One, Kant explicitly rejects what experience seems to teach us about our moral nature (i.e., some form of Latitudinarianism) and instead claims that "it must be possible to infer *a priori* ... an underlying evil maxim" (6:20). Further, Kant refers to the possibility of a "formal proof that there must be ... a corrupt propensity rooted in the human being" (6:32), though he chooses to "spare" us of it "in view of the multitude of woeful examples" (6:32) that can on their own make the case that the human species is evil. Thus, it seems that Kant did intend an a priori approach in Part One, and presumably at least *some* elements do require it. But that need not be true of all.

For example, it may be a priori that the imperative mood of the moral law entails that within us there is something that competes with its authority. However, there are various possible sources of such competition and it seems an empirical rather than a priori claim that for human beings, what competes with the authority of morality is inclination. Further, Kant's choice to follow the Rousseauian distinction between the Predispositions to Animality and Humanity also seems an empirical move. Only one of these Predispositions would be necessary for the argument that we have a force within us that competes with morality. The claim that there are two, or that our inclinations are divided into two domains, is based upon anthropological observation.

We ought, therefore, to consider Part One as having both a priori and empirical elements; and just as importantly, we should not assume that only the former permits universal theses. Various Kantians, including Sharon Anderson-Gold, Patrick Frierson, and Allen Wood, all defend the moral anthropology developed in Part One, yet do not assume that all of its theses rest upon a priori proofs. In fact, all three avoid the trap of presuming that all claims of universality would be, according to Kant, a priori. For example, using the illustration above, Kant claims that all of humanity has *both* a Predisposition to Animality and a Predisposition to Humanity. This is a claim that is universal, yet it is not one that is established through an a priori argument.

Some might see this as an error on either Kant's part or on that of the interpreter. It would be for Michalson an illustration of Kant's "wobbles," where his Enlightenment philosophy would demand that all universal claims have an a priori foundation, and yet for the sake of his interest in Christianity, he is forced into a compromise. But this accusation overlooks Kant's own distinction between two types of universal claims. As Frierson in particular makes clear, Kant also has a place for "empirical universal judgment" (Frierson 2003: 38).

One might presume that it is a cornerstone of the *Critique of Pure Reason*'s account of universality that it must be based upon an a priori cognition, but this is, in fact, not what is claimed. In its Introduction, Kant writes that "[n]ecessity and strict universality are therefore secure indications of an *a priori* cognition, and also belong together inseparably" (B4). However, the point being made here pertains specifically to "strict universality" (*strenger Allgemeinheit*). Kant recognizes as well a looser counterpart, which he calls "comparative universality" (*comparative Allgemeinheit*) (B3). In addition to the *Critique of Pure Reason*, this distinction can also be found in various other texts, including the *Critique of Judgment* (CJ: 5:213) and the *Anthropology* (AN: 7:242).[9] We should, thus, at least for now, consider it an open question as to whether or not his claims regarding the universal moral status of the species have strict or comparative universality.

In due time, I will argue that there is an a priori argument underlying Kant's claim that we must universally bear a Propensity to Evil. But, as we shall see, that argument does not on its own also establish that the human species is universally evil. This is, in part, because a distinction must be drawn between the Propensity to Evil and the evil *Gesinnung*. Even with an a priori argument for the Propensity to Evil, since it is innate and unchosen, the liability for our moral status depends instead upon the *Gesinnung* choice. But since this choice is free, nothing stronger than a claim of comparative universality can be assigned to it. In fact, given the possibility of a Change of Heart, even if Kant wants to claim that all of humanity passes through a stage of being evil, not everyone must remain within it.

A neglect of either the general distinction between strict and comparative universality or, more specifically, how this distinction feeds into the difference between the Propensity to Evil and the evil *Gesinnung* has had dire consequences for how *Religion* as a whole is assessed. I briefly noted Gordon Michalson's overall cynical assessment of the text. It has also led to various other missteps, including numerous criticisms of internal contradictions (Quinn 1986 and Wolterstorff 1991), claims that its philosophical theology is an outright "Failure" (Hare 1996), and even some defenses that have done to it as much harm as good – including what is probably the best known a priori argument for the Propensity to Evil.

In *Kant's Theory of Freedom*, Henry Allison is committed to the strict universality of the Propensity to Evil. He does not examine the possibility that it could be just a "comparative" or empirical generalization, and instead asserts that if we are to take it seriously, it must be a priori and so founded upon a formal proof or deduction. He presents his proof in the form of a *reductio* against what he considers to be the only other option for human nature, *viz.*, that we would instead bear an innate propensity to good: "The key to this deduction is the impossibility of attributing a propensity to the good to finite, sensuously affected agents" (Allison 1990: 155).

Allison defines this propensity to good as "a kind of spontaneous preference for the impersonal requirements of morality over one's own needs as a rational animal with a built-in desire for happiness" (Allison 1990: 155) and infers from it that "there would be no temptation to adopt maxims that run counter to the law, and, therefore, no thought of the law as constraining" (Allison 1990: 155). In other words, according to Allison, a propensity to the good is incompatible with the imperative mood of the moral law.

Allison then associates this propensity with Kant's concept of a holy will (Allison 1990: 156). As described in the *Groundwork*, a holy will is one where the moral law is not an imperative, but rather a law determining action without any possibility of deviation from what morality commands. Such a will is "of itself necessarily in harmony with the law" (GR: 4:414). This is presented more fully in the Lectures on the Philosophical Doctrine of Religion:

> *Holiness* is the absolute or unlimited moral perfection of the will. ... It must be *impossible* for it to will something which is contrary to moral laws. So understood, no being but God is holy. For every creature always has some needs, and if wills to satisfy them, it also has inclinations which do not always agree with morality. Thus the human being can *never* be holy, but *of course* [he can be] *virtuous*. For virtue consists precisely in *self-overcoming*.

(LR: 28:1076)[10]

His *reductio* then concludes that since creatures such as ourselves are subject to the moral law as an imperative, and so deviation from it must be possible for us, as we cannot have a holy will, it therefore follows that we cannot have a propensity to good. By way of its a priori strategy, this argument does present the Propensity to Evil as having strict universality. However, it only achieves its conclusion by way of a conflation between a moral propensity and the moral status of the *Gesinnung*. His argument presumes that a propensity to good is the same as the adoption of a supreme maxim that is aligned with the moral law. But one's supreme maxim is what defines the moral status of the *Gesinnung*. If it is impossible for us to have a good supreme maxim, then it is impossible for us to undergo a Change of Heart.[11]

The Propensity to Evil is, according to Kant, both universal and inextricable (6:51). It plays a vital role in what supreme maxim we adopt, but if it were the same as the *Gesinnung* or if it necessitated what supreme maxim one has, then a good *Gesinnung* would not be a possibility. As we have discussed, it is not uncommon for interpreters to put far too much weight on Part One, and so skew Kant's moral anthropology into one that is far too grim. Of course, Part One does contend that the human species is evil, but this claim, like the doctrine of Original Sin, sets the stage for our redemption (in Kant's language, for the Change of Heart). Hence, an argument that gains a priority and strict universality at the cost of the possibility of a Change of Heart is an unacceptable compromise, as the aim of *Religion* is not to show that we have an evil propensity, but rather to show that *despite it*, we can become morally good through a Change of Heart. Just as the Christian doctrine of Original Sin is tailored to the soteriological function of the Crucifixion, so by analogy we should see Part One's development of the Propensity to Evil as introduced for the sake of Kant's soteriology. The latter does not claim that we are transformed into beings with holy wills, nor does it claim that either temptation or the imperative mood of the moral law are eliminated. The Change of Heart, rather, realizes exactly what Allison up front tells us is not a human possibility: a will that prefers morality over self-interest. But rather than dismiss this possibility, we need to understand it in such a way that does not lead to Allison's *reductio*s.

Unfortunately, it seems that, like many other readers of *Religion*, Allison has not paid enough attention to Parts Two through Four, and so has not fully registered the extent to which the doctrines of Part One are part of a larger project.

Another consequence of Allison's interpretation (and one that could easily befall other a priori strategies) is that in its pursuit of strict universality, it is forced to deflate the freedom of the will. Allison recognizes this implication and chooses to reconcile universality and freedom by rendering the latter merely "in terms of a causality of reason rather than a general capacity to do otherwise" (Allison 2002: 343). Accordingly, the pursuit of a formal proof for the Propensity, at least in its most famous example, results in (a) a conflation between a holy will and one that gives priority to morality over self-interest; (b) a failure to distinguish the Propensity from the *Gesinnung*'s supreme maxim; (c) the impossibility of the Change of Heart; and (d) a deflation of our freedom into what has been called the "freedom of the turnspit." This is a freedom that does not require our capacity to do otherwise – and quite ironically, the *otherwise* here would be to make a choice that *is* in accordance with morality!

Given the above problems, I think we should take care not to so hastily presume that the argument for the Propensity to Evil is out and out a priori. Allison's argument, as we have seen, took it as such, but at too high a cost. Other attempts may advance more palatable interpretations of what the Propensity is, but we should guard against overstating how much of Kant's argument for the Propensity is a priori.[12] As noted, claims of universality do not always demand a priori proof, and there are some aspects of Kant's moral anthropology that ought to be understood as empirical. With these considerations in mind, I hope to offer an account of the Propensity that involves some a priori steps, but I do not presume to call it a formal proof. Rather, my aim will be to reconstruct what Kant says about the Propensity to Evil, offering an account of it that meets all of the following interpretative *desiderata*:

- The Propensity to Evil is a universal feature of the species (innate/part of human nature).

- The Propensity to Evil is chosen/we are responsible for it/and we are morally blameworthy because of that choice.
- The philosophical relationship between the Propensity and the Predispositions must be clear.
- The Propensity is conceptually/explanatorily distinct from and antecedent to the *Gesinnung* choice (i.e., the Propensity to Evil is not the same as the choice of the supreme maxim).
- The Propensity to Evil is compatible with the Change of Heart (i.e., a new *Gesinnung* choice whereby the individual is deemed morally good).

THE FIRST DESIDERATUM: UNIVERSALITY

As discussed above, Kant distinguishes between claims of strict universality (and necessity) where "no exception at all is allowed to be possible" (B4) and comparative universality. The former demands an a priori demonstration as "[e]xperience teaches us ... that something is constituted thus and so, but not that it could not be otherwise" (B3). The latter, on the other hand, has a looser character, akin to a generalization, such as one might make through empirical induction. Accordingly, we should not presume that the universality associated with the Propensity to Evil is strict rather than comparative. Just as Kant could not have filled in his account of the Predispositions to the Good without empirical considerations that cannot be established through purely a priori demonstration, so we should also remain open to the possibility that some aspect of his claim that the whole human species is evil is not a matter of strict universality.

When we consider how he presents the Propensity to Evil, he repeatedly states that it is a universal feature of the species (6:25, 6:29, 6:30, 6:32, 6:33, etc.), that it is "woven into human nature" (6:30) and that "it cannot be eradicated" (6:31). However, he does not directly indicate whether or not this is a case of "strict universality." One might take strict universality to be implied by his claim that there is a formal proof (6:32). Yet he does not supply us with this proof. Further, in one passage he describes the propensity as "contingent for humanity in general" (6:29) and then later denies that it has objective necessity, stating instead that "we may presuppose evil as subjectively necessary in every human being" (6:32).

What Kant means by "subjective necessity" here is that we have a practical need to hold to a particular claim, as we also do with the Highest Good and the Postulates. Because of this need, a need that presumably all of humanity shares since we share the same faculties, we must all see ourselves as carrying a Propensity to Evil. It is not objectively necessary, as it is not "inferred from the concept of ... a human being in general" (6:32). Although he does describe it as "woven into human nature" and as an attribute that "cannot be eradicated," we should regard the Propensity as still like a practical postulate, rather than gaining its justification from some theoretical analysis of human nature. Thus, even if we take this postulate as having strict universality, the ground of such a claim rests upon its subjective rather than objective necessity. To better understand what this subjective necessity is, and so why according to Kant there is a practical need through which we must attribute to ourselves a Propensity to Evil, let us take a moment to consider an alternative view to what we find in *Religion*, a view that Kant might have wrestled with earlier in the Critical Period.

In his 1783–84 Lectures on the Philosophical Doctrine of Religion, we find an account of human evil quite distinct from what is most clearly articulated in *Religion*. The discussion begins with a classic theodicy, where the Divine attributes seem to exclude the possibility of any evil in the world, either natural or moral (LR: 28:1076). To avoid the danger of God being responsible for the evil that we do (as a result of how He created us), the text asserts that there is no positive principle within human nature that is the cause of the evil that we do. "Evil has *no special* germ" (LR: 28:1078), and so God did not create some attribute within us that is the seat of moral evil. Evil is here rather portrayed as a "*mere negation*," an "*incompleteness in the development of the germ toward the good*" (LR: 28:1078).

This view may also be imported into the *Groundwork* and the *Critique of Practical Reason*, as they share an account of our unruly inclinations and the development of moral worth in relation to their mastery. This is especially clear in the latter's argument for immortality, as it supports this Postulate on the basis of our need to eternally strive towards the *"complete conformity* of dispositions with the moral law" (CPrR: 5:122). Moral evil is thus portrayed in relation to our *"incompleteness in the development of the germ toward the good."* It is, accordingly, a "negation" on our part, a failure of autocracy.

However, this is not how Kant portrays moral evil in *Religion*, as it there gains its own "seed," something within us that is "active and opposing" to morality. Whether Kant outright changed his view or whether prior to *Religion* he had not yet come to a stable account of moral evil, I will leave as an open question. Textually, I do not think we can gain a definitive answer. But we can, nevertheless, point to where Kant is quite frank about what is wrong with the view articulated in the Lectures. Once we gain an understanding of why there must be a seed to evil, we will be able to explain why there must be a universal Propensity to Evil.

In his 1791 essay "On the Miscarriage of All Philosophical Trials in Theodicy" Kant returns to the problem of how to account for evil without degrading God's goodness or power. But rather than supporting the earlier privation account, he argues that such an account undermines moral responsibility. In the Lectures we find: "if we ask where the evil in individual human beings comes from, the answer is that it exists on account of the limits necessary to every creature" (LR: 28:1079). However, in the "Theodicy" Kant draws out the implication that if moral evil were due to a limitation in our nature, then it would be outside of our control.[13] Thus, he concludes, "since it could not be attributed to human beings as something for which they are to be blamed, we would have to cease calling it 'a moral evil'" (MT: 8:259).

So, to preserve our moral responsibility, Kant rejects the privation account of evil in favor of an evil seed — a cause of evil present within human nature that actively opposes the moral law. A consequence of this is that God is no longer vindicated, but this is part of the general thrust of the "Theodicy" since its goal is to demonstrate that all attempts to reconcile the Divine attributes with the presence of evil have failed (and will continue to fail). In other words, the "Theodicy" accepts the incompatibility between the Divine attributes and moral evil. Either God must be held liable for the evil we do (threatening his omnibenevolence) or moral evil must dissolve into frailty. This is, at least, the conclusion that theoretical reason should come to – and on its basis, he declares a "miscarriage of all philosophical trials in theodicy."

Out of this we can actually see one of the a priori elements in Kant's argument for the claim that the human species is evil by nature. If we are to hold ourselves as morally responsible for evil, we cannot defer to a privation model that treats it as a consequence of our failure to more adequately cultivate our seed of goodness. There must, rather, be within us something that in its own nature (and so in ours) opposes morality. By arguing that moral evil requires the presence of such a principle, Kant has gained an a priori argument for why there must be a Propensity to Evil. It is the "seed" that serves as the precondition for the actual evil that we may will, and it allows Kant to assert that any being who is capable of moral evil must have within them an evil seed.[14]

This does not directly prove that all human beings have a Propensity to Evil, but it does prove that *if* all human beings are capable of moral evil, then all human beings have this propensity. The antecedent remains, however, without a strict proof. The "multitude of woeful examples" (6:32) can, nevertheless, serve as the basis for a claim of comparative universality. The examples illustrate the prevalence of evil deeds and so this capacity is generalized to the species. Yet no argument has been made to show that perhaps some human beings are incapable of moral evil. The possibility of a Change of Heart does not do this, since first, it implies that there has been a change from an evil *Gesinnung*; and second, even with a Change of Heart, there remains the possibility of recidivism (6:94).

To be as clear as possible on this issue, let me restate: the Propensity to Evil is a universal and necessary condition for moral evil. With it, we have strict universality. But Kant has not yet argued that human beings are necessarily (and so with strict universality) morally evil. He, in fact, cannot claim this. It cannot be the case that we necessarily have an evil *Gesinnung*, for if that were so, then the possibility of a Change of Heart would be lost. It also cannot be the case that the species is morally evil *because* of the putative innateness of the Propensity to Evil. The Propensity is a necessary condition for moral evil, but not a sufficient condition. The latter demands a choice on our part.

THE SECOND DESIDERATUM: FREEDOM

Kant writes that the Propensity to Evil, though innate and universal through the species, can be "thought of" as "*brought* by the human being *upon* himself" (6:29). That is, even though it is a "natural propensity" (6:29) and something that everyone has, "even the best" (6:32), we can represent it as freely chosen and "something that a human being can be held accountable for" (6:32). As we have discussed, Kant maintains that moral evil depends upon a seed of evil, a cause that actively opposes the moral law. This seed is, presumably, innate within us. But as innate, it is unchosen. Hence, outside of our choice, there is a principle within us that actively opposes the moral law – or put differently there is within us a principle that biases us in favor of adopting an evil *Gesinnung*. However, it is this adoption that sets our moral status. It is where choice enters. The Propensity to Evil drives us towards this choice, but it is only through our endorsement of it and what it entails about the relative priority of self-interest over morality, that we become morally evil.

We should thus draw a distinction between the facticity of the Propensity to Evil and what we do with that fact. Just as we have Predispositions to the Good whose facticity is unchosen by us, but whose influence we do have choice over, so the same can be claimed regarding the Propensity to Evil. That we have this Propensity, just as we also have our Predispositions, is an inherent feature of what it is to be a human being. What, however, the human being has "brought ... upon himself" is what role he allows the Propensity to have in his life. It is in this way that we can reconcile Kant's dual claims about the Propensity as innate and as chosen. We can understand the mere facticity of the Propensity as a characteristic in parallel with Kant's Predispositions to the Good as unchosen. It is part of human nature and like the Predispositions, it "cannot be eradicated" (6:31). It will endure even after the Change of Heart, and so we cannot then consider its facticity as fully responsible for our moral condition. Yet it is up to us whether or not we align ourselves with it, reinforce it and allow it to flourish, or pull away from it, separating ourselves as best we can from its influence.

Before moving on to the next desideratum, let us take a moment to consider Kant's claim that *peccatum originarium* (Original Sin) is "an intelligible deed cognizable through reason alone apart from any temporal condition" (6:31). This and similar passages have led many to posit a noumenal counterpart to our phenomenal selves, an agent outside of time who makes the most important decisions regarding our moral lives. But we do not need to move into such arcana and can read phrases such as the above without turning to the noumenal. To say that the *peccatum originarium* is cognizable through reason does not mean that we have to step outside the conditions for experience and extend our concepts into the noumenal realm. Rather, like his Rigorism and other a priori steps in his moral anthropology, the claim being made here is not something that can be established through experience. That is, it is a rationally grounded claim rather than one that is empirically grounded. It is merely in this sense that it is cognized through reason alone.

Similarly, Kant's claim that the Propensity is cognized "apart from any temporal condition" does not require that we introduce some noumenal agent acting outside of time. It rather means that the *peccatum originarium* predates any particular moral choice we can point to when reflecting on the past. No matter how far one may go back in one's personal history of moral choices, the Propensity, like the *Gesinnung* choice, must always be taken as temporally antecedent to any other *moral* choice. In fact, if we look carefully at his language when he discusses the establishment of our "subjective ground," he characterizes the choice in a way that suggests something far less metaphysical and more mundane. He writes, for instance, that a person's moral disposition has "been the one way or the other *always, from his youth on*" (6:25). Similarly, he also writes that if we were to seek out a beginning in time, "we must trace the causes of every deliberate transgression in a previous time of our life, all the way back to the time when the use of reason has not yet developed" (6:42). So, rather than shift to some mysterious noumenal counterpart to our phenomenal selves, let me offer a developmental account of the Propensity to Evil, one that has it emerge in time, though "all the way back to the time when the use of reason has not yet developed" (6:42).

THE THIRD DESIDERATUM: FROM PREDISPOSITION TO PROPENSITY

Kant claims that we have three different innate Predispositions and one innate Propensity. As innate, they must in some sense already be present in us at birth, but their presence does not entail that they have an active role in our practical lives right from the start. We find Kant claiming in various texts that we first become cognizant of the moral law sometime between the ages of eight and ten (cf. CPrR: 5:155; TP 8:286). Thus, our Predisposition to Personality is still inert, and since the Propensity to Evil is understood as reactive to the moral law, it too must not yet have become active. They reside only *in potentia* during our earliest years, and then emerge as our rational capacity matures to a level where we can deliberate about right and wrong not merely in relation to social conventions but through a process of formal justification.

Readers who prefer to take Kant's comments about intelligible deeds and independence from temporal conditions as pointing to a noumenal agent will likely not find this chronology important (or correct), but as noted above there are a number of passages where he describes the Propensity to Evil as having a temporal origin, during our youth, "when the use of reason has not yet developed." In this section, I will follow the lead of Sharon Anderson-Gold and Allen Wood, who present the Propensity to Evil as a consequence of the Predisposition to Humanity. Although the psychological account that is to come does not offer the sort of a priori argument that some prefer, it should nevertheless bring out the inner workings of this Propensity and how it emerges within our practical lives.

To begin, let us consider again the Predisposition to Humanity: "the inclination *to gain worth in the opinion of others*" (6:27). We have a natural desire for a positive sense of self-worth and, according to Kant (following Rousseau), we depend upon the approval, acceptance, and praise of others in order to gain this sense of self. If we meet their expectations, we will tend to receive praise and so feel good about ourselves. If we do not meet such expectations, our desire for praise and so our need for a positive sense of self will likely go unfulfilled. The issue I would like to focus on is how, out of the mechanics of the Predisposition to Humanity, we respond in such instances.

One possible response is greater competitiveness. We may be spurred on to try harder in the future, which in turn may lead others to do the same, and in this way, the Predisposition to Humanity can help to stimulate progress, as Kant mentions in his "Idea for a Universal History." But in *Religion*, he focuses on the more negative aspects: the insecurity, anxiety, fear, and jealousy that come from our need to gain worth in the opinion of others. This darker side of our humanity underlies many of our cultural vices (hate of the other, avarice, etc.). It is also, as I will now argue, the source of our Propensity to Evil.

Before the moral law becomes manifest to us, we still recognize social norms, and it is in relation to these norms that we will seek to gain worth in the opinion of others. In some cases, we succeed and when we do so, we experience the satisfaction and positive self-esteem that we have been seeking. With such reinforcement, we will tend to take on those norms as part of our sense of self, what we value, and who we are (as so famously depicted through the Freudian super-ego). But when we fail, especially when we do so regularly (or are made to feel that way), rather than internalizing the norms, it is not at all uncommon that we will instead rebel against them, downplaying or rejecting their legitimacy in order to diffuse the psychological impact of failure. We may tell ourselves (both in childhood and even still as adults) that the challenge was not really worth our effort. We may even think ill of others who did meet them, so as to undercut, at least in our own minds, their social ascendancy.

Thus, when we succeed, we will tend to align ourselves with the norms that reinforce our sense of self-worth; and when we fail, we will tend to downplay the norms that threaten it. We generate, accordingly, various "inner lies" through what Kant calls "the vice of subreption." He describes this vice as taking place when we treat a subjective principle as if it were objective (cf. A509/B537; CPrR: 5:116). This is, further, the core basis for all error, according to Kant. It occurs in metaphysics when we treat the conditions for our experience as if they were transcendentally real, and in the practical realm, it occurs through a representation of some subjective desire as if it were an objective law. Similarly, with regards to our present topic, subreption occurs when we adopt some social convention and treat it as an objective norm. Anderson-Gold associates this specifically with the Propensity to Evil (Anderson-Gold 2001: 39), but I differ slightly. Although it is relevant to the Propensity's manifestation in us, I take this psychological phenomenon as temporally prior to the first dawning of the moral law in childhood, and so at least at first, this subreption lacks a moral target (though it does eventually gain one). Children form their identities in relation to their successes and failures, and consequently judge others, "objectifying" them, as Anderson-Gold describes, in the service of their ego's needs.[15]

This process further corresponds to Kant's general account of cognitive bias, not only in its employment of subreption, but also in more specific ways. For example, in his various discussions of intellectual prejudice, he distinguishes between the "prejudice of the prestige of the multitude" and "logical egoism" (JL: 9:78–81). The former refers to what now is sometimes called the Fallacy of Popularity: i.e., when the fact that something is commonly believed is used as a warrant for its truth. Such a prejudice may arise when one has met with widespread approval and so wants to raise up the authority of the masses. It may also arise if one comes to acquire "a mistrust of learnedness" (JL: 9:78) and in its place "seeks it now in the common understanding" (JL: 9:79). This, actually, in Kant's view, is the more common path to this prejudice. What biases we have "often arise from opposed causes" (VL: 24:875), such as we can see as well in the case of Logical Egoism. Although our Predisposition to Humanity inclines us to seek the approval of others, the emotional harm that comes from criticism can lead one to dismiss the judgment of others as irrelevant, choosing instead to take the mere fact that one believes a claim to be a warrant for its truth.

There is no doubt that contemporary psychology would offer a more sophisticated account of our ego development, but I presume that the essence of Kant's account nevertheless holds true: that we seek a sense of self-worth and deceive ourselves as needed to secure it. If we fail a test, we will tell ourselves that the skills it was meant to evaluate are not worth the effort. If we find ourselves rejected by our peers, we will either find a new group and seek their acceptance or in other ways engineer a new image in order to conform. We will want to persist in the state when it fits our ego's needs and reject what comes along that may challenge it. We will resist reflection about the values and world-view in which we have found comfort, giving in to the "laziness and cowardice" (WE: 8:35) that come from an "*inclination towards* [the] *passive use of reason*" (JL: 9:76).

Given this interpretation of the dark side of the Predisposition to Humanity, let us consider how our drive to establish and sustain a positive sense of self-worth impacts our first encounter with the moral law. As noted earlier, Kant believes that somewhere around the age of eight or nine our rational capacity has matured to the point where we become aware of the moral law; and as described in the *Critique of Practical Reason*, this awareness will generate feelings of both humility and respect. When we act upon the latter, we take on the moral law as the subjective ground of our action (i.e., *acting from duty* as characterized in the *Groundwork*). But with the awakening of respect for the moral law, there comes as well a "negative effect" upon a person's "opinion of his personal worth" (CPrR: 5:78) and a feeling of humility or "humiliation" (*Demüthigung*) that is supposed to "thwart" our inclinations and "strike down self-conceit" (CPrR: 5:73).

If the child's initial awareness of the moral law brings with it these attacks on his ego, what should we expect the child's response to be to this "infringement upon the inclinations" (CPrR: 5:73)? After having struggled through much of his short life to secure a positive sense of self-worth, and after having cultivated cognitive biases and techniques of self-deception to rebuff challenges to it, would not the child take this first encounter with the moral law, with its humiliating provocation, as yet just another threat? Kant acknowledges that even once we have matured, we will still constantly "quibble" with morality (GR: 4:405) and commit many self-serving "inner lies" in the service of our inclinations and sense of self-importance (MM: 6:430). So, at the first glimmerings of our moral vocation, while our grasp of it is still weak and its authority still murky, the child will look upon it as a danger to his sense of self-worth. Its call will be treated as yet another threat and just as one does in response to other psychological threats, it will be dismissed, its claims will be undercut through some inner act of "dishonesty, by which we throw dust in our own eyes" (6:38).

This reaction can be thought of as a natural consequence of the Predisposition to Humanity, analogous to how Kant describes the production of transcendental illusions by the rational faculty. In both cases, there is an innate capacity that begets illusions of one sort or another. In one case, the illusions are produced through the faculty's pathological drive to the "unconditioned condition" and this "does not cease even though it is uncovered" (A297/ B353). It "cannot be avoided at all, just as little as we can avoid it that the sea appears higher in the middle than at the shores" (A297/B353). Likewise, the Predisposition to Humanity carries the inclination to secure a sense of self-worth and will generate what illusions are necessary for its sake. This drive is behind such phenomena as the confirmation bias, rationalizations, wishful thinking, and the many specific inner lies we tell ourselves daily. We are causally responsible for all of this, and even if we choose to confront the lies we have told ourselves, neither does the Predisposition to Humanity cease to be, nor do its ego-protective processes.[16] These processes are active in childhood, at a time before we can be held morally responsible for them, and will continue to react against the moral law's demand upon us, with quibbles and illusions, whether or not we choose to allow them to deceive us. Thus, the facticity of these mechanisms that are active and opposing to the moral law will endure, regardless of what we will.

Yet just as we can come to see transcendental illusion as the result of reason's pathology, so likewise we can come to see what we have been doing in response to the moral law. As Kant puts it in the *Metaphysics of Morals*, one cannot help "waking up from time to time" (MM: 6:436), and when one does, one can either take measures to help curb one's inner lies or descend back into them, choosing to perpetuate or even strengthen their delusory powers. It is, I contend, in how we choose to respond to this process of inner lies, rooted ultimately in the Predisposition to Humanity, that the Propensity to Evil becomes something for which we are to be held responsible. Its existence is outside of our control. We do not will its coming into existence and we lack the power to eradicate it. But we can decide whether or not to keep it in check or to let it reign over us. As such, its mere facticity should not be taken as the basis for determining our moral worth. That, instead, depends upon the *Gesinnung* choice, for it is through that choice that we decide whether or not to take up the illusions offered by the Propensity to Evil and give in to self-interest.

THE FOURTH DESIDERATUM: FROM PROPENSITY TO *GESINNUNG* CHOICE

As noted above, it is not uncommon to find in the secondary literature interpretations of Part One that posit a noumenal agent and associate it with the adoption of our Propensity to Evil and/or the *Gesinnung* choice. Comments about "an intelligible deed, cognizable through reason alone" (6:31) and a "determining ground not in time" (6:39) have been taken as evidence that our moral status is the result of some noumenal event. Yet these comments, when taken in context, convey a different, far more mundane picture. Kant repeatedly explains that some choices are assigned to us as a matter of rational deduction rather than introspection. Just as we may retroactively ascribe to ourselves a particular maxim after we have observed how we have behaved and seek to explain it, so likewise the choice(s) that ground our moral status are "representation(s) of reason" (6:39) in the sense that "if we wish to engage in an explanation of evil with respect to its *beginning in time*, we must trace the causes of every deliberate transgression in a previous time of our lives, all the way back to the time when the use of reason had not yet developed" (6:42–43).

Note here that Kant does not trace the cause of our transgressions back to something outside of time, but rather "all the way back *to the time* when the use of reason had not yet developed" [my emphasis]. As he puts the point: each person's *Gesinnung* "has been the one way or the other *always, from his youth on*" (6:25). The moral law first becomes manifest to us in our childhood, and so it is at this time, "when the use of reason had not yet developed" or at least not fully developed, that we begin to respond to it. As I have described the emergence of the Propensity to Evil above, when the moral law first becomes manifest to us, we will react against it as yet another threat to our sense of self-worth and so generate various inner lies to rebuff its humiliating effect.

Given Kant's Rigorism, it is not unreasonable to claim that the first time we make a choice about whether to accept our inner lies, our *Gesinnung* has been set. But I do wonder, and offer for speculation, that if the moral law's first appearances are murky, perhaps we would not at first be certain of its absolute authority. Although it comes to be "apodictically certain" for us (CPrR: 5:47), it may be that when it first manifests between the ages of eight and ten, we cannot yet be certain whether or not it is a legitimate principle of practical reason or an excessive and artificial stricture. Thus, there may be a period in our youth where we do not simply choose for or against the moral law, but may choose for or against taking its first appearances seriously. Through these uncertainties, the Propensity to Evil can gain a foothold, for it can exploit our initial uncertainty and preserve it as a tactic to cast doubt on the moral law in the future, even after our rationality fully matures.

Eventually, however, a principled response to the moral law is established and we may retrospectively then attribute to ourselves a choice of this principle. Our delusory maneuvers inevitably lead to a choice through which we give priority to self-interest over morality. This then is what finally determines the status of our *Gesinnung* as evil. The Propensity leads us to it, but we still have to will it. In doing so, the Propensity to Evil is given dominance and will presumably gain even greater power over us as we habitually rebuff the moral law as an obnoxious intrusion into our pursuit of personal happiness. In this way, the Propensity and evil *Gesinnung* are mutually reinforcing. The former shapes our psychology such that we choose the latter, and the latter then promotes the continuing activity of the former.

The Propensity to Evil is, thus, distinct from the evil *Gesinnung*. The former logically and causally precedes the latter, even though they do seem to converge once we choose to give the former rule within our *Gesinnung*. But this convergence is through an act of will whereby a practical principle is installed within our will. If the two were treated as actually the same, as it seems Henry Allison did in his attempt to establish a formal proof of the moral status of the species, we would lose the possibility of a Change of Heart. This is not a minor issue, a sideline in how *Religion*'s account of evil is to be rendered. Part One, read in isolation, may suggest this, but the whole of *Religion* is about the transformation of the individual and society from evil to good. Accordingly, this transformation is essential, and so, however the Propensity to Evil is interpreted, the possibility of a Change of Heart must be preserved.

THE FIFTH DESIDERATUM: THE CHANGE OF HEART

We will discuss the Change of Heart at length in the next chapter. Our focus here is specifically on how it should shape the interpretation of the Propensity to Evil. As stated above, it is a common mistake to overlook the relevance of the Change of Heart to the Propensity to Evil. Just as the Christian doctrine of Original Sin was developed to explain what the Crucifixion offers redemption from, so likewise the account of evil in Part One sets the stage for the Change of Heart introduced in its General Remark and discussed more fully in Part Two. Any interpretation of Radical Evil should therefore be guided by its relationship to the Change of Heart and, certainly, must preserve its possibility.

That becomes far more difficult if one chooses to merge the Propensity to Evil with the evil *Gesinnung*, for the former is clearly presented as ineliminable; and so if one were to say the same about the latter, the possibility of a Change of Heart is undermined. Accordingly, the interpretation here presented does separate these two aspects of Kant's doctrine of Radical Evil, holding that even though the former "cannot be eradicated" (6:31), the moral status of one's *Gesinnung* rests upon and is transformed through a "restoration of the original ethical order among incentives" (6:50).

Regrettably, the Change of Heart has received relatively little attention by comparison to the Propensity to Evil, and, egregiously, hardly has anyone seen Kant's interest in moral redemption as the motivation behind his examination of the nature of evil. Rather, our evil Propensity is often treated as the highlight of *Religion*'s moral anthropology, thus skewing its depiction of human nature into something far more grim. By contrast, if Kant's claim that the species is by nature evil is understood as part of a larger moral story, then we may see *Religion* as not only a text filled with hope, but with awe, for its primary aim is not to articulate the depths of our depravity, but rather the augustness of our rise beyond it.

THE THREE GRADES OF EVIL (6:29–32)

Kant describes our Propensity to Evil as having three grades (*Stufen*). The first is called "the frailty of human nature" and is described as "the general weakness of the human heart in complying with the adopted maxims" (6:29). The second is an impurity of motives, where we "adulterate moral incentives with immoral ones." The third is given a number of different names: "depravity," "corruption of the human heart," and "perversity." It is characterized as "the propensity to adopt evil maxims" (6:29), "the propensity of the power of choice to maxims that subordinate the incentives of the moral law to others (not moral ones)," a heart that "reverses the ethical order as regards the incentives," and a corruption of the mind's attitude "at its root" (6:30).

In what sense we have different "grades" is not easy to determine. Kant's language suggests that they are worsening degrees, and this in turn may lead some to assume that we progress from one to the next as our evil *Gesinnung* drives us farther and farther away from morality. Consider, however, the similarity between the third grade of evil and what it is to have an evil *Gesinnung*. In both cases, there is a corruption whereby we adopt evil maxims and subordinate morality to self-interest. Moreover, consider that one implication of the first grade is that we deceive ourselves regarding the nature of our own agency. As an act of self-deception, the first grade seems to presuppose the depravity of the third. Thus, I do not think we should treat the three grades of evil as worsening degrees. It may be granted that in depravity there is a greater consciousness of one's stance towards the moral law, a "deliberate guilt (*dolus*), and is characterized by a certain *perfidy* on the part of the human heart (*dolus malus*) in deceiving itself as regards its own good or evil disposition" (6:38). However, this stance is still implied in the two other grades, and so to both those grades we must still assign a maxim that gives priority to self-interest over morality.

We may instead consider these three grades as parallels to the three Predispositions to the Good. In frailty, we tell ourselves that we are too weak to not give in to some desire. This correlates well with the Predisposition to Animality and the vices that may be "grafted" to it. Our bodily desires can be very intense and may provoke the feeling that they may sometimes be beyond one's control.

Similarly, impurity can be linked to the Predisposition to Humanity. As the Predisposition to Humanity is centrally responsible for our social structure, our public institutions legislate regarding our conduct rather than our intent. Hence, they tolerate (or even expect) that our obedience does not come from anything other than self-interest. In impurity, we tell ourselves that acting from duty is inessential to our moral worth and that our obligations can be fulfilled through our behavior, regardless of motive. The impure agent hence finds an excuse to forgo his inner moral struggle in society's demand that one need only act in conformity with duty, and so exchanges the call of morality for the esteem of others, an approval he hopes to gain through outward appearance.

Lastly, depravity correlates with the Predisposition to Personality. Where the Predisposition to Personality pertains to the bindingness of the moral law upon us, so depravity denies the law's rightful status. The depraved agent may thus tell himself that the commands of morality lack supreme authority over the will, are not overriding, or do not pervade the whole of life. As I suggested above, even the frail and impure are depraved in that they take on an inner perfidy that just as well qualifies their relationship to morality. Moreover, they, like the depraved, have subordinated the incentive of the moral law to self-interest. But if we are to read depravity as more extreme in some way, it may be taken as a more conscious rejection of the moral law's stature.

The frail agent does not admit to himself that he has subordinated the law, and rather perpetrates an inner lie about his inability to carry out his duties when desires pull him in a different direction. The impure agent lies to himself that the call of morality can be fulfilled through how one behaves rather than through the motives upon which one acts. The depraved agent, however, just more directly and more explicitly prioritizes self-interest, granting it dominance while downgrading the moral law.

DIABOLICAL EVIL (6:35–39)

In addition to the above three grades of evil, Kant mentions one more: diabolical evil. He describes it as the "corruption of the morally legislative reason" or simply "evil reason" (6:35). It occurs when "resistance to the law would be … elevated to incentive" (6:35). However, Kant considers this grade as beyond what is possible for us: "The human being (even the worst) does not repudiate the moral law, whatever his maxims, in rebellious attitude (by revoking obedience to it)" (6:36). It is, rather, the form of evil that demons (if any were to exist) would presumably have.

When we choose to prioritize self-interest over morality, we do not reject the latter outright. Even if we understand the prioritization of self-interest as a rebellion against the moral law, we do not outright revoke obedience to it. Even in depravity, the third grade of evil discussed above, the agent wantonly declares his interests as having more worth than morality, but does not consider the latter to be of no or negative worth. Of course, an agent might delude himself into thinking that he has followed Milton's Satan in declaring "Evil be thou my good," but according to Kant this is not something we humans can do. Even the most evil among us will still experience the moral law within, its pressure upon our self-conceit and its authority to direct our action.

This exclusion of diabolical evil may, however, seem naive. Given the litany of horrors that humans have perpetrated, explanations that come down to mere self-interest may seem just too languid. Even if self-interest drives most instances of immorality, it is hard to accept that no one has ever so rebelled against morality that they chose to commit an action just for the sake of its badness. Yet, according to Kant, we cannot do evil for evil's sake. That option is only available, it seems, for Satan and his legion.

Trying to prove why this is the case – why human beings cannot be diabolically evil – is difficult. An argument may be given that total renunciation of the moral law is not even a possibility. Alternately, it may be argued more modestly that it is just not a possibility *for us.* The former seems to argue for too much, as it would also exclude the possibility of non-human diabolical agents.[17] The latter, however, is hard to sustain given that in the "Theodicy" and *Religion*, Kant expresses the importance of rendering human evil in terms of an active and opposing principle. We do not merely fail to act morally, as a result of some lack of inner development.

We also seem to have here a different position than the one usually rendered out of the *Metaphysics of Morals'* claim that "the possibility of deviating from it [the moral law] is an incapacity" (MM: 6:227). If the possibility of deviation from the moral law comes from "an incapacity," we fall back into the problem from which the "Theodicy" sought to extricate us. Moreover, if this statement applies generally to all rational beings, and not just humanity, then it also seems to threaten the possibility of diabolical evil. So, assuming we want to preserve the diabolical evil of non-human agents, we need an argument that is specifically tailored to human agency – what it is about us in particular that excludes the possibility of diabolical evil. Of course, much of the evil that we do may come out of self-interest and its prioritization over morality. But if the diabolical is not a possibility for us, then we must find a way in which it is barred only for us versus for all rational agents.

If it is argued that rational agents are necessarily subject to the moral law because it offers a formal condition for practical justification, then once again, we may not be able to sustain the possibility of the diabolical. If practical rationality requires that choice is rooted in justificatory criteria and justification necessarily involves as part of its formal structure the demand that maxims are universalizable, then how could a being capable of liberating himself from the incentive to morality still retain his rationality after doing so? One might suggest that Satan's rebellion did dislodge the moral incentive, but if so, could we still consider him rational?

Thus, if we want to explain why the diabolical is not possible for human beings, we risk undoing its logical possibility altogether. Assuming that the latter is not an acceptable option (though one might argue that it is), then whatever reasoning is used to satisfy Kant's claim that the diabolical is not possible for us must be duly tempered so as to preserve its logical possibility. One strategy here is to treat Satan's rebellion as a sort of polarity shift in the motivational significance that is tied to the moral law. The diabolical will may neither give up freedom or rationality, but inverts the effect that justification has upon the will. That is, a diabolical agent may still test to see if his maxims are universalizable, but when he discovers that they are not, he is motivated to act upon them (Samet-Porat 2007).

This strategy can be drawn out in various ways, depending upon whether or not one wants to read Kant and his understanding of the diabolical in terms of motivational internalism or externalism, and also what place is given to moral feeling as perhaps an affective mediator between the intellect and the will. But I will leave the issue here. Kant does seem to recognize the logical possibility of a diabolical will, even though it is not a possibility for humanity. However, I am not persuaded that an adequate argument can be given. *If* it is possible for a free and rational demon, then the Kantian would be hard pressed to show (without just begging the question) that it is merely not possible for us.

ORIGINAL SIN AND *RELIGION*'S EXPERIMENT (6:39–44)

I am going to defer commenting on the "General Remark" (6:44–53) until the next chapter because its topic, the Change of Heart, is also the main topic of Part Two. Instead, let us take a moment to consider how well the experiment of *Religion* has fared in Part One. As Kant explains in the Second Preface, *Religion* seeks to determine the extent to which traditional Christian doctrine overlaps with the Pure Rational System of Religion.

In Part One, the doctrine at issue is, of course, Original Sin, and as this part comes to a close, Kant compares what he has said to the story of Adam and Eve. He is not interested in the story's historical veracity. He recommends agnosticism about this because the question of its veracity is immaterial to what is of genuine religious importance (6:43n). What really does matter is instead its moral meaning. So, read as an allegory, Kant interprets the initial innocence of Adam and Eve as symbolizing our freedom to refrain from immoral conduct. Although the story presents us with a transition from innocence to corruption, Kant wants us to use its imagery as a reminder that in every misdeed, we fall anew. So, rather than claiming that humanity moves from innocence to sin either as a species or in the course of each person's life, he rather asserts that we should see our innocence as enduring along with our freedom, since just prior to every misdeed, we are as yet not guilty of it. Accordingly, he writes that we may consider each evil deed as if we "had just stepped out of the state of innocence into evil" (6:41).

In addition, Kant puts the story to a second use. After rejecting the view that our sin is to be understood as inherited from Adam and Eve (6:40), he uses the story to help depict our moral condition. As Adam and Eve were tempted by "sensory inducements" (6:42), so we are too, and like them, we "rationalize downgrading ... obedience to the command." The adage from Romans

5:12 "in Adam we have all sinned" (6:42), is thus interpreted by Kant as allegory for "what we do daily" (6:42).

The above interpretative positions may seem to some peculiar, but Kant has a reason for them. As religion is most fundamentally about moral improvement, he reads the Bible in terms of allegories and symbols that can be of use in our efforts to progress morally. He says this quite directly with regards to various interpretations of the afterlife (6:69n; ET: 8:329), and elsewhere suggests that we disregard some doctrines because they have no such practical value (6:80n, 7:39). He even recommends that authorial intent can be put aside if there is some other way to read the passage that would better contribute to our moral growth (7:64). Thus, when he considers the story of Adam and Eve, he sees its greatest practical value in its reminding us that in each violation of morality, it is as if we fall anew from "the state of innocence into evil." Rather than take the story as about something in the past, something already done, the story better serves as a reminder in the midst of life of what we ought to do and what we are forsaking when we fail.

Kant's allegorical analysis then concludes by noting that any rational account of evil will be incomplete as there remains something "inexplicable" in the Propensity to Evil (6:43). He expresses perplexity at the fact that "[e]vil can have originated only from moral evil ... yet the original predisposition ... is a predisposition to the good" (6:43). He recognizes that this Predisposition is corrupted by us, but prior to its having been corrupted, we are without the moral evil that could lead to the corruption. This mystery is accordingly represented in Genesis by the addition of some other being, "a *spirit* of an originally more sublime destiny" who tempts us (6:44). If we draw this point back to our previous discussion of the Propensity to Evil, the tempting spirit can be seen as something within us. As "spirit" Kant gestures towards his repeated claim that bodily inclinations are not the source of evil, and as a tempting *force* within us, we must not presume (as the "Theodicy" makes clear), that evil comes from "the limitations of our nature" (6:43). It is thus not the body and its desires, nor a negation or privation that simply lacks the strength to heed morality. There is rather an inward and active principle that is the cause of evil – a positive principle of corruption, a serpent coiled in the human heart.

NOTES

1 *Gesinnung* is often translated as "disposition." In Pluhar's translation of *Religion*, he chooses "attitude." Stephen Palmquist argues for "conviction" in his forthcoming commentary on *Religion*. But none of these quite capture the German. A more literal translation might be something like "mentality" or "state of mind," but I take the term to have a similar meaning to "character." However, we cannot use this term since Kant uses *Charakter* in the *Anthropology* to represent a principled and stable practical orientation, though one that does not necessarily reflect either a moral or immoral status. In lieu of any strong options in English, I have decided to retain the original German.

2 By "radical" Kant does not mean an extreme degree of evil. Rather, the German word *radikal* derives from the Latin word *radix*, which means "root."

3 Note that the argument for Rigorism in *Religion* is an argument by elimination – through a rejection of the empirical alternatives, Kant takes Rigorism to be suitably established. The core of this argument captures the central philosophical theses that (a) there is a singular supreme maxim; and (b) that supreme maxim must be either good or evil. Kant's case for (b) is rooted in the nature of the moral law, which commands unconditionally. Hence, a supreme maxim that downgrades or qualifies the authority of the moral law is in violation of it.

4 Although it is fairly common to view this thesis as applying to Kantian agency from the *Groundwork* onwards, I am not persuaded that this is so. We have examined this issue to some extent in Chapter 1. Further, as we will discuss below, in the 1780s Kant routinely described our immorality in terms of a limitation on our part or a failure to fully develop our capacity to be moral. This suggests that he may have viewed inclination as capable of moving the uncultivated will, or at least more powerful inclination as sometimes exceeding our self-control. Consequently, I regard his understanding of moral agency as developing through three stages. The first is (predominantly) pre-critical, though it can also be found in the *Critique of Pure Reason*. We examined this in Chapter 1. Then, he comes to regard pure practical

reason as itself able to move the will, yet insofar as he describes evil as a product of our limitations, it may be that he saw us as susceptible to the determining influence of inclination. Lastly, in the 1790s, as a result of the reflections upon the relationship between freedom and evil found in the "Theodicy," he saw that evil must (just like morally good actions) be positively chosen. Additional clarity on this point may underlie *Religion*'s articulation of the Incorporation Thesis.

5 Of course, we are not always conscious of our maxims. But this does not mean that our actions do not still stem from them. Much of what we do is through habit, but habit, for Kant, is still the product of our acting on maxims. They become so established within us that our choice to activate them hardly flickers in our consciousness. Nevertheless, we can always reflect upon our behavior after the fact and identify the principles of volition we have employed.

6 It does not follow from this, however, that all the content of all our maxims are somehow derived from the supreme maxim. Maxims obviously contain various empirical contents. But as we know from the *Groundwork* and elsewhere, maxims must be tested against the moral law. It ought to be the gatekeeper for whatever it is we do, and the supreme maxim we adopt reflects how fully we commit to it.

7 One might wonder how Kant's division of human nature into Predispositions *to the Good* and a Propensity *to Evil* is compatible with Latitudinarian Syncretism. If our natures carry some good and some evil principles, does it not follow that there is within the sort of "coalition" that Syncretism proffers? It certainly does seem that we do have a mixed moral nature, and so at root, human nature should neither be seen as absolutely or fundamentally good or evil. A response to this question can be given by considering the role of choice with regards to our predispositions and propensities. According to Kant, the former are not chosen by us. Although we might choose whether or not to act on them, they are simply facts about what it is to be a human being. The Propensity to Evil, likewise, is both in one sense an innate fact beyond our choosing, while in another sense, what role we allow it to have in our lives is chosen (see 6:29). As facts of human nature, we may see neither as on their own making us morally culpable. Since we do not choose what it is to be a human being, we cannot be held responsible for these characteristics. We can, however, be held responsible for what we do with them, and so, following Kant's

argument for Rigorism, we must have a supreme maxim. That supreme maxim will either harness the moral good within us (our "seed of goodness" or Predisposition to Personality) or give ourselves over to the bad.

8 Note that Di Giovanni sometimes translate *Keim des Guten* as "seed of goodness" (e.g. 6:20) but other times as "germ of goodness" (6:45). The German is, however, the same.

9 Frierson also notes that Kant sometimes also distinguishes between "general" (*generale*) and "universal" (*allgemein*) propositions (Frierson 2003: 39). In addition to the passages just cited, see (AN: 7:242) and (JL: 9:102).

10 Such a will goes beyond the Second *Critique*'s characterization of moral perfection as a "*complete conformity* of dispositions with the moral law" (CPrR: 5:122). This would still be an impressive achievement, but one that falls short of a holy will, as it does not necessitate compliance with the moral law. Moral perfection reflects, rather, the ideal of virtue: someone who has fully mastered his inclinations and optimally adapted them to the demands of morality. But the relation remains contingent. Evil remains a possibility in such a case, though it is just never willed.

Virtue is something that we cultivate bit by bit through our lives, it involves a "constant *progress* from bad to better" (6:48). It is a gradual reform whereby we gain greater control over our inclinations and adjust them so that they better accord with morality. We may begin this process while still in sin, while self-interest reigns over morality in our *Gesinnung*, and we may continue with it long after having a Change of Heart (see 6:75n). The inclinations never go away, nor do our Predispositions, and nor does the evil Propensity. The Change of Heart may realize a good *Gesinnung*, but this refers specifically to the change in supreme maxims to one that gives priority to morality over self-interest. It does not do away with the finite nature of our wills or its flaws. It does not guarantee moral compliance either, as we can still be tempted, fail, and even come to forsake the Change of Heart under the enduring influence of the Propensity to Evil and the corrupting influence of others. We will return to this issue in Chapters 5 and 7.

11 Moreover, if having an evil Propensity does not undermine the possibility of occasional moral action, then having a good Propensity should not undermine the possibility of occasional immoral actions.

Propensities do not fully determine our wills as Allison's argument implies, and so he should not treat a good Propensity as the same as a holy will.

12 As for other a priori strategies, they may not make these specific errors, but they do carry difficulties of their own. For instance, in "The Missing Formal Proof of Humanity's Radical Evil in Kant's *Religion*," Seiriol Morgan presents an interpretation that has many details in common with the one I will develop below, but he regards his argument as a priori, revealing the "Missing Formal Proof," and describes the proof as moving "from some accepted phenomenon [i.e., moral evil] to the reality of its conditions of possibility" (Morgan 2005: 86). Similarly, Stephen Palmquist, in his "Kant's Quasi-Transcendental Argument for a Necessary and Universal Evil Propensity in Human Nature," claims that Kant is moving from the general experience of moral evil to the Propensity (Palmquist 2008: 281). Both are, I believe, correct. However, the inference from a given phenomenon to its conditions is not always going to be a formal, a priori argument. Moving from some given phenomenon to its conditions is the basic form of transcendental arguments, but it is also the form of merely abductive arguments as well.

13 One might offer the retort that if we have control over our level of limitation, we can be held morally responsible for the deeds that come as a result. Let's say, for example, that I cannot stop myself from drinking when I get angry, but it is within the scope of my powers to change this. I could through therapy or mere self-discipline learn to manage my anger differently. Hence, it seems that even if some wrong is outside of one's present level of control, insofar as that level can be adjusted, one remains culpable. It may be responded that whether or not one has gained control over oneself in various regards is itself a matter of one's various limitations. So, if I have not gained control over my drinking when I get angry, that may be due to some other moral weakness on my part, which in turn has not been overcome because of yet another weakness. To illustrate this point, let's say that at the age of ten, one first comes to awaken to the moral law and recognizes thereby that one ought to cease taunting one's younger sibling. But at the age of ten, one has gained very little self-discipline and so ignores the demand of morality. These initial conditions may cascade through future issues of self-discipline and so if it is granted

that there ever is some drive that is at a given time beyond one's control, the logical space has been opened to the problem of moral responsibility that Kant hopes to redress in the "Theodicy." This, at least, is an expressed worry in 1791 and so I suspect that this marks when he turned from the earlier privation model to an active and opposing cause of evil.

14 Because our inclinations need to be mastered should not be taken to mean that Kant saw our inclinations as evil. Just as in *Religion*, in the texts of the 1780s our inclinations play a role in why we deviate from the moral law but still that deviation comes about through a voluntary accession to our inclinations. The key difference I am here pointing to is that prior to *Religion*, Kant tends to model our moral deviations in terms of some privation on our part. As mentioned, this is quite evident in the Second *Critique*'s discussion of our eternal striving in the afterlife as well as in the *Groundwork*'s characterization of our inclinations as a "counterweight" to morality. In both texts, immorality is explained in terms of a failure of autocracy. However, in *Religion*, and I suspect as a result of the reflections we find in Kant's "Theodicy," Kant recognizes that such a privation model of evil is replaced with the "active and opposing" cause tied to the Propensity to Evil. Thus, in my view, the introduction of the "Propensity to Evil" in *Religion* does not merely give name to some notion that was already *fully* present in the *Groundwork* or Second *Critique*. It should, rather, be seen as either the maturation of something still inchoate in earlier texts or an actual advance in Kant's theory of evil.

15 A similar point is made by Andrews Reath in his analysis of self-conceit. Although he does not develop this analysis in relation to the Propensity to Humanity as robustly as Anderson-Gold or Wood, he nevertheless recognizes that "the object of self-conceit is best described as personal worth or esteem, or importance in the opinions of others. It is a desire to be highly regarded, or a tendency to esteem oneself over others." (Reath 1989: 292).

16 Kant claims that the Propensity to Evil is inextricable (6:51) and so even after a Change of Heart, it remains possible for it to again dominate our practical lives (6:93–94). Thus its mechanisms will remain active, just as the mechanisms that lead to transcendental illusion also remain active even after we have liberated ourselves from their errors.

17 Matters could be made much simpler if Kant thought that diabolical evil was in itself impossible, but the text does not bear this out. Kant tells us that a diabolical agent would harbor "a reason exonerated from the moral law"; "resistance to the law would thereby be elevated to incentive ... and so the subject would be made a *diabolical* being." On the one hand, this may be taken as "absolutely impossible" as it implies reason can "extirpate within itself the dignity of the law itself" (6:35). But Kant goes on to state that this is just something that is not "applicable to the human being" (6:35). Moreover, both Kant's continued remarks through Part One and his long excursus on the personification of the evil principle in Part Two (6:78–84) should indicate that he did not see the diabolical agent as self-contradictory. This problem of reconciling the possibility of diabolical agency with its impossibility *for us* is borne out in the ample literature on Part One. See, for example, Muchnik 2009: 109–19, Sussman 2009 and Samet-Porat 2007.

4

PART TWO OF *RELIGION*
THE CHANGE OF HEART

Part Two begins with a reminder of Part One's thesis that there must be a positive principle behind moral evil, an "active and opposing cause of evil" (6:57). As we have discussed, Kant's "Theodicy" rejects the view that our moral failures should be understood through a privation model whereby our misdeeds are the result of a limitation, incapacity, or a deficient development of the "seed of goodness." At the start of Part Two, Kant also reiterates his earlier claim that it would be a mistake to treat our natural inclinations as the principal cause of our immorality. He further adds to this that those who do see immorality in this way are not merely making a philosophical error, but a practical one. Even though moral continence is relevant to Kant, and is central to his understanding of virtue, this is not where our fundamental moral struggle lies. Thus, those who struggle to master their appetites are engaged in more of a side skirmish rather than the central battle against their Propensity to Evil.

This is an important issue for Part Two. At its focus is how we become well-pleasing to God, i.e., come to be worthy of membership in HG$_i$, Kant wants to make sure that readers know their enemy. The nature of evil is not something that was always clear to Kant, or at least not something that he always saw in the same way. For example, the *Critique of Practical Reason* presents our moral mission in terms more amenable to virtue theory, for in its discussion of the Postulate of Immortality, Kant claims that through the afterlife, we are to strive to better align our inclinations with morality. This, however, is not the position advanced in *Religion*. In its polemic against virtue, a polemic we began to consider in Chapter One, Kant wishes to distinguish the path laid out by the Stoical "watchword" *virtue* (6:57) from the path he develops through Parts One and Two.

As discussed earlier, in Part One, Kant represents virtue in terms of the development of habits and traits that remain "in conformity with the prized principle of happiness" (6:47). Likewise, at the opening of Part Two, he reprises this polemical use of virtue, claiming that the Stoics, with their emphasis on courage and continence, "mistook their enemy" (6:57). Neither are our inclinations in themselves evil, nor are they "the really true enemy" (6:58n). They may "invite transgression" (6:58n) and their mastery is something that Kant continues to regard as important. But we must take care not to follow the many who "mistook their enemy" and thought that their battle was against inclinations, fought on the plains of virtue. Our true enemy is far more insidious. It "hides behind reason" (6:57) and "secretly undermines the disposition with soul-corrupting principles" (6:57).

This point should not be overlooked, for despite there being a place for virtue in Kant's practical philosophy, it is important to recognize that the cultivation of various felicitous traits is of secondary importance to our true moral project. So, despite his use of "virtue" elsewhere,[1] in *Religion*, Kant repeatedly points out that our fundamental moral worth is not a matter of virtue, but a function of the order of incentives within our supreme maxim. This does not mean that virtue is of no importance, but in *Religion*, Kant emphasizes that virtue's call for autocracy (and other adjustments of inclination) is not the same as the Change of Heart. We can choose to pursue virtue as a consequence of our deepening commitment to morality, or we can choose it simply out of self-interest. We may decide to master various appetites, delay gratification, or even cultivate philanthropic interests solely for the sake of our own happiness. Thus, Kant wants to make clear, virtue is quite compatible with having an evil *Gesinnung*. As he states in Part One:

> not the slightest *change of heart* is necessary for this; only a change of *mores*. A human being here considers himself virtuous whenever he feels himself stable in his maxims of observance of duty – though not by virtue of the supreme ground of all maxims, namely duty, but [as when], for instance, an immoderate human being converts to moderation for the sake of his health; a liar to truth for the sake of reputation; an unjust human being to civic righteousness for the sake of peace of profit, etc.
>
> (6:47)

All virtues can thus remain "in conformity with the prized principle of happiness" (6:47). They are developed through "gradual *reform*" of our habits as well as the management and adjustment of our inclinations, but remain distinct from the "*revolution* in the disposition of the human being" (6:47) whereby our supreme maxim is transformed. Accordingly, our moral exemplars should not be the courageous, the just, or even the beneficent. We may have other things to learn from them, but we should not consider the virtuous as our moral exemplars. In "the battle of the good against the evil principle for the dominion over the human being" it is not the stoic wise man whom we should follow, but, as Kant now contends, it is Jesus Christ.

KANT'S CHRISTOLOGY (6:60–78)

THE PERSONIFIED IDEA OF THE GOOD PRINCIPLE (6:60–62)

This section begins with a statement about the Highest Good that echoes the theme of §84–87 of the *Critique of Judgment*: "That which alone can make a world the object of divine decree and the end of creation is *Humanity* (rational beings in general as pertaining to the world) *in its full moral perfection*, from which happiness follows in the will of the Highest Being directly as from its supreme condition" (6:60). Similarly, in §84 of the *Critique of Judgment*, Kant raises the question of what is the final end "of creation itself" (CJ: 5:434), then in succeeding sections answers it by claiming that this end is "rational beings under moral laws" (CJ: 5:444) and, more fully, "a happiness of rational beings harmoniously coinciding with conformity to the moral law" (CJ: 5:451).

Kant then shifts from the general "Humanity in its full moral perfection" to the particular "[t]his human being, alone pleasing to God" (6:60) and proceeds to a series of New Testament phrases, primarily from the Gospel of John: "in him from all eternity," "God's only-begotten Son," "the Word," etc. In the second paragraph, we can see why Kant makes this shift, for the general "Humanity in its full moral perfection" is the expression of an Ideal or "prototype [*Urbilde*] of moral disposition [*Gesinnung*] in its entire purity" (6:61). Kant's allusions are clearly meant to have the reader think of Jesus Christ, and he continues to encourage that association as he writes that the *"prototype* has *come down* to us from heaven," has "taken up humanity," is the "Son of God," and has suffered "the most ignominious death, for the good of the world and even for his enemies" (6:61).

Finally, Kant calls for our *"practical faith in this Son of God"* (6:62), and so the text here carries the impression that Kant is endorsing a very traditional Christian conception of Jesus Christ. Yet this should provoke immediate suspicion, for such an endorsement is far more metaphysical than what an astute reader would expect from the father of Transcendental Idealism. For example, the claim that there is an eternal "prototype" *existing* in Heaven that has come to the world seems too much like Christian Platonism. But we must not forget that in keeping with its experiment of comparing Christian doctrine with Pure Rational Faith, *Religion* moves back and forth between the two. "The Personified Idea of the Good Principle," read in isolation, disconnected from the overall strategy of *Religion*, and separated even from its succeeding section "The Objective Reality of This Idea," does yield the impression that Kant is endorsing orthodox Christology if not one tinged with Christian Platonism. However, the next section, "The Objective Reality of This Idea," should disabuse careful readers of such presumptions.

But before we move to it, let us briefly consider Kant's use of "prototype" (*Urbild*). Some have taken the term to indicate a "Platonic turn" in Kant or a "Transcendental Platonism" (Firestone and Jacobs 2008: 157f). First, *Bild* is the German word for image and the *Ur* of *Urbild* denotes something's origin or an original versus a copy. So, *Urbild* and *Bild* convey a distinction between an original and its copy. Second, in the *Critique of Pure Reason*, Kant briefly discusses the Platonic *Urbild*, and though he praises Plato's turn from the empirical with regards to morality, Kant regards the hypostatization of the *Urbild* to be an "exaggerated expression" (A318/B375). *Urbilder* are, more mundanely, just entities of the mind, instruments of regulative judgment through which "the understanding is directed towards a certain goal" (A644/B672). Kant does not claim that *Urbilder* have a transcendent existence, nor does he presume that their non-empirical character demands that they exist in the way Plato suggests.

Rather, reason produces "ideals," individuated representations of general ideas, "determined, through the idea alone" (A568/B596). We may have the idea of what it would be like to manage a business, and out of that idea, we can envision an ideal working environment, staff, etc. The same applies to the ideal of a perfect spouse, pet, garden, etc. We can take our ideas and frame from them ideals, representations of a perfected form that help offer us practical guidance.

But they are just images we utilize in our pursuit of various goals. A passage from the *Critique of Practical Reason* is particularly helpful here:

> If I understand by an *idea* a perfection to which nothing adequate can be given in experience, the moral ideas are not, on that account, something transcendent, that is something of which we cannot even determine the concept sufficient or of which it is uncertain whether there is any object corresponding to it at all, as is the case with the

> ideas of speculative reason; instead, the moral ideas, as archetypes [*Urbilder*] of practical perfection, serve as the indispensable rule of moral conduct and also as the *standard of comparison*.
>
> (CPrR: 5:127n)

Accordingly, the Prototype of *Religion* is one such ideal of practical perfection. We find in the Gospels a representation that helps us grasp moral perfection and so helps guide us in our own efforts. This does, however, mean that Kant took the historical Jesus to in fact be the embodiment of the Prototype. Even if he achieved moral perfection, we should not conflate this with a metaphysical claim about the ideal becoming flesh. As ideals are products of reason, "no appearance can be found in which they may be represented *in concreto*" (A567/B595).

Kant certainly regards the Gospels as representing an ideal of moral perfection in its depiction of a life that "spread[s] goodness ... as far wide as possible through teaching and example" even when subject to "temptations and afflictions" (6:61). But we should not presume this to mean that he regards the actual person known to us as Jesus of Nazareth as an embodied Prototype. This would, first, run afoul of how he generally uses "*Urbild*"; and second, even if the principle of Hypostatic Union did obtain, or Jesus Christ was what Kierkegaard calls the "absolute paradox," these claims still rest upon the historical and so would not for Kant be proper objects of faith. We will discuss Kant's reasoning in greater detail when we get to the "Remarkable Antinomy" in Chapter 5, but in short he argues that religion does not (or should not) require a Historical Faith in the historical veracity of the Gospels. That is an empirical issue and Kant denounces any soteriological requirements that fall outside of what reason alone can establish.

Thus, despite the dramatic Johnnian language that begins this section, Kant is not proclaiming Jesus to be the Prototype *in concreto*, nor is he advancing a metaphysical claim, accepting the divinity of Jesus, or the doctrine of Hypostatic Union. He is, however, progressing with his experiment, considering the Bible's more "vivid mode of representing things" (6:83) and considering to what extent it correlates with the principles of Pure Rational

Faith. Whatever ties they have to actual historical events, the Gospels offer a depiction of a rational ideal. Our *"practical faith in this Son of God"* (6:62) is therefore not a faith in the Gospels' historical truth, but rather, as *practical*, it refers instead to its value for our moral lives: "The living faith in the prototype of a humanity well-pleasing to God (the Son of God) refers, *in itself*, to a moral idea of reason, insofar as the latter serves for us not only as guidance but as incentive as well" (6:119).

THE OBJECTIVE REALITY OF THIS IDEA (6:62–66)

In the *Critique of Pure Reason*, "objective reality" refers to whether or not a concept or idea can apply to objects of possible experience. Metaphysical ideas lack objective reality as they are not possible objects of experience. Monads and Platonic ideas, the soul and God, freewill and eternity are all outside of possible experience and so they lack objective reality – at least as the term is used in the *Critique of Pure Reason*.

However, in Kant's practical writings, "objective reality" is used differently: a concept or idea gains objective reality in relation to the moral law and the "needs of pure practical reason." This is explained in the Preface to the *Critique of Practical Reason*:

> the reality thought of here does not aim at any theoretical *determination of the categories* and extension of cognition to the supersensible but that what is meant by it is only that in this respect an *object* belongs to them, because they are either contained in the necessary determination of the will a priori or else are inseparably connected with the object of its determination.
>
> (CPrR: 5:5)

Similarly, Kant explains in the *Critique of Judgment* that there are ideas which "cannot be proved adequately in any experience possible for us ... but the use of which is nevertheless commanded by practical pure reason" (CJ: 5:469).

Most metaphysical ideas will lack objective reality in both the theoretical and practical sense, as they not only are not possible objects of experience, but also are not requirements of pure practical reason. However, as freedom, God, immortality, and the Highest Good are "indissolubly connected" with pure practical reason, they do qualify for objective reality in the practical, though not theoretical, sense. They may (or rather must) therefore be affirmed, though not as matters of either knowledge or opinion, since (as we discussed in Chapter 1) these are epistemic modes of assent that should be limited to the theoretical domain of objective reality. They are, instead, objects of faith (*Glaube*) as their ground of assent lies within the needs of practical reason.

Applying the above to the question of the objective reality of the Prototype, it is clear that the practical rather than theoretical standard should apply. As mentioned in the preceding section, the Prototype is an ideal, and ideals, presumably, can never be met with *in concreto*. Nevertheless, Kant realizes that some will want the Prototype to have objective reality in the theoretical sense. They will not be satisfied with its practical objective reality, and will instead want to find grounds for affirming it as a possible object of experience. Thus, they will seek epistemic standards, such as empirical evidence, and so will look to "miracles as credentials" (6:63). However, Kant contends, anyone who does this "thereby confesses to his own moral *unbelief*, to a lack of faith in virtue which no faith based on miracles (and thus only historical) can remedy" (6:63).

One might wonder as to why an interest in the Prototype as empirically real entails moral unbelief. Is it not possible for someone to *both* take its practical objective reality as a matter of faith and also have an interest in its empirical reality? To this one might respond simply by reiterating the point that ideals cannot be found in experience, and so one who is looking for evidence of it in empirical reality is looking for something that cannot truly be an ideal. It thus displays a misunderstanding of what the Prototype is, and so implies a failure to grasp its importance "as a model already in our reason" (6:62).

However, this does not seem to capture the tone of Kant's criticism. The error here is not simply theoretical in nature, but one that, for Kant, has practical implications. His concern is that those who want to answer the empirical question are probably interested in it because they are not convinced that the ideal "resides in our morally-legislative reason" (6:62) and/or that it residing in this way is adequate to the purpose(s) it is supposed to serve. That is, they are not convinced that our moral transformation fully resides on our own shoulders. Instead, they turn to miracles as evidence that supernatural aid is available.

Kant further rebuts such an appeal to evidence as irrelevant. Even if *per impossible*, the Prototype could be present in experience, experience "does not disclose the inwardness of the disposition" (6:63). Hence, miracles cannot testify to whether or not Jesus was the Prototype. Second, miracles are irrelevant because whatever evidence they yield, our moral transformation still will depend upon whether or not we appropriate the rational ideal as a representation that helps guide us morally:

> even if there never had been one human being capable of uncondi-
> tional obedience to the law, the objective necessity that there be such
> a human being would yet be undiminished and self-evident. There is
> no need, therefore, of any example from experience to make the idea
> of a human being morally pleasing to God a model to us; the idea is
> present as a model already in our reason.
>
> (6:62)

In sum, the objective reality of the Prototype pertains solely to its status as a rational ideal. Our faith in it has nothing to do with its presence in experience, but rather in our commitment to it as something that can guide us in our quest to become well-pleasing to God. We do not need an outward example, nor can one ever be proven. Consequently, neither do we have "cause to assume in him [Jesus] anything else except a naturally begotten human being" (6:63), nor is any such supposition of benefit to us "since the prototype which we see embedded in this apparition must be sought in us as well" (6:63).

So, despite his use of Johnnian imagery at the opening of "The Personified Idea of the Good Principle," we can now see how far removed Kant's actual views are from the implied metaphysics found in this Gospel. As he does on various occasions throughout *Religion*'s examination of the overlap between traditional doctrine and the Pure Rational System of Religion, he begins with a more "vivid mode of representing things" that is *"suited to the common people"* (6:83), then removes this "mystical cover" (6:83), and in so doing conveys what he regards as the proper rational meaning behind traditional doctrine. Thus, in this case, once the "mystical cover" of the Johnnian imagery is removed, Kant wants us to see that (a) the Prototype as an ideal is incompatible with there being an actual embodied example; (b) even if the historical Jesus were somehow more than "a naturally begotten human being" (6:63), neither could we possibly know this to be the case, nor would it be of practical value for us; and (c) what is really of soteriological importance is the Prototype as it resides in our reason since it, rather than its putative historical instantiation, is what guides us in our pursuit to become well-pleasing to God.

Kant further adds a fourth and even more radical claim. In an astoundingly bold move for one living in the eighteenth century, and one for which a price was paid, Kant actually presents us with a practical argument *against* the divinity of Jesus. Although he has been arguing that we have no need for an objectively real instantiation of the Prototype, this should not be taken to mean that actual examples of moral perfection are of no practical value. First of all, there is a "natural need of all human beings to demand for even the highest concepts and grounds of reason something that *the senses can hold on to*" (6:109). Secondly, Kant also recognizes the importance of examples in moral education. For instance, earlier in *Religion*, he writes that "the predisposition to the good is cultivated in no better way than by just adducing the *example* of good people" (6:48). Thus, the Gospels' portrayal of a morally perfect life can help us gain a clearer grasp of what perfection entails and can also help inspire our own moral improvement.[2]

However, the value one might get out of an example depends upon one's being able to identify with it. If its purpose is to facilitate our grasp of the *"Idea* (of humanity), with man as he ought to be" (MM: 6:480), we must be able to see ourselves in relation to the challenges it depicts and see its protagonist in struggles that reflect our own. So, as Kant characterizes its contents, we see in the Gospels a tale of a man who "spread[s] goodness about him as far wide as possible through teaching and example, but also, though tempted by the greatest temptation, to take upon himself all suffering, up to the most ignominious death" (6:61).

This example could inspire us to better ourselves and persevere amidst great adversity, but only if the protagonist of the Gospels were like us. The value of his example would be lost if he were regarded as "superhuman," "a Holy One above every frailty of human nature" (6:64). Though Kant arguably overlooks the doctrine of Hypostatic Union,[3] he maintains that by representing Jesus as more than human, we lose the basis through which we can draw inspiration from the Gospels. By assigning him instead a Divine nature, we would be treating his perfection as a product of that nature, and so would read his successes as a result of knowledge and/or powers that we lack. We would then no longer take Him to be *"an example to be emulated"* since "[t]he consequent distance from the natural human being would then again become so infinitely great that the divine human being could no longer be held forth to the natural human being as *example*" (6:64).

This section closes with an allusion to Philippians 3:9, stating that in the Prototype there is "a righteousness which is not our own" (6:66). On the one hand, we may be said to partake of this righteousness insofar as we have this ideal as a "model already in our reason." But the phrase also has a second meaning, one that is more typically associated with the doctrine of Vicarious Atonement, a doctrine that is "fraught with great difficulties" (6:66). In the next section, Kant considers these difficulties.

THE THREE DIFFICULTIES (6:66–78)

Kant presents three difficulties that stand in the way of our becoming well-pleasing to God. The First Difficulty concerns the infinite distance between our sinful state and what we must achieve in order to be well-pleasing to God. It addresses the question of how we can, while in a state of sin, undergo a transformation through which morality gains priority in our supreme maxim. Although the fact that we ought to undergo such a transformation entails that we are capable of it, Kant struggles with its possibility and in Part One states that it "surpasses every concept of ours" (6:45).[4] As we shall see, this difficulty reflects the soteriological principle that leads Christians to introduce the doctrine of Sanctifying Grace, but it leads Kant into what appears to be a concession (or at least a partial concession) to Pelagianism. The Second Difficulty concerns our ability to discern whether or not we have undergone a Change of Heart, and the dangers that both certainty and uncertainty pose to our moral motivation. To solve it, Kant makes a surprising use of the Postulate of Immortality, one that is quite different from what we have seen in previous texts. The Third Difficulty concerns the seeming impossibility of our wiping out our debt of sin. Again, this reflects a key issue in soteriology, one that corresponds to what the doctrine of Justifying Grace is intended to solve. However, once again, Kant rejects the standard Christian approach to this issue. As we shall see, he not only rejects the doctrine of Vicarious Atonement, but even the idea of Divine forgiveness in general.[5]

THE FIRST DIFFICULTY: THE INFINITE DISTANCE BETWEEN A GOOD AND EVIL *GESINNUNG* (6:66–67)

Kant describes the First Difficulty as follows:

> The law says: "Be ye holy (in the conduct of our lives) as your Father in Heaven is Holy," for this is the ideal of the Son of God which is being placed before us as a model. The distance between the goodness which we ought to effect in ourselves and the evil from which we start is, however, infinite, and so far as the deed is concerned – i.e. the conformity of the conduct of one's life to the holiness of the law – it is not exhaustible in any time.
>
> (6:66)

The solution that Kant offers to this problem in the Second *Critique* comes by way of the Postulate of Immortality. A future life is there postulated because our worthiness to receive happiness demands that we struggle "in an *endless progress*" (CPrR: 5:122) towards a "complete conformity with the moral law" (CPrR: 5:122). However, Kant further notes that even with an eternity of moral striving made possible through this Postulate, we will still fall short of that perfection and not be "fully adequate to God's will" (CPrR: 5:123). Thus, he here follows the tradition that humanity is unable to become genuinely worthy before God and so depends upon His forgiveness, taking our efforts through eternity "as [equivalent to] possession" (CPrR: 5:123n).

It is not uncommon for readers to assume that the above view from the Second *Critique* is of a piece with *Religion*, but there are many important differences between the soteriologies presented in each text. One key difference concerns what is required of us in order to become well-pleasing to God. As we have discussed, in the Second *Critique*, Kant presents our moral worthiness as based upon the pursuit of a perfection akin to the acquisition of virtue. Whereas in *Religion*, although we still have this duty, it is not the standard by which God judges us. That, rather, has become the Change of Heart.

There is also a second important difference between the two texts. As the Second *Critique*'s soteriology requires our "complete conformity of the will with the moral law," it commits us to something that we cannot possibly achieve, even with an eternity to work towards it. Thus, its solution to *Religion*'s First Difficulty follows the traditional Christian view on Justifying Grace, for we will inevitably fall short and so must depend upon Divine forgiveness. To be clear, this forgiveness does not raise us up to the standard of perfection, but rather is an act of mercy on God's part, awarding us beyond what we deserve.

By contrast, in *Religion*, we find a soteriological standard that can actually be met. In the previous chapter, we examined Kant's claim that we grant self-interest priority over morality in our supreme maxim. This is how the Pure Rational System represents the state of sin, and through the Change of Heart, we make a second *Gesinnung* choice, one that grants morality its rightful priority over self-interest. This change does not require that we strive through eternity in order to (at best) asymptotically approach it. Rather, it is something that can actually be achieved in life, through a spontaneous "revolution" (6:47) through which our *Gesinnung* transitions from evil to good.

Critique of Practical Reason	**Religion**

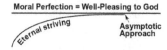

Moral Perfection = Well-Pleasing to God

Eternal striving

Asymptotic Approach

Soteriological standard = Moral Perfection*

* Neither through our own striving nor through Divine aid can we achieve moral perfection. God, however, accepts our <u>effort</u> as equivalent to possession (CPrR: 5:123n).

Self-interest / Morality →spontaneous revolution→ Morality / Self-interest

Soteriological standard = Change of Heart*

* Through a spontaneous "*revolution*" (6:47) in this life (6:71n), the moral incentive is given priority over self-interest. Note also that our "gradual *reform*" (6:47) through the pursuit of moral perfection remains a duty, but is distinguished from the soteriological standard of the Change of Heart (6:47, 6:67, 6:75n).

Figure 3 Critique of Practical Reason versus *Religion* on the soteriological threshold

Although the Change of Heart offers a soteriological standard that can actually be achieved, we still have the question as to whether or not this change is something we can do on our own or whether Divine aid is still needed. It is needed in the Second *Critique* because its soteriology has us inevitably falling short of what is required for our salvation. Divine aid is therefore required in order that our efforts (through eternal striving) are accepted as a substitute. However, in *Religion* this particular need for Divine assistance is removed. With the introduction of the Change of Heart, we do not need to be forgiven for falling short of a standard that cannot possibly be realized, for it is a standard that is actually within our reach. Nevertheless, this does not preclude some other necessary role for Divine aid. But unfortunately, the text is notoriously unclear on this point, with various passages conveying different views as to whether it is still in some way necessary, or whether we can accomplish the Change of Heart fully on our own.

In *Religion*, this issue first emerges in the General Remark of Part One, where Kant discusses the possibility of some sort of "supernatural cooperation" (6:44). However, the key phrase is ambiguous. In German, it reads "*Gesetzt, zum Gut-oder Besserwerden sei noch eine übernatürliche Mitwirkung nöthig ... .*" George di Giovanni has translated it as "Granted that some supernatural cooperation is also needed in becoming good or better." By translating *Gesetzt* as "Granted" the natural reading suggests that we do need Divine aid. Pluhar, however, has a different interpretation of *Gesetzt* and translates the German into the subjunctive: "Supposing that, for him to become good or better, a supranatural cooperation were also needed" (6:44). In this alternative, it is not "granted" that Divine aid is required, but rather the passage takes the possibility of Divine aid as more of a conjecture to be pondered.[6]

The sentence then continues by stating that, even if there were some "supernatural cooperation," "the human being must nonetheless make himself antecedently worthy of receiving it" (6:44). This cooperation, moreover, does not have to be in the form of aid that directly facilitates our transformation. It might instead be less direct, "the diminution of obstacles" (6:44) or a positive assistance through setting up external conditions that can help us confront our inner perfidy, though still leave it up to us as to how well we take advantage of the opportunity God has given to us.

Those who favor the interpretation that is suggested by the di Giovanni translation find further support in a passage that follows just a few sentences later. It reads "[h]ow it is possible that a naturally evil human being should make himself into a good human being surpasses every concept of ours" (6:44). This may be taken to imply that we cannot achieve the Change of Heart on our own because it is not even something we can comprehend. According to this reasoning, if this is something whose performance we cannot comprehend, then it is something that we cannot do. Yet Kant then states that "the fall from good into evil ... [is] no more comprehensible than the ascent from evil back to the good" (6:45). So it seems that both directions, our fall into sin and our ascension out of it, surpass our comprehension. Presumably, Divine (or diabolical) aid is not required for the former, and so an appeal to what "surpasses every concept of ours" in order to reinforce the *need* for Divine aid is overly presumptuous.[7]

A key point in favor of the alternate view, i.e., that we can through our own efforts undergo a Change of Heart, arises from Kant's commitment to the logic of *ought implies can*. If the Change of Heart is genuinely morally required of us, then Divine aid is not necessary. It may or may not be available, but if we are to hold consistently to the demand that *ought implies can*, if this inner transformation is something that we ought to accomplish, then it is something we can accomplish. As discussed in Chapter 1, this is also how we should understand our duty to promote the Highest Good (HG_d), for it is through this transformation that we become well-pleasing to God and thus worthy of membership in His Kingdom. Additionally, Kant recognizes the practical importance of our conceiving of ourselves as fully responsible for our moral endeavors since a belief in Divine aid may lead us to put in less effort. As he writes, we should not "take them [miracles] into consideration in the employment of our reason" (6:87). Rather, "[a] human being's moral improvement is ... a practical affair incumbent upon him," and so he should "act as if every change of heart and all improvement depended solely on the application of his workmanship" (6:88).

Thus, in *Religion*, Kant rejects two possible solutions to the First Difficulty: the soteriological standard of the *Critique of Practical Reason* has been replaced by one that can actually be realized; and (despite the translation offered by di Giovanni) he also opposes the view that we need Divine aid in order to undergo a Change of Heart. On the latter, the logic of *ought implies can* offers a theoretical basis for rejecting it, and the risk of moral laziness offers us a practical basis. Correspondingly, we may see Kant as distancing himself from both the Christian doctrines of Justifying Grace and Sanctifying Grace. The former concerns Divine forgiveness so that we are considered by God justified before Him; the latter concerns Divine assistance in our efforts to become morally worthy. Although he does allow for the possibility of Divine aid, perhaps forms of aid such as arranging circumstances so that opportunities for transformation are made available or offering protection from circumstances that would hinder our moral efforts, his philosophical commitments bar him from taking Divine aid as a condition without which the transformation of the Change of Heart would not be possible.

Kant's actual solution to the First Difficulty (as well as to the Third Difficulty) does, nevertheless, make a certain use of grace, but one quite different than those mentioned. In *Religion*, as elsewhere, when discussing the standpoint of Divine justice, Kant couches his phenomena/noumena distinction in the Leibnizian terminology of a Kingdom of Nature and a Kingdom of Grace.[8] For instance, in the *Critique of Pure Reason* he writes: "Leibniz called the world ... in accordance with moral laws under the rule of the highest good, the realm of grace, and distinguished it from the realm of nature, where, to be sure, rational beings stand under moral laws but cannot expect any successes for their conduct except in accordance with the course of nature in our sensible world" (A812/B840); and it is "in the realm of grace, where every happiness awaits us" (A812/B840).

From our human perspectives, we can tally up what actions we have done that conform to the moral law and what actions are in violation of it. We can likewise keep a journal of our desires and reflect upon the extent to which we have learned to control them. We can chart all this over time and gain some impression of whether or not we are becoming more or less virtuous. We can compare ourselves against the appropriate ideals and see what progress we have made. But as Kant here writes, our project of moral improvement "is not exhaustible in any time" (6:66) and as we learn from the Second *Critique*, even with an eternity available to continue to strive towards these ends, we will still fall short.

However, from the "sight of a divine judge" (6:74), from the standpoint of one looking at us from the Kingdom of Grace, a different judgment can be rendered. God can see more than how many actions we have taken and how many are performed from one incentive or another. He can also judge the moral status of our *Gesinnung*. This is something that we cannot do, just as we cannot know even with regards to a particular action whether or not we have acted merely in conformity with duty or performed the action from duty. We lack access to our own hearts as well as those of everyone else. But God, "through his pure intellectual intuition" (6:67), can know whether or not our supreme maxim gives priority to morality or self-interest.

Thus, the First Difficulty presents us with a problem of infinite distance "between the goodness which we ought to effect in ourselves and the evil from which we start" (6:66), a problem that sounds similar to what we have seen in the Second *Critique*. But here in *Religion*, Kant shows how to overcome it in this life and without the demand for infinite striving. We may be "unavoidably restricted to temporal conditions" (6:67), and so may see ourselves as constantly needing improvement, but God can judge our *Gesinnung*. Depending upon which incentive has priority over the other in our supreme maxim, we are either good or evil – and so to God, we are either deserving of punishment or well-pleasing to Him. Accordingly, this Difficulty of infinite distance is solved by distinguishing between two standpoints. From our human perspective, we will see ourselves as always needing improvement. But God can judge our *Gesinnung*. It is, as Kant has argued, the true ground of our moral status and thus is the proper basis for moral assessment. Such assessments are, of course, beyond our human capacities, but for God "this disposition count[s] for the deed itself" (6:66).

THE SECOND DIFFICULTY: CONSCIENCE AND COMMITMENT (6:67–71)

The Second Difficulty is not as succinctly expressed as either the First or the Third. It involves the question of how confident we ought to be regarding whether or not we have become well-pleasing to God, and intimates some worries about what implications doubt and certainty would have for our moral motivation. On the one hand, Kant is concerned that too much confidence about one's moral status can lead to backsliding. While on the other hand, he also worries that "without *any* confidence in the disposition once acquired, perseverance in it would hardly be possible" (6:68).

In one way, the solution to this Difficulty is obvious: we should secure some intermediate level of confidence about our moral status, neither too much nor too little. Full certainty is rejected since, as discussed in the solution to the First Difficulty, from our human standpoint, we can never know if we have undergone a Change of Heart. This point is also restated towards the end of this discussion, with Kant adding "nor, so far we can see, [is it] morally beneficial" (6:71).

Too much confidence here further suggests self-deception. Most people tend to think too highly of themselves and, as discussed in the previous chapter, entertain delusions that reinforce their sense of self-worth. If one sees one's moral transformation as a *fait accompli*, the humiliating effect of the moral law can be cast aside and replaced by a delusory pride. The result of such contentment is inaction. Confident that one has already met with success, further efforts are unnecessary.[9]

On the other side of this spectrum, Kant notes that there is the risk that without any confidence, one will not be able to persevere morally. This concern echoes the *Critique of Judgment*'s Parable of the Righteous Atheist, which presents the Highest Good as a motivational supplement needed to fend off despair in the face of all the suffering and injustice that one encounters through life. The "evils of poverty, illness and untimely death" (CJ: 5:452) will eventually undermine the Atheist's moral resolve for without the hope of some ultimate justice, all his efforts will be swamped by the "purposeless chaos of matter" (CJ: 5:452). So some middle ground is needed, one that preserves "fear and trembling" about one's own moral status, but also offers some way to connect one's sense of self with the deserts of the Highest Good. But given the cautions that Kant has raised regarding our ability to discern our moral status, how do we gain any assurance? The answer to this question comes by way of a surprising avenue: by appeal to the Postulate of Immortality.

Kant's turn to the Postulate may at first seem like a digression on his part, and may be quite disorienting to those who have built their understanding of it and the Highest Good primarily from the Second *Critique*. As discussed in Chapter 1, although the *Critique of Practical Reason* has become the *locus classicus* for Kant's discussions of the Highest Good and the Postulates, this is more an accident of the secondary literature than a product of it being an apt portrayal of his mature views.

With the exception of the Second *Critique*, Kant primarily uses the Postulate of Immortality as the platform for the Highest Good's distribution of happiness in accordance with moral worth. It is this use that is here employed, but with a particular twist. Kant realizes that we will tend to distort our moral self-assessment, usually exaggerating our worth: "one is never more easily deceived than in what promotes a good opinion of oneself" (6:68).

This is not something that we can outright prevent, but we can help curb it if we take more seriously what is at stake. So, by contemplating the "*boundless* future" (6:69) that awaits, one that is "either a blessed or a cursed *eternity*" (6:69), the hope here offered is that we will be pressed to be more honest with ourselves. Although there will still be no certainty on the matter, if our self-deception can be curbed, Kant proposes that we can make practical use of our conjectures about our moral status and what afterlife fate awaits.[10]

This is then Kant's solution to the Second Difficulty. He claims that we are going to be more honest with ourselves once we attend to what is at stake in the afterlife. With this added assurance, we can "legitimately assume" (6:68) that our judgment about ourselves is correct. Although we remain far from certain in this matter, Kant thinks that we can trust our conscience enough for what is here needed: to gain a modicum of confidence about where we stand morally, at least enough to help us persevere in our struggles.

IMMORTALITY IN *RELIGION* (6:69N–71N)

Before we proceed to the Third Difficulty, let us discuss the long footnote beginning on 6:69 and how it relates to Kant's other discussions of the Postulate of Immortality. As noted above, the Second *Critique* is very much an outlier on this issue. Unlike nearly every other text, it builds its case for the Postulate primarily by way of what is required to become worthy of happiness, rather than what is required for happiness to be distributed to the worthy.[11] By contrast, in the 1790s, with the introduction of the *Gesinnung* and with our moral desert most fundamentally tied to whether or not we have undergone a Change of Heart, the Postulate again (as it was in the First *Critique*) primarily serves to explain how there can be a proportionate distribution of happiness in accordance with moral worth (what in Chapter 1 I referred to as PPD).

However, Kant does not fully close the door to moral improvement in the afterlife. Dying with a good or evil *Gesinnung* is correlated with either a blessed or cursed afterlife. Hence, it seems that he merely divides our fates in two. Yet it could still be that there are degrees of happiness corresponding to a second standard of moral assessment. Our *Gesinnung* determines whether we deserve punishment or *any* reward. But it may be that there is still a proportionate distribution of happiness in accordance with our degree of virtue/perfection. As we discussed in Chapter 1, Kant never explicitly merges these two aspects of what our future life may hold, but as he does claim in *Religion* and "The End of All Things" both a bifurcation into a "blessed or a cursed *eternity*" (6:69) as well as the possibility of some sort of improvement in the afterlife, they may be reconciled along with PPD into a unified doctrine.

Another significant consideration is that in the 1790s, Kant began to consider more carefully how we conceive of the afterlife. In the 1780s, the Postulate was used to solve philosophical problems: how PPD can obtain, and (in the Second *Critique*) how we can approach moral perfection. But in later texts, greater focus is given to its motivational importance. Of course, this was already present in the First *Critique*, but it reappears in the Third *Critique*, and is compounded in *Religion* with both its use in relation to the Second Difficulty and, in an extended footnote, an examination of what may and may not guide our speculations about the world to come.

Although the footnote begins by stating that it would be "childish" to presume that we can ever reliably predict what the afterlife is really like, it goes on to consider what motivational benefits various conceptions could have. That is, while Kant opposes any pretenses to theoretical evaluation, he does see practical reason as providing us with a methodology through which we can assess the merits of one afterlife conception over another. This is illustrated in his discussion of the opening question of the footnote: "Will the punishment of hell be finite or everlasting?" Rather than defending one view or another in relation to what is required by the Highest Good's demand for justice, Kant instead considers the *practical consequences* of each option. If the first is chosen, then we should worry that many will say to themselves, "Well, I hope that I will be able to last it out" (6:69n). Hence, a threat of merely finite punishment will, according to Kant, fail to have the motivational effect of infinite punishment and so many will continue to live an immoral life. On the other hand, if we were to conceive of punishment as everlasting, the result would be the unintended consequence that soft-hearted clergy would offer deathbed absolutions, which again would undermine the motivational potential of the Postulate.

It is not as if Kant thinks that such absolutions would actually expunge one's guilt and make one worthy of a reward instead of a punishment. His concern is rather that this conception of the afterlife would militate against moral improvement since such absolutions would give people an excuse to continue on in sin. Accordingly, Kant recommends a third option. Following a common pattern of argumentation, Kant explores two initial options and finds deficiencies in each. He then moves on to an alternative by way of the introduction of a new distinction. In this case, he differentiates between two ways in which punishment can be infinite: it may either be infinitely enduring or it may be qualitatively "immeasurable." The former, as we have seen, can undermine the motivational potential of the Postulate due to the unintended consequence discussed above. By contrast, a qualitatively "immeasurable" punishment can satisfy the demands of Divine justice, offer a salve to the soft-hearted as it leaves open the possibility of something in the next life other than just punishment, and can still have the "same moral effect ... as can be expected from proclaiming the eternity of evil, without however entailing the disadvantages of the dogma of this eternity" (6:69). That is, fear of "immeasurable" punishment, Kant presumes, can do as much for us as a fear of everlasting punishment, without the pitfalls.

Barely a year later, in "The End of All Things," Kant reconsiders some of the specifics of this argument and, even though he follows the same root methodology, comes to different conclusions. As in *Religion*, he explicitly opposes the adoption of any dogmas regarding the afterlife, but still allows for speculation guided by what practical value the Postulate may have. So even though the Postulate itself is supposed to be certain, affirmed as an object of faith, that assent concerns its core structure as the vehicle for PPD. Beyond that, our conceptions must be more tentative. Overall, we should withhold judgment, except insofar as there may be a practical advantage to one conception over the other.

In *Religion*, Kant claims that an afterlife conception with an "immeasurable" though not everlasting punishment is preferable. However, in "The End of All Things" he reconsiders. When he returns to the idea of eternal damnation in this text, he again presents his case in relation to "the *practical* aims of every human being" (ET: 8:329). But here, he asserts that those who die in sin should expect that they will forever remain under the dominion of the evil principle (ET: 8:330). If one were instead to allow everyone to receive happiness in the afterlife, the worry is that it would "lull us too much into an indifferent sense of security" (ET: 8:330). Whether Kant began to worry that the position found in *Religion* would also lull us, or whether he simply overlooked it when writing "The End of All Things," we do not know. It may be that he continued to vacillate over these issues in the 1790s, or it may be that the details were not of great importance to him and could potentially vary (as he opposed any dogmas on this issue) depending upon social circumstances and what given those circumstances would be of greatest motivational benefit.

THE THIRD DIFFICULTY: THE INFINITE DEBT OF SIN

The Third "and apparently greatest" Difficulty concerns our debt of sin. Kant follows Christian tradition by representing Original Sin as incurring upon us an infinite debt to God, one that cannot be repaid through our deeds. This is, in part, because of its magnitude. It is also because there is nothing we can do to accrue any "surplus merit" for its repayment. Good life conduct is simply what we already should be doing and no further value can be gleaned from it to repay our debt. Thus, it seems that even one who "has entered upon the path of goodness, [is] still a reprobate in the sentencing of his entire life conduct before a divine *righteousness*" (6:72).

The traditional Christian solution to this problem comes by way of the doctrine of Justifying Grace. Whereas Sanctifying Grace refers to the Divine aid that we may receive in our striving to become morally better, Justifying Grace pertains to the repayment for our debt of sin. More specifically, this repayment is held to have been made through the Crucifixion, for the infinity of the debt demands that what is offered in payment is likewise of infinite magnitude. Christ, as a being of infinite worth, provides this payment on behalf of all mankind, substituting himself for us and satisfying God's demand for repayment. This, at least, is how the Satisfaction Theory of Atonement interprets the Crucifixion, a theory that has its roots in Saint Anselm's *Cur Deus Homo*, is also adopted by Luther, and pervades the Lutheranism of Kant's day.[12]

The Satisfaction Theory is one that Kant was certainly aware of through his Pietist upbringing and is quite clearly targeted in his examination of the Third Difficulty. Although he acknowledges the infinite magnitude of the debt of sin, he does not consider Satisfaction Theory a viable reading of what happens to this debt. Unlike other types of debt, Kant asserts that the debt of sin is "the *most personal* of all liabilities … which only the culprit, not the innocent can bear" (6:72). Unlike financial debts "where it is all the same to the creditor whether the debtor himself pays up, or somebody else for him" (6:72), our relation to this debt is one that "cannot be erased by somebody else." It is not a *transmissible* liability which can be made over to somebody else, in the manner of a financial debt. Thus, he rejects not only Satisfaction Theory, but even more broadly, the doctrine of Vicarious Atonement.[13]

This rejection has been interpreted by some as a devastating problem for Kant's soteriology. According to John Hare, for example, without it, or more generally without the possibility of Divine forgiveness, Kant has trapped himself in such a way that the entirety of *Religion* becomes a "Failure" (Hare 1996: 64). He claims that Kant has shouldered himself with the "stoic maxim" that we are each fully responsible for the resolution of our sin while also maintaining that the Propensity to Evil is ineradicable. Unlike how in Chapter 3 I distinguished between the Propensity and the *Gesinnung*, Hare merges them in such a way that "Kant is therefore left with an incoherence in the pure religion of reason" (Hare 1996: 65). Hence, as we also saw in Allison's interpretation, a merger of the two leads to the impossibility of salvation.

Hare is correct, that if (a) we alone are responsible for our salvation, while (b) our salvation depends upon our liberation from the Propensity to Evil, Kant would truly leave us with a failed soteriology. However, this interpretation does not follow the actual text. First, as we have discussed, we must distinguish between the Propensity to Evil and the moral status of our *Gesinnung*. The former is, Kant claims, ineradicable. But, contrary to Hare's reading (Hare 1996: 65), the latter can be changed. Second, Hare claims that Kant denies the possibility of Divine aid. But that is inaccurate. As we have discussed, Kant is agnostic as to whether or not such aid is given in our individual moral struggles, but he recommends for practical reason that we ought to act "as if every change of heart and all improvement depends solely on the application of his own workmanship" (6:88).[14]

Another, and even more prevalent line of criticism, appears in works by Gordon Michalson, Philip Quinn, and Nicholas Wolterstorff. Contrary to Hare's view that Kant does not waiver from his "stoic maxim," they maintain that he concedes to a "Divine Supplement" through which we are both Sanctified and Justified. Michalson, for instance, has suggested that God is willing to "treat our moral progress as a kind of promissory note" (Michalson 1989: 268).[15] We must still strive as best we can towards a Change of Heart, but in addition to our striving, there is a "divine 'supplement'" that takes care of the rest. Quinn and Wolterstorff likewise have interpreted Kant to be suggesting that we must "take the initiative" but then God forgives our inevitable falling "short of compliance with the moral law's demand for perfect obedience" (Quinn 1990: 425).[16]

As we have discussed, the logic of the Second *Critique* would have required Kant to turn to a Divine supplement since the soteriological standard presented therein is something we cannot ever satisfy. Thus, Kant must there appeal to Divine forgiveness in order that our progress towards moral perfection is accepted as equivalent to possession (CPrR: 5:123n). But this changes in the 1790s. First, we see in the "Theodicy" an opposition to the privation account of evil, and in *Religion*, with the introduction of the *Gesinnung*, it is our supreme maxim that determines our moral standing. Accordingly, it is the Change of Heart through which the moral incentive is given priority over self-interest in our supreme maxim that we become justified before God. There is reason enough to think that this transformation is something that we can accomplish on our own, and thus the objections of both Hare and those who claim that Kant was forced to concede to a "Divine Supplement" do not hold.

It is also through this turn that Kant gains his solution to the Third Difficulty. Even though he does use "grace" (*Gnade*) in the passages where he develops his solution, this should not be mistaken for an appeal to Divine aid. Rather, just as we saw in his solution to the First Difficulty, Kant draws upon an epistemic distinction, one that parallels the Leibnizian distinction between the Kingdom of Nature and Kingdom of Grace. Kant writes that "[t]he resolution to this difficulty rests on the following consideration. The judicial verdict of one who knows the heart of the accused must be thought as based on the universal disposition of the latter, not on the appearance of the disposition" (6:72–73), and once again, he states that our "disposition takes the place of the deed" (6:74). That is, from the Divine perspective, God is able to see our inner worth, the moral status of our *Gesinnung*, and so is able to assess our worth in a way that we cannot.

Given the changed dispositions of the "new man," "punishment cannot be considered appropriate to his new quality (of thus being well-pleasing to God)" (6:73). This is "imputed to us *by grace*" (6:75), but this does not mean that Kant reverts to an appeal to Divine mercy. Rather, it is an imputation that comes out of the epistemic or perspectival distinction between how we can assess ourselves and how God can assess us. Moral effort, good works, and so on cannot repay our debt of sin since (a) these are already duties required of us; and (b) as our debt is infinite, we cannot through a series of (finite) acts redeem ourselves. Hence, Kant suggests that through the objects available for our assessment, there seems no way to overcome the debt. But God can judge more than our deeds. He can also judge whether or not we have a changed heart. In this additional perspective, Kant finds "that surplus over the merit from works for which we felt the need earlier, one which is imputed to us *by grace*" (6:75).

This "surplus" is not, though, something handed to us from God. Rather, the surplus is to be understood as the further perspective that God employs to judge our *Gesinnung*. From our perspective "we indeed have no rightful claim (according to the empirical cognition we have of ourselves)" (6:75), but from God's perspective, where "disposition takes the place of the deed" (6:74), a judgment can be passed upon the *Gesinnung* of the new man, finding him "well-pleasing" *and* "relieved of all responsibility" (6:76) for the old man's debt of sin. Unfortunately, this decree has been routinely interpreted as an act of forgiveness on God's part, but this is not what is claimed in the text. Kant's use of "grace" here, as in "decree of grace" (6:76), pertains merely to the Divine perspective. The text is actually quite clear on this point as the term is employed specifically to articulate the contrasting judgments "according to the empirical cognition we have of ourselves" (6:75) versus the "idea of an improved disposition of which, however, God alone has cognition" (6:76).

Moreover, to be "relieved of all responsibility" does not mean that from the Divine standpoint the new man is relieved of something that he still ought to bear. Quinn and Wolterstorff have rightly claimed that that would run afoul of Divine justice, something that would, indeed, have been a very clumsy mistake for Kant to have made here, given that in these very pages he is emphasizing the importance of Divine justice. Fortunately, though, we do not have to shoulder him with such an error.[17]

The new man is "relieved" of responsibility for the old man's debt – but it does not follow from this that the debt is forgiven. The English does not convey the point well, but to be "relieved" (*entschlagen*) of responsibility is different from being forgiven (*vergeben*). When Kant quotes conventional views about forgiveness, he uses *vergeben* (e.g. 6:70n; CF: 7:47). But *entschlagen* has a different meaning. When a judgment is dismissed, or a statute struck down, it is not that the guilty are forgiven – rather, the change in evaluation occurs at a deeper level than with forgiveness. The forgiven are guilty, but treated mercifully. The "relieved" are no longer guilty.

Through the Change of Heart, the subvening conditions upon which the debt of sin depended no longer obtain. As discussed earlier, since sin does not actually harm God, it is a mistake to imagine the debt in monetary terms or as compensatory damages. The debt is not like a judgment imposed upon a civil tort, nor is it to be treated as if it were a line item to be managed by an accountant. These are just metaphors and we have exceeded their limits. More aptly, the debt of sin supervenes upon a (mis-) relation between the sinner and God, and once there is a change in that relationship, and the subvening conditions no longer obtain, the "strike" (*der Schlag*) upon one is "un-struck" (*ent-schlagen*).[18]

This is the solution to the Third Difficulty. The debt of sin is not somehow repaid in the suffering that goes along with the Change of Heart. It is not repaid through Christ's Vicarious Atonement. It is not forgiven through a "Divine Supplement." And the Pure Rational System of Religion is not a "Failure" as Hare contends. More conservative readers may not like what Kant has to say, but an answer is given that satisfies Kant. From the standpoint of grace, where "disposition takes the place of the deed" (6:74), God judges the *Gesinnung* of the new man. He has successfully reoriented his fundamental incentives, corrected his relationship with God, and thereby no longer bears the debt of sin. In this there is no supererogatory forgiveness. Nor is there any need. God sees one's true *Gesinnung* and judges it accordingly.

CORPOREAL INHERITANCE AND VICARIOUS ATONEMENT (6:75N)

Towards the close of the Third Difficulty, Kant adds a footnote that provides a glimpse of his vision of the life of someone who has undergone a Change of Heart. Continuing with the Pauline distinction between the old and new man, Kant focuses on the worldly liabilities transferred from the old to the new. One might imagine that the old man, leading a life dominated by self-interest, caused various harms to other people, had failed and dysfunctional relationships, may have neglected his long-term interests when pulled by various impulses, etc. Thus, the new man begins, so to speak, with all the worldly consequences of sin left to him by the old man.

Of course, the new man cannot know that he is no longer (morally speaking) the man that he was, since via the "empirical cognition we have of ourselves" we cannot know the status of our *Gesinnung*. This is something that only God can see (6:75). Thus, the new man cannot disclaim ownership of the corporeal liabilities left to him by the old man – nor, presumably, would he want to dissociate himself from the misdeeds of his past. Empirically, he remains the same person, and even if he were to regard his moral identity as distinct from that of the old man, he would nevertheless see his inherited liabilities "as so many opportunities to test and exercise his disposition for the good" (6:75n).[19]

The promises made by the old man, he will see as his own; the tainted or broken relationships with friends and family, he will see himself as required to restore; and the history of bad habits written into the old man's body will be ones that he will proudly undo. Whereas the old man would see acts of atonement as burdens and punishments, they become for the new man "opportunities to test and exercise his disposition for the good" (6:75n).

In the above, one might further see a parallel to the doctrine of Vicarious Atonement that Kant rejects in the Third Difficulty. This is most likely not a coincidence, but rather something that he meant to intimate. However, as should be abundantly clear, we should not mistake the corporeal atonement of the new man for the old as also the atonement for his infinite debt of sin. Kant clearly follows Luther's rejection of works as the means for Justification. Not only is the debt infinite in magnitude, but as we have discussed, there is no "surplus merit" to be accrued from performing deeds that one was already under obligation to perform (6:72). Nevertheless, there is an evocation here of the grander problem of atonement, though it is one that operates not at the scale of our infinite debt, but merely upon our far more mundane transgressions.

Lastly, despite Kant's rejection of Vicarious Atonement, and with it a central tenet of Luther's account of Justification, we can see in Kant's portrayal of the new man ample affinity with Luther's depiction of Sanctification. Luther holds that Christ is active in both our Justification and Sanctification, so having explored the former, Kant at least briefly considers the form of the latter. For Luther, the new man is one who not only has been Justified through Christ's death, but also receives the living Christ whereby he partakes of an "alien righteousness" (Luther 1883: 1.2.145). Kant's new man, similarly, has brought forward the Prototype within, which he likewise depicts via the Pauline phrase of "a righteousness which is not our own" (6:66).[20]

In both, the new man's character is aligned with this righteousness, and for both, morality "begins to be a joyous thing" (Luther 1883: 1.46.662). While we have distinguished between the Change of Heart and the polemical use of virtue that dominates Parts One and Two of *Religion*, the former nevertheless instills in the new man a desire to improve himself in ways that accord with virtue. He will accept it as his duty to improve his self-control and to cultivate inclinations that are more conducive to morality. In so doing, the new man partakes of the righteousness of the Prototype, alien to him only in the sense that it remains an ideal in contrast to which he "always remains deficient and infinitely removed" (6:75n); and yet, in his exercise of his newfound disposition for the good, a desire to observe morality will evolve. Out of this desire, the new man "gladly takes upon himself" (6:75n) the liabilities of the old man, and can find in his struggles "the contentment and *moral happiness* inherent in the consciousness of his progress in the good" (6:75n).[21]

SECTION TWO: THE EVIL PRINCIPLE'S RIGHTFUL CLAIM TO DOMINION OVER THE HUMAN BEING (6:78–84)

In this brief section, Kant discusses what Pure Rational Faith has to say about Satan, the personification of the evil principle. Like his presentation of the personified idea of the good principle, Kant begins in the "vivid mode of representing things." Satan has rebelled against God and having "lost whatever estate he might have had in heaven" (6:78), replaced what was lost by establishing through the fall of Adam and Eve a "Kingdom of Evil ... here on earth" (6:79).

He thereby made all of humanity his subjects and establishes his reign unchallenged until the time of Jesus. As we shall discuss more fully in Chapter 5, Kant reprises the common Christian view that Judaism is (or was) a religion of "burdensome ceremonies and observances" (6:79), concerned merely with "the goods of this world," and without concern for our moral condition. Thus, Judaism "did no substantial injury to the realm of darkness" (6:79) and so it was not until Jesus that the "sovereignty of this prince was ... put in jeopardy" (6:80).[22]

Continuing with this symbolism, Satan challenged Jesus to combat, tempted him, and caused him to be persecuted and eventually put to death. Kant notes that from one perspective "which belongs to the senses" (6:81), Satan was clearly victorious since Jesus' life came to an untimely and gruesome death. However, since the combat was over principles rather than worldly matters, the more apt perspective passes a different judgment on the battle. Though Jesus was put to death, his life manifested "the good principle, that is, of humanity in its moral perfection, as example for everyone to follow." Thus, in the end, the good was victorious since "by exemplifying this principle (in the moral idea) that human being opened the doors of freedom to all" (6:82).[23]

In the final paragraph of this section, Kant finally "divest[s] of its mystical cover this vivid mode of representing things ... *suited to the common people*" (6:83). As in his discussion of the good principle, he moves from the symbolism of personification to a philosophical commentary having to do with the principle's objective reality. As discussed previously, a positive principle of evil is one that we must posit in order to sustain our culpability, and as he also reminds us this principle "is surely not the so often blamed sensibility" (6:83). Evil, rather, arises from and is sustained by "a certain self-incurred perversity" (6:83) – a point that is symbolized in the depiction of Satan as having no interest in "earthly and corporeal objects" (6:79) but rather sought "to establish dominion *over minds*" (6:79).

Kant then ends this discussion by reinforcing the philosopher's right to interpret the Bible, asserting that it is not only permissible but a duty to "find a meaning in the Scriptures in harmony with the *most holy* teachings of reason" (6:84). Thus we have the principles of good and evil within us, personified in Jesus and Satan, and allegorized through the Bible's more "vivid mode of representing things ... *suited to the common people.*"

GENERAL REMARK: ON MIRACLES (6:84–89)

The General Remark at the end of Part Two considers the practical and epistemological status of miracles. Kant begins by discussing the relevance of miracles presented in the Gospels, and though he has various cautions about believing in them as well as their becoming religious tenets, he is willing to concede that they may actually have taken place and may have aided in the establishment of Christianity. Nevertheless, he remains agnostic on this matter, as we cannot know whether their reports are true or false and so recommends that we "leave the merit of these miracles, one and all, undisturbed" (6:84).

Kant then moves on to discuss what it is to be a miracle and asks how we should understand the term. He begins by defining miracles as "events in the world, the causes and *effects* of which are absolutely unknown to us and so must remain" (6:86). He later adds that they are deviations from the laws of nature that God "from time to time" seems to allow (6:86). This marks them as quite different from how Kant understands freedom of the will, which also has its basis in a causality distinct from the order of nature, nevertheless do "not contradict any of the concepts we have to form of appearances and of a possible experience" (A538/B566).

On practical grounds we are justified in claiming that we are capable of action determined through the "causality of reason" rather than that of natural laws. But as is explained in the solution to the Third Antinomy of the *Critique of Pure Reason*, what on the one hand can be rendered in accordance with the laws of nature, on the other can be understood as a consequence of practical deliberation. Although Kantians hold very different positions on how freedom and nature are related, most heed his claim that free actions, unlike miracles, do not interrupt the causal order of nature.

Miracles, on the other hand, are understood as a causal intrusion of the Divine into the order of nature, and thus stand in violation of the conditions for possible experience as depicted in the *Critique of Pure Reason*. In the Second Analogy, Kant argues that in order for an object's changes of state to be changes of the same object, rather than the passing away of one and the spontaneous appearance of another, the changes must be governed by a rule that brings the two states into relation and secures them as changes in the self-same object. However, insofar as a miracle violates this principle, the turning of water into wine, for instance, it cannot be taken as a change of water but rather a replacement of one for the other. The same presumably would follow for miraculous healings, resurrection, the parting of the seas, etc. Miracles thus threaten Kant's conditions for numerical identity.

This is not, however, the place to deal with this interesting question of transcendental philosophy. Although Kant might have dismissed miracles as impossible on the basis of the above, in *Religion* we see a more tentative stance, accepting that "[h]ere reason is paralyzed" (6:86) and that we "must renounce cognition of that which brings about effects according to these laws" (6:88) – i.e., that we cannot comprehend how they are possible. Kant further adds that even if a miracle did occur, we could never prove it. We have no positive criteria to demonstrate that one has happened since what appear to be deviations from the laws of nature might only be special circumstances that can be explained through more advanced scientific knowledge. We do, however, have a negative criterion, or at least a partial negative criterion through which we can reject some claims.

Kant distinguishes between "theistic" and "demonic miracles," and further distinguishes in the latter both "angelic" and "satanic miracles." From what he has said, we have no definite criteria, either positive or negative, regarding satanic miracles. Even actions that are in accordance with duty or that help some individuals in the path towards moral transformation may just be means within some dastardly plot. But we can disconfirm theistic (and perhaps angelic) miracles. Any putative miracle or revelation that is incompatible with the moral law is one for which God could not be responsible. Thus, according to Kant, God would never have commanded Abraham to sacrifice his son. It could not possibly have been God who commanded it as either God would then be commanding murder or would be deceiving Abraham. Either way, the moral law would be violated, which is something that a being with a holy will would never, and could never, do.

In the final paragraph of the General Remark, Kant applies what has been discussed to the issue of moral improvement. As in Part One, he is willing to accept the possibility that there is some cooperative "heavenly influence" (6:88), but no one is able "to distinguish with certainty such influences from the natural ones, nor how to bring them and so, as it were, heaven itself down to himself" (6:88). Moreover, it would be a mistake to expect a miracle or presume that Divine aid will be offered. Doing so could lead one to make less than a whole-hearted moral effort. Even those who claim that we must first do our utmost before Divine aid is offered still face a practical danger. With the belief that Divine aid is forthcoming, we may underestimate our own potential and too readily decide that it is now God's turn. Accordingly, Kant writes that one who is truly devoted to morality does not "*sanction* miracles but rather ... conducts himself as if every change of heart and all improvement depends solely on the application of his own workmanship" (6:88).

ADDENDUM: PART TWO AND *RELIGION'S* EXPERIMENT

As we did at the end of the last chapter, let us again take a moment to consider how well Kant's experiment has fared in this part of *Religion*. In Part One, Kant offered a philosophical account of evil that was meant to correspond to the Christian doctrine of Original Sin. Then in Part Two, he moves on to Christianity's conception of redemption, including how we can become well-pleasing to God and what becomes of our debt of sin. However, on these issues, he diverges significantly from the prevailing Christian views.

Christian theology has traditionally regarded the historical event of the Crucifixion as essential to our salvation. It is viewed as an actual occurrence in space and time, whereby a sacrifice was offered on behalf of all mankind. Yet as we have seen (a) Kant rejects the transmissibility of the debt of sin; and (b) affirms (at least practically) that we ought to regard ourselves as fully capable of moral transformation through our own efforts. In these, he modifies the traditional views of Sanctifying and Justifying Grace to reflect just an epistemic distinction between our perspective and that of God.

Consequently, it seems that *Religion*'s experiment has revealed a divergence between traditional Christianity and the Pure Rational System of Religion. Whereas the tradition claims that Divine aid is necessary for our moral transformation and the sacrifice of Christ is necessary for the repayment of our debt of sin, Kant offers a soteriology that revises both these core doctrines. Yet Kant did not, I presume, see this. Instead, he saw himself as divesting the "mystical cover" from the Gospels and traditional doctrines, disclosing the true meaning that lies within. For Kant, the heart of the Christian story is that "there is absolutely no salvation for human beings except in the innermost adoption of genuine moral principles in their disposition" (6:83). Accordingly, he sees this in the teachings of Jesus, and reads both Genesis and the Gospels symbolically in such a way that they fit with this view. Hence, he did not see himself as rejecting Christian doctrine, but rather getting to its core, a core that is also available to the Pure Rational System of Religion.

Lastly, we see in Part Two greater use of the Bible than in Part One. In addition to various references to Genesis, Kant makes significant use of the Gospels, especially the Gospel of John. As noted above, part of what he was doing, at least as he saw it, was revealing the true teachings behind the "mystical cover." But in doing so, he is clearly interpreting the Bible. Thus, despite the claims in the First Preface regarding the proper domain of biblical versus philosophical theology, the actual experiment of *Religion* encroaches upon the former, following a hermeneutic that distinguishes between what is just an outer veneer versus an inner truth that corresponds with reason. The experiment, consequently, does not just borrow felicitous passages or identify correlations between doctrine and the Pure Rational System. Rather, insofar as Kant employs a hermeneutic shaped by philosophical principles, is he not contravening both claims made in the First Preface and in his response to the royal rescript, where he contends that he "make[s] no *appraisal* of Christianity" (CF: 7:8) and merely "cite[s] some biblical texts to corroborate certain purely rational teachings in religion" (CF: 7:8)? In short, however philosophically compelling *Religion* may be, we must wonder whether the Prussian censors were legally in the right, as Kant was in fact trespassing into the domain of biblical theology and public doctrine.[24]

NOTES

1 See note 20 of Chapter 1. I generally follow the reading of virtue found in Baxley (2010). However, while Baxley tends to see Kant as holding to a stable account of virtue through the Critical Period, we see in the polemics of *Religion* something quite different from the Second *Critique*. In the *Metaphysics of Morals*, we see some tension between these two views. See for example 6:394 versus 6:407.

2 Of course, it is generally taken for granted that Jesus was morally perfect – or at least his portrayal in the Gospels is of a morally perfect agent. Kant's reasons for seeing Jesus as such are given at 6:61, 6:64, and 6:159–62. We can summarize the features Kant mentions as follows: Jesus gave priority to morality over self-interest; devoted himself to spreading "goodness about him as far wide as possible"; and though he had the same natural inclinations we do, mastered them so fully that neither the "greatest temptation" nor the "most ignominious death" lead him to give in to them. In this we can see the conjunction between a good *Gesinnung* and the virtuous traits that, in addition, we ought to develop.

3 This is the thesis that Jesus Christ is fully human and fully divine. Kant comments briefly upon it at CF: 7:39. In his view (at least as expressed in *The Conflict of the Faculties*), just as the doctrine of the Trinity has no practical value, he makes the same claim about the ideal of a "Divinity 'dwelling incarnate' in a real human being." One may further wonder whether the doctrine of Hypostatic Union can overcome Kant's practical argument against the divinity of Jesus. Even if, following this doctrine, Jesus felt all the desires we do, and even carried the

Propensity to Evil, if he knew of his second nature, that would bring with it a significant difference from the ordinary human being, one with practical relevance to the struggle against sin.

4 In retrospect, we can see this as hyperbolic. Perhaps when writing the essay that became Part One Kant had not yet fully formulated what he was going to say in Part Two. But now, although it is a "difficulty," it is given an explanation.

5 This is clearly one place where Kant does diverge from both Luther and the Lutheran tradition. That Luther subscribed to the doctrine of Vicarious Atonement is broadly accepted and well documented. See Althaus 1966: 202–11. I discuss this issue further in note 12 below. See also my discussion of the issue in Pasternack 2012.

6 We might say that Kant was not merely agnostic about whether or not there is Divine aid, but struggles over whether or not through our own efforts we can overcome our state of sin. He certainly acknowledges a problem with conceptualizing how this is possible (6:45) and at times seems to seriously consider the possibility that aid is needed (6:143). I will return to this issue periodically through the book and will address directly the question of Pelagianism in Chapter 7.

7 Moreover, I regard these claims as somewhat hyperbolic. How a person driven by self-interest could while in that state choose to leave it is definitely a quandary. But to claim that it is beyond our comprehension is going too far. In various texts, Kant considers how the moral law impresses itself upon us, "waking [us] up from time to time" (MM: 438; see also CPrR: 5:72–78). This may not provide a full account as to how we can overcome this seeming "catch-22," but it does give us some significant comprehension of what is involved.

8 For the use closest to what is under discussion, see A812/B840. Kant also uses the nature/grace distinction quite broadly to refer to either an epistemological distinction between our mode of cognition and God's or a metaphysical distinction between the causal order of nature and supersensible/divine causation. All, of course, reflect different elements within the Leibnizian nature/grace distinction. See also: 6:173–74; CF: 7:24, 7:43, 8:250, 29:629, etc. In his "Kant's History of Ethics," Allen Wood characterizes the *Groundwork*'s account of our membership in an intelligible world as a further allusion to Leibniz's "realm of grace." Perhaps so, but it is not explicit since Kant does not use *"Reich der Gnade"* or a similar phrase in the third chapter of the *Groundwork*.

There have been various enumerations of different uses of *Gnade* in *Religion*. Byrne, for example, distinguishes between distributive grace, transforming/sanctifying grace, and justifying/atoning grace (Byrne 2007: 140), all of which can be seen as connected to the Leibnizian *Reich der Gnade*. In his introduction to *Religion within the Boundaries of Mere Reason*, Robert Adams briefly discusses Kant's views on grace and distinguishes between Prevenient, Sanctifying, and Justifying grace. According to Adams 1998 (and I concur), Kant rejects the first. He also holds that Kant accepts the second and gives "cautious embrace" to the third (see xxi–xxiii).

9 For a related approach to the Second Difficulty, see Palmquist 2010.

10 Kant is here certainly putting considerable trust in our conscience, which he does as well in Part Four (cf. 6:185–90) and in the *Metaphysics of Morals*, where he quite boldly claims that "an *erring* conscience is an absurdity" (MM: 6:401). Kant explains that we can always make mistakes regarding our judgment about whether something is a duty or not, but this is matter for the faculty of understanding and not conscience (6:186; MM: 6:401). Conscience's task is, rather, to scrutinize ourselves: what maxims we are actually employing and our motives for employing them. It does not, however, follow from this that an erring conscience is not possible, and though Kant claims that the faculty of practical judgment cannot err with regards to itself, he nevertheless still accepts that we have a duty to cultivate our conscience and sharpen our "attentiveness to the voice of the inner judge" (MM: 6:401).

11 In the *Critique of Pure Reason*, we do not have a direct statement regarding the standard determining our moral deserts. Then, in the *Lectures on the Philosophical Doctrine of Religion* of 1783/4, Kant at times associates what we deserve directly with our conduct, but at other times with "moral perfection" and "corruption" (LR: 28:1084–87). Hence, we might see the mid 1780s as a period where Kant saw the afterlife as necessary for our pursuit of moral perfection and that pursuit was seen as necessary for our becoming worthy of happiness. These points also correlate quite well with the privation account that, it seems, Kant held to until the "Theodicy": our moral status was based upon our degree of cultivation of the "seed of goodness" and the evil that we do is the result of the degree to which we have failed to fully cultivate it.

12 See *Cur Deus Homo*, I. 11–15, and 21. In Chapter 11, our debt of sin is described in terms of "not rendering to God his due" and as a "debt of honor." It is similarly described in Chapters 13–15. Thus, commentators often interpret Anselm's account of the debt as a violation of the honor due to God. Chapter 21 as well as Chapter 6 of Book II characterize the magnitude of the debt.

Readers familiar with Luther and the Lutheran movements up through Kant's time will likely find this non-controversial. However, for readers less familiar with this period of theology, let me offer some textual support for the entrenchment of the doctrine of Vicarious Atonement in Lutheranism. First, in Luther, the point is evident from the Second and Third Articles of the Small Catechism. But as a second example: "Christ, the Son of God, stands in our place and has taken all our sins upon his shoulders ... He is the eternal satisfaction for our sin and reconciles us with God, the Father" (Luther 1883: 1.10III.49). See also 1.10I.720; 1.17II.291, etc.

Althaus, accordingly, writes: "Luther, like Anselm, views Christ's work in terms of satisfaction ... This is true because satisfaction can occur only through substitution. Jesus Christ takes our place. In a 'wonderful exchange' he takes upon himself all men's debts and guilt before God. He achieves that satisfaction which men were not able to produce for themselves" (Althaus 1966: 202–3).

From the Lutheran Scholastics, we have: "because sin is an offence, wrong, and crime against the infinite God, and, so to speak, is Deicide, it has an infinite evil, not indeed formally ... but objectively, and deserves infinite punishment, and, therefore, required an infinite price of satisfaction, which Christ alone could have afforded" (from Quenstedt's *Theologica Didactio-Polemica*, III, 228); "For by His acts Christ expiated the crime which man had committed against justice" (*Theologica Didactio-Polemica*, III, 244); "Christ most exactly fulfilled the divine Law in our stead, in order that penitent sinners, applying to themselves, by true faith, this vicarious fulfillment of the Law, might be accounted righteous before God, the judge" (from Hollaz's *Examem Theologicum Acroamaticum*, 737); "By the passive obedience, Christ transferred to Himself the sins of the whole world" (*Examem Theologicum Acroamaticum*, 737).

From the Pietists: "for Christ alone has made satisfaction for us by his sacrifice, and he who wishes to add to it his own sacrifice for atonement blasphemes the sacrifice of Christ" (from Spener's *The Spiritual Priesthood*); from Franke: "If you wish to enjoy the foretaste of eternal life, you must believe above all that there is no power or ability in your own nature to gain it ... we can do nothing without him [Christ]" (from Franke's *The Foretaste of Eternal Life*). Lastly, from Arndt, who precedes Pietism but was the Lutheran Scholastic of central influence to the later movement: "Through this faith (in Christ) we receive forgiveness of sins, in no other way than through pure grace without any of our own merits (Eph. 2:8) but only by the merits of Christ ... See to it indeed that your righteousness is the grace and gift of God that comes before all your merit" (from *True Christianity*). Scholastic quotations are from Schmid 1889; Pietist quotations are from Griffin and Erb 2006.

13 Although Satisfaction Theory has become the dominant interpretation of the Crucifixion, other interpretations have been offered that still employ the idea of Christ as a vicarious substitute. Perhaps the best-known alternative is the Penal Theory of Atonement where Christ's death is not understood as a sacrificial repayment, but rather as an act of suffering, taking on the punishment that we deserve. In the *Metaphysics of Morals* Kant also indicates his opposition to the view that sin causes an injury to God, as if our debt is then incurred in a way akin to a civil tort. There is no "*compensatory justice (iustitia brabeutica)* in the relation of God to men" (MM: 6:489). God cannot be injured, cannot be harmed, and so the debt of sin cannot be understood in terms of compensatory damages.

14 If our moral transformation is fully on our own shoulders, and so Divine aid, even if available, is not necessary for the Change of Heart, one may see Kant as offering a Pelagian view of salvation. We will return to this issue in Chapter 7.

15 Some of Michalson's comments suggest that the Divine supplement is merely that God sees us as a "completed whole." Though Quinn and Wolterstorff also take note of the distinction between our perspective and that of God, Michalson seems to take the latter as God's act of grace. But if so, it is not clear why this helps our cause. As a "completed whole," have we repaid our debt of sin or, as Quinn and Wolterstorff suggest, is there still a forgiveness for our falling short? Unfortunately, I do not find Michalson clear on this issue. Nevertheless, there is – as I shall discuss below – something important to

be taken from the distinction between our perspective and God's. See also Michalson 1990: 107–24.

16 See also Quinn 1986: 455, and Wolterstorff 1991: 44–45. Kant actually offers two reasons why we inevitably fall short. One is, obviously, that the debt is infinite. The other actually parallels a point made by Anselm in *Cur Deus Homo* I.20. Just as Anselm states, so we find in Kant the position that since we are already obligated to do all we can morally, there is no "surplus" available from our moral obedience to be used to repay the debt. See 6:72.

17 Quinn and Wolterstorff are correct that forgiveness is incompatible with Kant's conception of Divine justice. Kant is quite clear about this point elsewhere. He states that the idea of a generous or merciful judge "in one and the same person is a contradiction." See: 6:141, 6:146n, 19:264, 27:171, 28:338, etc.

18 There is one further argument supporting the position that the new man does not inherit the old man's debt of sin. When Kant discusses the Change of Heart in Part Two of *Religion*, he states that from God's perspective, the new man is "*morally* another being" from the old. In "the emergence from the corrupted disposition into the good" (6:74), Kant states that the old man dies and the new man is a "new creation," a "rebirth," etc. (see 6:47). Similarly, in *The Conflict of the Faculties* Kant describes the moral transformation as "a conversion by which one becomes another, new man" (CF: 7:54), and a few lines later, "the end of religious instruction must be to make us *other* human beings and not merely better human beings" (CF: 7:54).

The moral status of the old and new man's *Gesinnungen* are fundamentally different, and it seems that by virtue of this qualitative difference, in both *Religion* and in *The Conflict of the Faculties*, Kant presents the old man and the new as numerically distinct. Through most of this section, I have argued that the new man, by virtue of his own moral characteristics, would not be burdened by the debt of sin. But if we follow Kant's language here and consider moral transformation as a change in numerical identity, we can again reject the idea that the new man carries the debt of sin through an inheritance from the old, for that would violate Kant's claims concerning transmissibility. It is a debt which "only the culprit, not the innocent, can bear" (6:72). We will return to this in Chapter 7. See also Pasternack 2012.

19 Whether the new man is bound by the promises of the old depends upon how one reads Kant's claim about the new man being "*morally* another being." If one holds that the old and new man are numerically distinct, then presumably promises do not carry through (though the new man may have other reasons to remain committed to them). However, my argument does not need their numerical distinctness. Once there is a *qualitative* change in the subvening relationship, the supervening debt ceases. So, if one wants to claim that the new man and the old man are numerically identical, the old man's promises are still binding for the new man as he is the same agent as the one who made them. On the issue of numerical identity, it should be viewed as a coda to my main argument. It offers a supplement and it presumably strengthens my conclusion. However, I am not making a metaphysical claim here about how to count noumenal objects. We posit the *Gesinnung* on practical grounds and so when Kant says that we regard the new man as "*morally* another being," he is similarly characterizing how we conceptualize the *Gesinnung* for practical purposes. I discuss this more fully in Pasternack 2012.

20 See note 4 of the Introduction.

21 We can find in Kant periodic suggestions of a form of happiness that is not corporeal but rather stems from one's moral efforts. In the Second *Critique*, Kant mentions an "intellectual contentment" and a "satisfaction with one's existence, an analogue of happiness that must necessarily accompany the consciousness of virtue" (CPrR: 5:117). Similarly, in the *Metaphysics of Morals*, Kant writes that "[w]hen a thoughtful man has overcome incentives to vice and is aware of having done his often bitter duty, he finds himself in a state that could well be called happiness, a state of contentment and peace of soul in which virtue is its own reward" (MM: 6:377). Nevertheless, Kant frequently cautions against "moral fanaticism," which is a commitment to morality out of some more self-interested desire (CPrR: 5:84), one which substitutes for our respect for the law and is really just "exaggerated self-conceit" (CPrR: 5:84). By contrast, the new man is motivated by respect for the moral law *and* as a result of his Change of Heart, he begins to find contentment and satisfaction in his observance of duty. The latter is granted as an effect of his commitment to morality and so may be distinguished from fanaticism, as an effect of rather than what motivates his action.

22 In Part Three, Kant has even harsher claims to make against Judaism, and we shall turn to this topic in Chapter 5.

23 In Mariña 1997, she uses this passage to suggest that Kant follows much more closely to the traditional Christian view regarding the importance of the event of the Crucifixion. That is, she reads 6:82 literally, taking Kant's view to be that the historical event of the Crucifixion is essential to our salvation, that it is an instance of Divine aid and without it, salvation would not be possible for us (cf. Mariña 1997: 395–98). However, in my view, this ignores the core analysis of Vicarious Atonement in Part Two as well as the Remarkable Antinomy of Part Three. See my comments on her interpretation in Pasternack 2012.

24 To compound this, we may also add that Kant offers various recommendations regarding how the afterlife should be understood, not on philosophical grounds, but on grounds that are explicitly shaped by how it will impact the public at large. We must avoid some interpretations because they will undercut the fear of punishment, avoid others because of how soft-hearted clergy may respond – and what we should adopt is because of its offering the greatest benefit to public morality. Contemporary philosophers and theologians would have no principled objection here, but clearly in Kant's time, this was a trespass into a domain that he too recognized was reserved for those formally charged with "the welfare of souls" (6:8). That is, it is a violation of what I designated as AD in Chapter 2.

For a more detailed discussion of Kant's battle with the Prussian Censors, see Hunter 2005; di Giovanni 1996: 41–48; Lestition 1993; Dilthey 1890; and Arnoldt 1909: vol 4, 32–37. I also have forthcoming a paper that examines the tension between Kant's initial claims about the boundary between biblical and philosophical theology and what actually transpires in *Religion*. See Pasternack 2015.

5

PART THREE OF *RELIGION*
THE KINGDOM OF GOD ON EARTH

Compared to Parts One and Two, Parts Three and Four have received very little attention in the secondary literature. Some work has been done on Part Three's "Remarkable Antinomy" and what Kant calls the "Ethical Community" is periodically mentioned. But there is little analysis of either Part Three or Part Four as a whole and no received understanding of how their content is related to Parts One and Two in a way that brings to *Religion* an overarching unity. To many, the second two parts dangle more like addenda to the main philosophical work accomplished in Parts One and Two.

This view, however, neglects the social issues pertinent to Kant's soteriology. Although Part Two does very much provide the impression that the quest for salvation is a solitary affair, even in Part One we see some indications that he saw our moral paths as deeply intertwined. As we discussed in Chapter 3, our reliance upon the judgment of others for our sense of self-worth prepares the way for the Propensity to Evil. Accordingly, it is sometimes assumed that to set ourselves on the moral path, we must make a turn inwards and disentangle ourselves from such dependencies. But this is not what Kant maintains. Despite its more pernicious effects, the Predisposition to Humanity is a fundamental component of who we are. So, rather than being denied or repressed, Kant wants to harness it and bring it into the service of the good.

This is how Part Three opens, with a dialectic that begins with the acknowledgment that the "assaults of the evil principle" (6:93) have little to do with "the instigations of nature ... what should properly be called the *passions*" (6:93) but instead with our social interests. They are instrumental in our initial corruption and, surprisingly, continue to have a pernicious effect upon even those who have undergone a Change of Heart. That is, Kant asserts not only that human beings "mutually corrupt each other's moral disposition" (6:94), but even those who have "escaped from the dominion of evil" will "still be held in incessant danger of relapsing into it" (6:94).

The latter claim in particular is surprising because in Part One, Kant describes the Change of Heart as "a single and unalterable decision" (6:48). By contrast, here, at the beginning of Part Three, it now appears that there is a risk of recidivism. As I argued in Chapter 3, we can understand Kant's ambivalence regarding the innateness of the Propensity to Evil by distinguishing between it being an innate and unchosen fact about what we are and a choice about how we deal with that fact. As an innate fact of human nature, the Propensity to Evil never leaves us, not even with a Change of Heart. Just as with the First *Critique*'s claim that Transcendental Illusion never ceases, even when we gain the tools through which we can avoid Transcendental Error, so likewise our evil Propensity remains with us even once we have pulled ourselves out from its governance. It still will beckon to us and is never silenced.

Reminiscent of Rousseau's critique of civilization, Kant discusses how the vices of envy, addiction to power, and avarice arise out of the Predisposition to Humanity's comparative sense of self-worth. To illustrate this, Kant notes that regardless of how financially comfortable one is, when around those who have greater wealth, one's financial contentment will give way (6:93). The same applies to nearly all social values that have taken root in our psyches. We can, when on our own, feel quite secure in ourselves, but when among those who have achieved more or have greater social standing, we will begin to compare ourselves to them, leading to insecurity, embarrassment, envy, etc.

Given this natural tendency, Kant realizes that our moral improvement also has a social dimension. Along our path to a Change of Heart, we might fight against the "malignant inclinations" that are so readily triggered when we are around others; and even once this change has taken place, the more negative aspects of our Predisposition to Humanity bring with it an "incessant danger of relapsing"(6:94) into sin. To mitigate these hazards, we need those around us to also take up a commitment to their own moral improvement. In doing so, there will be a shared interest that transcends each individual's selfish desires. Accordingly, Part Three progresses from the individual-focused soteriology of Part Two to one that deals with how society itself must change. That is, in addition to our duty as individuals to undergo a moral revolution, there must as well be a transformation of society through which is established "an *ethical state*, i.e. a *kingdom* of virtue" (6:94) – what Kant calls the "Ethical Community."

DIVISION ONE: THE FOUNDING OF A KINGDOM OF GOD ON EARTH (6:95–124)

THE ETHICAL VERSUS JURIDICAL STATE (6:95–96)

Division One examines the formal characteristics of both the Ethical Community and what Kant refers to as the "True Church" or "Universal Church." It begins with the former, contrasting it against the social order in which we currently dwell, the juridical (juridico-civil) state. In our social system, laws primarily concern how we conduct ourselves in relation to others. It imposes external constraints that seek, or presume to seek, a balance between our mutual safety and our individual liberty. Such constraints are for Kant considered justified because by limiting some actions, there should be an overall optimization of the freedoms we can all enjoy (6:98; MM: 6:231).

However, the state can only compel us to act in conformity with the law. It lacks the capacity to also compel us to act from the right motives. Since "a human judge cannot penetrate into the depths of other human beings" (6:95), there is no way to determine what motives are in play, nor who deserves to be rewarded or punished. We are, thus, in a sort of inner state of nature. Kant calls it an "ethical state of nature" as our human institutions are unable to impose upon us the "laws of virtue" (i.e., laws not of our outward behavior but of the inner processes through which we choose how to act).[1]

It is, nevertheless, possible to augment the juridical with the ethical. This cannot be done through coercion, since ends must be freely chosen. Additionally, unlike the political divisions traversing the juridical communities of the world, the ethical "concern[s] the entire human race" and so "the concept of an ethical community always refers to the ideal of a totality of human beings" (6:96). But it is important not to confuse what Kant is here introducing with the cosmopolitanism of Perpetual Peace, for that still concerns merely external conduct and not matters of an inward nature. Cosmopolitanism may be conducive towards the realization of an Ethical Community, and it may further help to prevent wars, facilitate trade, foster the exchange of ideas, etc. But these remain at most an outward expression of a human totality rather than the inward moral transformation essential to the Ethical Community. To reduce it to cosmopolitanism would be to reduce it to the secular ideal of a social utopia rather than an eschatological hope, as the titles of both Part Three and its First Division indicate. The Ethical Community is "the founding of a Kingdom of God on earth" (6:93, 6:95).[2]

THE FOUNDING AND FUNCTION OF THE ETHICAL COMMUNITY (6:96–100)

Kant introduces the Ethical Community specifically in response to the problem of moral recidivism. As noted above, despite an earlier claim that the Change of Heart is "unalterable" (6:48), Kant now offers a different position, stating that even those who have undergone a Change of Heart face an "incessant danger of relapsing" into sin (6:94). The Propensity to Evil remains, as does the susceptibility to unsocial sociability, and so Kant warns us that the mutually corrupting influence we have on one another not only catalyzes our evil Propensity but also can lead those who have had a Change of Heart back into sin.

Even a gathering of individuals who have all undergone a Change of Heart will, according to Kant, continue to have this malignant influence upon one another – or at least they would if not for the addition of some unifying principle of volition. Through the Predisposition to Humanity, we are drawn to one another because we want to *"gain worth in the opinion of others"* (6:27); but in the Ethical Community, whose members have undergone a Change of Heart, there is a common commitment to the Highest Good as "a principle which unites them" (6:97).

In earlier texts, the Highest Good seemed more of an aggregate of individuals rather than an interdependent unity. Likewise, in previous texts, Kant presented moral worthiness as a solitary venture, a self-regarding duty that is unrelated to the moral development of others. Although Kantian morality obviously includes many other-regarding duties, those duties do not include one another's moral development. But here, in *Religion*, he acknowledges that one's own moral status does depend upon others. This holds with respect to both our original corruption as it is instigated by the social needs of the Predisposition to Humanity, as well as to the realization and stability of the Change of Heart. Unsocial sociability collectively corrupts, whereas the Highest Good unites humanity in such a way that can secure one another's moral transformation.

This moral interdependence is also reflected in one's supreme maxim. In Chapter 2, we examined Kant's claim in the First Preface that we have a practical need for the Highest Good as the principle of reconciliation between our conflicting ends of morality and happiness. Those who fail to give morality its proper status reject the ordering principle it offers and substitute for it a principle of selfishness. By contrast, those who choose as their supreme maxim one that gives priority to morality over happiness thereby commit to the Highest Good, a commitment that is not only a "special point of reference for the unification of all [one's own] ends" (6:5), but also, as we now begin to see, what directs the individual out of their self-interested perspective to one where they unite with others in a communal project to raise up all of humanity (cf. Muchnik 2009).

Nevertheless, as elsewhere, Kant recognizes that the Highest Good's realization is still beyond what we as humans can achieve. God remains in charge of the distribution of happiness in accordance with moral worth. He alone "knows the heart ... the most intimate parts of the dispositions of each and everyone" (6:99). It is ultimately "a work whose execution cannot be hoped for from human beings but only from God himself" (6:100). But we still "have a duty *sui generis*, not of human beings towards human beings, but of the human race towards itself" (6:97). This is because although God rules the ideal state of the Highest Good (HG_i), it is up to us to populate it. That, as discussed in Chapter 1, is the essence of our duty to promote the Highest Good (HG_d). This is why Kant claims that "human beings are not permitted ... to remain idle in the undertaking [of the Highest Good] and let Providence have free rein" (6:100), and why "Each must ... so conduct himself as if everything depended on him" (6:101).[3] Without our efforts, HG_i would be like an empty shell. If a day of judgment were to come and we did not strive to become worthy of God's blessings, then that judgment would bring with it a justice that offers only punishment. In such, there still would be a proportionate distribution of happiness in accordance with moral worth, but that distribution would confer no happiness as no one would have come to be worthy of it. Hence, while the justice of HG_i is in the hands of God, populating HG_i with anyone worthy of happiness depends on us.

THE UNIVERSAL CHURCH (6:101–2)

Kant now turns to the Christian distinction between the visible and invisible church. As these terms have traditionally been used, the visible church refers to the actual institutions of the church, its offices and laity. The invisible church, by contrast, refers to the true believers, the elect or those who have found salvation. According to most theologians, membership in one does not entail membership in the other, for one can be part of a Christian assembly yet only masquerade as a believer, or one can be a true believer but have no involvement with existing religious institutions.

As membership in the visible church does not entail that its congregants are true believers, the distinction gained a polemical character during the Reformation, often associating the visible church with Catholicism versus the emerging reformers as the authentic Christians. But Kant is not following what by his time was a fairly common rhetorical use of the distinction. Instead, he identifies the church invisible with the Ethical Community, as "the mere idea of the union of all upright human beings under direct yet moral divine world-governance" (6:101). It is the "archetype" for any actual manifestations in the world, but "is not the object of a possible experience" (6:101). This is an important point with regards to the Ethical Community as Kant is making it clear that it, just like the Highest Good, is an ideal not to be instantiated within the natural order.

By contrast, the visible church is an actual union of human beings "that displays the (moral) kingdom of God on earth inasmuch as the latter can be realized through human beings" (6:101). Insofar as the term is used by Kant to specifically refer to human beings who have undergone a Change of Heart and are committed to the Highest Good, it actually corresponds to the traditional use of the "church invisible." That is, if Kant's use is essentially shaped by a moral principle rather than history, geography, etc., then the visible church may include members who have no ties to any physical organization. Of course, an actual congregation is possible, and it is still important to Kant's hopes for humanity, but as the condition for membership in the visible church is an inward moral one, its members need not be part of any outward organization.

After the above definitions, Kant then moves on to enumerate four characteristics of the True Church. In parallel to the divisions of quantity, quality, relation, and modality, as used, for instance, in the First *Critique*'s Table of Categories, he presents these characteristics as follows:

1. Universality. Kant is not clear as to whether membership in the church is gained through the Change of Heart or, more modestly, through a sincere commitment to strive for this transformation. But either way, membership must be, in

principle, open to all. Its qualifications do not extend beyond what is required of us morally, without the need to pass through special rituals, without nationalist or ethnic restrictions, etc.

2. Purity. The principles of the True Church must be composed of nothing other than morality, "cleansed of the nonsense of superstition and the madness of enthusiasm." Its official doctrines, insofar as we can say that it has any, extend no farther than the dictates of reason. Its members must be committed to the church "under no other incentives" other than its importance to our moral efforts (individually and collectively).

3. Freedom. A church that requires doctrinal commitments beyond those dictated solely by reason forces beliefs upon its members that they in good conscience cannot really affirm (see 6:185–90). Such a church is, as Kant discusses in Part Four, "despotic" and makes faith into something that is "slavish."

4. Unchangeableness of its constitution. As the church of Pure Rational Faith, its principles are not contingent upon external historical or social circumstances. Nevertheless, Kant acknowledges that it will still have some "accidental regulations" that can vary. He mentions those that concern its administration, but as he discusses later this may be extended to symbols, myths, rituals, and other accoutrements that are of instrumental value.

THE EPISTEMOLOGICAL RELATIONSHIP BETWEEN PURE RATIONAL FAITH AND HISTORICAL/ECCLESIASTICAL FAITH (6:102–3)

Religion's experiment has so far compared the contents of Pure Rational Faith to the Christian doctrines of sin and salvation. Now, as we move more deeply into Part Three, Kant turns to ecclesiology and, with it, begins to draw out in greater detail the relationship between Pure Rational Faith and Historical/Ecclesiastical Faith. This distinction has, of course, been active throughout the text, but it has not been discussed directly since the Second Preface. Now, finally, we see Kant not only further articulating what each side of the distinction involves, but also finally arguing for some vital commitments that have all along shaped the experiment.

He begins by considering to what extent each form of faith can be "convincingly communicated to everyone" (6:103). This is an important standard for Kant as it undergirds the rationale for *Religion* as a whole. As in many other contexts, including epistemology, ethics, and aesthetics, Kant uses the standard of universal agreement as the basis for distinguishing between legitimate and illegitimate forms of assent. His general term for legitimate assent is "conviction" (*Überzeugung*), and illegitimate assent is called "persuasion" (*Überredung*).

Kant explains the latter form of assent as the product of an individual's biases, idiosyncrasies, or psychological needs. As such, it has "only private validity" (A820/B848) since its grounds have to do with "the particular constitution of the subject" (A820/B848). Depending upon our individual temperaments, we will be prone to various cognitive biases or emotional drivers such as wishful thinking or peer pressure. However, we are usually unaware of the subjective character of our grounds and instead delude ourselves into thinking of them as objective.

Given this delusion, we will expect universal agreement, but if we actually were to try to communicate our grounds of assent to others, we would (or should) fail since a ground that has mere private validity would not be one that would be convincing to others. There is always the local problem that a group of individuals may share the same cognitive biases, and so we can have a false positive in the test of communicability. We can also end up with false negatives, such as when legitimate grounds are communicated to a biased audience. Thus, we cannot consider the test definitive. Rather, it is a mere "touchstone [*Probierstein*] of whether taking something to be true is conviction or mere persuasion" (A820/B847).

Nevertheless, the touchstone provides us with a way to explore whether "the grounds that are valid for us have the same effect on the reason of others" (A821/B849) and serves as a crucial (albeit imperfect) test for our own cognitive activity. It should be clear from what was discussed in Chapter 3 that we constantly deceive ourselves and are so deeply engulfed in self-deception that we cannot rely upon ourselves alone to separate out legitimate objective grounds from subjective delusions. This point is integral to the call upon us in "What Is Enlightenment?" to "make *public use* of one's reason in all matters" (WE: 8:36), and is expressed even more directly in "What Does It Mean to Orient Oneself in Thinking?": "how much and how correctly would we *think* if we did not think as it were in community with others to whom we *communicate* our thoughts, and who communicate theirs with us!" (WO: 8:144).[4] Similarly, in the Blomberg Logic we find: "Man needs this communication of his cognitions very much in order to be able to pass judgment on them rightly" (BL: 24:151).

By contrast, conviction is characterized as "universally valid" (BL: 24:202), "valid for everyone merely as long as he has reason" (A820/B848), "necessarily valid for everyone" (A821/B849), and objectively valid (5:461).[5] Unlike persuasion, conviction's grounds of assent are such that they hold for all and so, if communicated, should lead others to assent as well. This applies to the more routine domain of objective grounds, such as those we use to support our knowledge claims. But it also applies, according to Kant, to matters of faith. Kant refers to this form of assent as practical or moral conviction and so also expects that its claims, although grounded in the needs of reason rather than evidence and theoretical argument, are still "necessarily valid for everyone" (see Pasternack 2011).

Thus, we see here that Kant builds into his conception of the true church his standard characterization of legitimate assent, for its doctrines must be "convincingly communicated to everyone." As these are doctrines of the Pure Rational System of Reason, their grounds are such that everyone should be able to recognize and affirm them. By contrast, Historical Faith is "merely based on facts, can extend its influence no further than the tidings relevant to a judgment on its credibility can reach" (6:103). In this case, testimony about facts serves as the basis for assent. But the authority of the testimony can only reach so far. Let us consider, for example, some testimony of a purported miraculous event, such as spontaneous healings of the blind or lame. First, as discussed in the General Remark of Part Two, we cannot know whether or not claims about some putative miracles or revelation are veracious. In fact, neither can we have knowledge (*Wissen*) nor even opinion (*Meinung*) on these matters. The latter is because the grounds for opinion involve (a) some background knowledge related to the issue at hand; and (b) probabilistic inferences drawn from (a). We can know that some sequence of events does not comport with our existing model of the natural order, but we must be agnostic as to whether there is an unknown natural law in play or whether the cause is supersensible. If we begin to speculate about the latter, we must concede that we have no background knowledge about how the supersensible operates such that we can evaluate the probability that the cause is not natural (cf. CF: 7:63; PT: 8:396n).

Nevertheless, we still can opine regarding the likelihood that the testimony is reliable. That is, we can opine as to whether or not the bare observation statements are to be trusted (e.g. that a blind man suddenly began to see). We may not be able to judge regarding the cause of the event in question, but we do know that the farther removed the testimony is from first-person accounts, the less reliable it is. If it is first-hand and/or if the testimony has been well corroborated, Kant holds that we can accept it "with the same certainty as if we had attained it through *facta* of our own experience" (JL: 9:72n, see also 9:68). But if the testimony is second or third hand, we should give it "only half as much credibility as the eyewitness [account]" (BL: 24:246).

Once we begin to distance ourselves even farther, such as across the decades extending from the actual events during Jesus' life to the writing of the Gospels (roughly 60 CE for Mark to 100 CE for John), and factor in as well the layers of translation in the original accounts (from Aramaic to Greek), the credibility of the Gospels' tidings must be significantly diminished. One who then has Historical Faith in their veracity is in a perilous epistemic state. It may not be unreasonable to carry a weak opinion that their contents have some modest credibility, at least with regards to what was observed by the original spectators, but there is no legitimate basis for assent to claims about supersensible causes. So, at best, a Historical Faith in the Gospels can take the form of weak opinion with regards to their portrayal of what the original spectators observed, but we should remain agnostic about whether the events observed actually had a supernatural cause.

THE NEED FOR HISTORICAL/ECCLESIASTICAL FAITH (6:102–10)

Despite Kant's call for agnosticism regarding the supernatural aspect of Historical Faith, he acknowledges that because of our human limitations "pure faith can never be relied on as much as it deserves, that is, [enough] to found a Church on it alone" (6:103). This does not mean that the doctrines of Historical Faith should be adopted by a church as if they were essential to our salvation or even taken in their literal form. All that God really wants from us, at least according to the Pure Rational System of Religion, is "steadfast zeal in the conduct of a morally good life" (6:103). However "human beings are yet not easily convinced [*überzeugen*]" of this and thus may use the symbols and rituals of Historical Faith as a sort of crutch.

Kant writes that there is a "natural need of all human beings to demand for even the highest concepts and grounds of reason something that *the senses can hold on to*" and so he accepts that "some historical ecclesiastical faith or other, usually already at hand, must be used" (6:109). Thus, there is a place within the religious life of individuals and communities for various symbols and rituals that fall outside of what reason alone can provide. They can help us grasp "the highest concepts," can help foster fellowship within a congregation, and in other ways can contribute to both individual moral struggles and the spread of the True Church. However, as we shall discuss in the next chapter, Kant sees these trappings of Historical Faith as precarious. Even though they can offer much, they also can become instruments for "counterfeit service" and "delusory faith." Thus, they can supplant (and often have supplanted) the moral core of religion.

So, although they are of potential value, Kant nevertheless pines for a time when the True Church of Pure Rational Faith has gained a sufficient footing "that in the end religion will gradually be freed of all empirical grounds of determination, of all statutes that rest on history" (6:121). For now, it seems, they must be used. But he imagines a time when "the pure faith of religion will rule over all" (6:121). Through the centuries, Historical Faith has served as a "vehicle" [*Leitmittel*] for the Pure Rational System of Religion, but he holds out hope that in time "finally we can dispense of that vehicle" (6:115).

Considered on their own, the elements of Historical Faith are "intrinsically contingent" (6:105) and "arbitrary precepts" (6:106). Whether one has built one's religious practices and imagery upon the tales of the Mahabharata or the Koran, whether one takes communion or dovens, these are all "at bottom morally indifferent actions" (6:106). They may help to mold a religious community, but it is important that the community recognizes that even if some of these instruments celebrate purported miracles or are based upon alleged revelations, they must be understood as contingent accoutrements. Although instrumentally valuable, they are not part of what is required of us to gain salvation.

Kant maintains this view because of his commitment to the thesis that we all must be capable of becoming Justified before God. So, if some element of Historical Faith were in itself necessary for our salvation, those who live in different historical and geographical circumstances, by accidents of their birth, could not be saved. Kant thus claims: "The only faith that can found a universal church is *pure religious faith*, for it is a plain rational faith which can be convincingly communicated to everyone, whereas, a historical faith, merely based upon facts, can extend its influence no further than the tidings relevant to a judgment on its credibility can reach" (6:102–3). A few pages later, we find this point reiterated: "a church sacrifices the most important mark of its truth, namely the legitimate claim to universality, whenever it bases itself upon a faith of revelation which, as historical faith ... is incapable of a transmission that commands conviction universally" (6:109).

Moreover, if our salvation were to depend upon forms of divine service that cannot be derived from reason alone, then religion would lose its universal ground and faith would no longer be free. Our choice to commit to that service would not be based upon a rational judgment about its intrinsic merits, but we would instead be forced to accept edicts that in good conscience we could never confidently determine as authentic. We could not know if they are truly what God demands, if the alleged sources, such as claims of revelation, are veracious. We instead would be expected to act against our own judgment, taking as true claims whose probability cannot even be measured. In doing so, we take on heteronymous and despotic rules which make faith into something "servile" and "slavish."

We should now better see what motivated the experiment of *Religion*. Following from Kant's view that both free action and assent must comport with reason and justification, the Divine service that is essential to our salvation must not extend beyond what we all can discern on our own. As in his moral theory, where our duties are grounded in the law that resides within the will itself, so likewise a faith that is free must stem from principles already present in our reason. This is why it was so important to Kant that the moral Prototype "is present as model already in our reason" (6:62). If it were not, if we had to look outside of ourselves for the model of what it is to be well-pleasing to God, then the possibility of salvation would fluctuate with the reach of Historical Faith's "tidings," and the moral force of the duty to become well-pleasing to God would be undermined. If we ought to become worthy of salvation, then the conditions upon which this is possible must be universally available. Accordingly, a church that is genuinely committed to human salvation and has the correct understanding of what is required for it must be guided by the universal principles of the Pure Rational System of Religion. It may clothe these principles in various historical vestiges, but must ensure that its members understand that ecclesiastical rituals and traditions are only of instrumental value, and their observance makes no direct contribution towards becoming well-pleasing to God.

SCRIPTURAL SCHOLARSHIP (6:110–14)

We saw in the First Preface a distinction drawn between biblical and philosophical theology and an injunction against the trespass of one into the other. Although the Prussian Censorship Commission saw *Religion* differently, Kant asserted that it remained "within the boundaries of mere reason" (6:9) and did not carry its "propositions over into biblical theology" (6:9). Likewise, in his response to the royal rescript of 1794, he defends his work, as making "no *appraisal* of Christianity" (CF: 7:8), merely citing biblical texts "to corroborate certain purely rational teaching in religion" (CF: 7:8).

Nevertheless, we have seen Kant interpret the story of the Fall, the ministry, temptation, suffering, and death of Jesus, and various other biblical tales and biblically based doctrines. In each case, he has told us how to interpret them, what their true meaning is, what we can set aside as "mystical cover," and even when to discount their veracity, such as the putative command of God to Abraham that he sacrifice his son. Guided by a hermeneutic rooted in his Pure Rational System of Religion, he even comes to tell us what the point of reading the Bible is: "the final purpose of even the reading of these holy books, or the investigation of their contents, is to make better human beings; whereas their historical element, which contributes nothing to this end, is something in itself quite indifferent, and one can do with it what one wills" (6:111; see also CF: 7:68–69).

Kant might have thought that this hermeneutic does in fact preserve the First Preface's distinction between philosophical and biblical theology, and he is correct that it does articulate *some* boundary between the two. After all, there is the historical element, "which contributes not to this end" and "one can do with it what one wills," whereas the philosophical core is supposed to "make [us] better human beings." Yet this hardly conveys the sort of deference to the biblical theologian suggested by the First Preface (what in Chapter 1 we called IP). Rather, it seems to hand over to the philosophical theologian the right to interpret the Bible's meaning. In fact, he claims as much in such statements as "the moral improvement of human beings – constitutes the true end of all religion of reason, it will also contain the supreme principle of all scriptural exegesis" (6:112) and "[t]here is, therefore, no norm of ecclesiastical faith except Scripture, and no other expositor of it except the *religion of reason* and *scholarship* (which deals [merely] with the historical element of Scripture)" (6:114; see also CF: 7:38 and 7:59–61).

What is left for the biblical theologian – issues of historicity, philology, translation, and other empirical matters – does help "preserve the authority of a church based on holy Scripture" (6:112) since its members will often want to be confident that their translated Bibles are accurate, their rituals have the etiologies they are thought to, and so forth. The scriptural scholar is thus responsible for the symbols and rituals that are instrumentally useful to the church. But they are to remain within this outer sphere as the underlying truth of religion "must always be based on reason" (6:112).

After addressing the proper (and very limited) role of the scriptural scholar, Kant very briefly takes issue with the presumption on the part of some governments who direct religion, forcing upon the clergy specific doctrinal views. He then moves on to a third "claimant to the office of interpreter" (6:113). Although there has been a long-standing view in Christianity that the Holy Spirit has guided both the Early Church in its discussions of the rightful Canon and also guides how a person of faith reads the Bible, Kant raises the challenge that "just as we cannot derive or convey the recognition of laws ... on the basis of any sort of feeling, equally so and even less can we derive or convey on the basis of a feeling sure evidence of a direct divine influence: for the same effect can have more than one cause" (6:114).

Assuming that the only way we can know whether or not the Holy Spirit is guiding our interpretation is through some sort of feeling, that feeling Kant sees as having no intrinsic relationship with its source. Feeling, for Kant, is "private to each individual" and "teaches absolutely nothing but only contains the manner in which a subject is affected as regards his pleasure or displeasure, and no cognition whatsoever can be based on this" (6:114). He makes a similar point in his 1796 "On a Recently Prominent Tone of Superiority in Philosophy," balking at the idea that "Philosophy has its secrets that *can be felt*" (PT: 8:395). Concepts, ideas, and claims cannot be felt. We may be excited by a new discovery or fearful of an implication, but these feelings more appropriately have to do with practical consequences: the prospects for one's career, for society, and so forth. We may also hold a claim with some degree of confidence, but these degrees (on the continuum of what he elsewhere calls subjective insufficiency to subjective sufficiency) have "only three stages of apprehension ... knowledge, belief, and opinion" (8:396).

The feeling of confidence, considered on its own, has no correlation with truth. It can just as well come from subjective and idiosyncratic causes as from those that are universal and objective. If we look to feeling as if it were a sign of truth, we are confusing the subjective with the objective, falling into persuasion through the commission of an act of subreption. So, despite the long tradition that has employed the thesis that the Holy Spirit can be felt and that feeling can guide interpretation, Kant ardently opposes our putting trust in our feelings. However authoritative they may feel, they are *schwärmerei*.

THE REMARKABLE ANTINOMY (6:115–24)

Despite framing *Religion* as an experiment that explores the scope of overlap between Historical and Pure Rational Faith, Kant has not conducted himself as an impartial investigator. He has not merely surveyed the overlap, but rather has guided the experiment through his existing commitment to the formula: Pure Rational Faith (*Reiner Vernunftglaube*) = Saving Faith (*seligmachender Glaube*). Hence, Parts One and Two have not merely informed us about what Pure Rational Faith has to say about sin and salvation, but, guided by the above formula, they have separated out what is essential in these topics from what is inessential.

Now, in Part Three, Kant finally comes to defend his use of the formula. The implied argument is that if salvation is to be available to everyone, then the doctrines that are essential to our salvation must come from reason rather than revelation.[6] The former is portrayed as universally communicable whereas the latter has limited reach (i.e., cannot convince those removed from the putative revelatory moment). Thus, in order to preserve the universal availability of salvation, Historical Faith can only be a vehicle for Pure Rational Faith, so that it contains nothing essential to our salvation that is not also present in the latter.

There are, of course, many who would reject this deflation of Historical Faith, revelation, miracles, and the soteriological importance of historical events. This is most evident in the Christian commitment to the Crucifixion as a historical event that is essential to our salvation, and one that cannot be adequately appropriated by the Pure Rational System of Religion. Taken as an actual event in time, the Crucifixion and the Justification the event is said to offer cannot be reduced. Whatever reason might say about the meaning of the event, its facticity – its actual happening – is not something that can be part of Pure Rational Faith. Reason trades in ideas and, as Kant claims, rational grounds must be universally communicable. But the facts of history are by their nature beyond the scope of rational demonstration. Accordingly, it is anathema to Pure Rational Faith to grant to any fact a necessary role in our salvation. Yet this is precisely what Christianity does claim about the Crucifixion – and Kant responds with an antinomy.

The "Remarkable Antinomy" concerns the order of priority between "two conditions for ... hope of blessedness" (6:116). The first condition is the "undoing" (*ungeschehen*) of the debt of sin and the second is the "conversion to a new life conformable to its duty" (6:116). These may be taken to correspond with Justification and Sanctification respectively – with the question posed by the Antinomy being which of the two is the condition for the other. Although Part Two may be seen as already giving us Kant's answer (viz., Justification precedes Sanctification), in the Remarkable Antinomy, he wants to present his case by contrasting it against the opposing perspective, one that claims that "a historical (ecclesiastical) faith must always supervene as an essential portion of saving faith over and above the pure religious one" (6:116). This perspective, arguably that of traditional Christianity, is committed to there being a fact at the heart of soteriology, one that is essential to our becoming well-pleasing to God.

The actual presentation of the Antinomy is somewhat difficult to follow. Although Kant numbers the paragraphs containing the Antinomy's thesis and antithesis, the arguments in each are hard to unravel. What we find in each is an alternation from thesis to antithesis, using one to generate an argument for the other. So we see in the first numbered paragraph, the introduction of one possibility, its rejection, and then a defense of the other option. Similarly, in the second numbered paragraph, an option is introduced and immediately challenged, then the other option is mentioned and given support.

Because the second option mentioned in the first numbered paragraph is the one that Kant first endorses, let me refer to it as the Antinomy's thesis, while its antithesis (though appearing initially in the first paragraph as well) is only defended in the second numbered paragraph. That is, put in terms of the text's order of presentation, we have in paragraph one, Kant introducing and rejecting the Antinomy's antithesis as a segue to the thesis; then through the first half of paragraph two, a case is made for the antithesis.

The Antinomy's thesis is that our moral improvement is a condition for partaking in the Atonement offered through the Crucifixion; and the antithesis is that only by first being freed through the Crucifixion can we hope to make moral progress. After it states the antithesis, paragraph one rejects it as something that no one can "seriously believe" (6:116) and insinuates that it is merely wishful thinking drawn from self-love: "No thoughtful person can bring himself to this faith, however much self-love often transforms into a hope the mere wish for a good ... lured by the mere yearning for it" (6:117). So, the more tenable option, the thesis that is endorsed in this paragraph, is that a person must "consider the improvement of his life conduct, as much as lies in his power, as having to come first" (6:117).

In the second paragraph, Kant returns to the antithesis, now defending it through the conjecture that "if humankind is corrupt by nature, how can a human being believe that on his own, try hard as he will, he can make a 'new man' of himself, one well-pleasing to God" (6:117). Under this conjecture, it seems that we will necessarily remain captivated by our self-interest since while guided by self-interest, we will never choose to set it aside in favor of morality.[7] The thesis, therefore, must be false since in the state of sin, we cannot make moral progress. In order to become well-pleasing to God, we must partake of a "foreign satisfaction,

¶ #1

6:116	Antithesis Stated
6:116-117	Antithesis Rejected
6:117	Thesis Stated

¶ #2

6:117	Thesis Rejected, leading to
6:117	Antithesis Stated
6:117	Antithesis Defended

6:118

| Antithesis | "Whether from Faith in what God has done for our sake" | First Alternative |
| Thesis | "From what we ought to do in order to become worthy of it" | Second Alternative |

"There is no hesitation in deciding for the second alternative"

Figure 4 The remarkable antinomy

and, through this faith ... capable for the first time to undertake a new life conduct" (6:117).

About midway through the second enumerated paragraph, Kant turns to the resolution of the Antinomy. He begins by stating that a theoretical solution is not possible since we can have no "insight into the causal determination of the freedom of a human being" (6:118). But from the practical point of view, we can say "whence ... we are to make our start" (6:118). The next sentence, though, can be confusing. It ends with "there is no hesitation in deciding for the second alternative" and we need to take a moment to clarify what alternative Kant means. A cursory reading may leave one in sheer confusion or one may mistakenly take the referent to be the option defended in the second of the enumerated paragraphs (i.e., the antithesis). However, Kant is rather referring to the order of presentation in the sentence itself, as this quote should make clear: "whether from faith on what God has done for our sake, or from what we ought to do in order to become worthy of it (whatever this may be), there is no hesitation in deciding for the second alternative" (6:118). Thus, the practical solution to the Antinomy endorses its thesis, that we must first do what is within our power.[8]

Nevertheless, this is still only the first gesture towards Kant's actual solution. Although he does endorse the thesis, it still has to be cast in a new form (just as the solution to the Antinomy of Practical Reason in the Second *Critique* endorses its second option once the Practical Postulates are made available to combine happiness and morality – see CPrR: 5:114–15). After a few remarks about some failed strategies of resolution, strategies that leave one with either "ritual *superstition*" or "*naturalistic unbelief*" (6:118), Kant finally moves on to more fully articulate his own solution to the Remarkable Antinomy.

He begins by recalling Part Two's presentation of the Prototype as "a moral idea of reason" (6:119) and uses it not simply to solve the Antinomy, but to dissolve it, showing that it is "only apparent" (6:119). Hence, unlike the antinomies of the *Critique of Pure Reason*, which are inevitable products of the rational faculty, the Remarkable Antinomy is not native to our cognition, but rather arises merely through a particular perspective, i.e., Christianity. By making our salvation dependent upon a historical event, the relationship between the two requirements of Saving Faith (the "undoing" of the debt of sin and the "conversion to a new life") becomes indeterminate. That is, we lack a principled solution as to which requirement is the condition of the other. However, by recasting these requirements through the position expressed in Part Two, so that the Prototype is "present as model already in our reason" (6:62), the two requirements are reunited: "we do not have two principles here that differ in themselves ... but only one and the same practical idea from which we proceed" (6:119).

In the Prototype, we have our model for good-life conduct, a model that is the "seed of goodness" which remains as incentive within us, despite the Propensity to Evil; and we also have the resolution to the debt of sin, for as examined in Part Two, through the restoration of the moral incentive to its rightful status, we as well restore our relationship with God. We no longer live in a way that dishonors God and so the conditions upon which our debt to Him depended no longer obtain. Of course, Kant's ultimate commitment to the Antinomy's thesis position (that moral improvement is the condition for the undoing of the debt of sin) is something he has telegraphed throughout the Antinomy (e.g. no "rational human being can seriously believe that he only has to believe the news of a satisfaction" (6:116), "there is no hesitation in deciding for the second alternative" (6:118)). But it is not until he returns to the rational nature of the Prototype that he provides the ground upon which the Antinomy can be resolved.

With this resolution to the Remarkable Antinomy, Kant believes he has settled once and for all the question of "whether a historical (ecclesiastical) faith must always supervene as an essential portion of saving faith over and above the pure religious one" (6:116). Accordingly, Kant believes he has, through this Antinomy, shown that there cannot be anything present within Historical Faith yet absent from Pure Rational Faith that is necessary for our salvation. Of course, he has not discussed every soteriological claim that Historical Faith may make, but he has targeted the historical moment that Christianity has traditionally taken as necessary for our salvation.

Even though there are, of course, other historical claims that are part of traditional Christianity (as well as other religions), the Crucifixion is typically seen as having a different status than all others. Claims of miracles and revelation, be they in Christianity or other faiths, are not touted as events that in themselves Justify humanity. Of course, a religion may draw from a historical claim some principle or other that is soteriologically relevant, but the Crucifixion is itself taken as *the* Justifying event. Kant has no problem with doctrines appropriated from history, so long as those doctrines can also be established through reason. The Antinomy is rather brought to bear against the claim that the event in time itself, rather than its meaning, what it symbolizes, or what principles we may glean from it, is necessary for our salvation. Thus, with his dismissal of the Crucifixion as a Justifying event, Kant is able to reaffirm his commitment to the formula Pure Rational Faith (*Reiner Vernunftglaube*) = Saving Faith (*seligmachender Glaube*) and restate his hope "that in the end religion will gradually be freed of all empirical grounds of determination, of all statutes that rest on history ... [and] at last the pure faith of religion will rule over all" (6:121).

DIVISION TWO: HISTORY AND THE UNIVERSAL CHURCH (6:124–37)

In such works as the "Idea for a Universal History with a Cosmopolitan Aim" and the "Conjectural Beginning of Human History" Kant approaches history as more than a narrative of events. In the former, he notes that he wants "to displace the treatment of history proper, that is written merely *empirically*" (ID: 8:30), and instead utilize some intelligible structure through which to reflect upon both human and natural history. To fulfil this goal, he represents both nature and culture as unfolding in accordance with some telos. He claims that human existence is "the ultimate end of nature" (CJ: 5:429) and, depending upon the text, characterizes our ultimate human end as individual moral perfection (CPrR: 5:123), "[h]umanity under moral laws" (CJ: 5:445), a "perfect civil union" (ID: 8:29), the "cosmopolitanism" of *Perpetual Peace*, or, of course, the Highest Good.[9]

In this division of Part Three, Kant applies teleology to the history of religion. He wants history to have a "principle of unity" (6:125), by which he means a way to bring together the "manifold and mutable forms" (6:124) of Historical Faith into one unified and purposive narrative. However, if we consider the development of various pantheons, or the evolution of Buddhism out of Hinduism, we hardly can see a fully unified teleology stretching across both the West and East. Thus, Kant acknowledges that not all religious developments are ruled by a common telos and so chooses to put aside all but "the history of the church which from the beginning bore within it the germ and the principles of the objective unity of the true and *universal* religious faith to which it is gradually being brought nearer" (6:125).

KANT'S CRITIQUE OF JUDAISM (6:124–28)

Although Kant's discussion of Christianity is preceded by a discussion of Judaism, he writes that "the *Jewish* faith stands in absolutely no essential connection, i.e. in no unity of concepts, with the ecclesiastical faith whose history we want to consider" (6:125). It may have immediately preceded it in time, and served as the "physical occasion for the founding" of Christianity (6:125), but Kant's historiography brings him to exclude Judaism from the actual history of the Universal Church of Pure Rational Faith. It stands outside the latter's conceptual history as it lacks "the germ and the principles of the objective unity of the true and *universal* religious faith." In fact, he characterizes the transition from Judaism to Christianity as "a total abandonment" of the former and "a total revolution in doctrines of faith" (6:127).

Jesus and his disciples may have come from the Jewish people. However, according to Kant, Christianity's religious views are fundamentally discontinuous with those of Judaism. This may seem quite strange, given that they are both monotheisms, that we find in the Gospels Jesus stating that he has come to fulfill the Law (Matthew 5:17), and that he is represented as the messiah prophesied in the Hebrew Bible. Yet these are all of little relevance for Kant. In his view, Judaism is "simply a union of a number of individuals who, since they belonged to a particular stock, established themselves into a community under purely political laws, hence not into a church" (6:125). Its laws "deal only with external actions" (6:126) and have no concern for our inner morality. As such, Judaism pays no regard to our *"moral disposition* (whereas Christianity later placed the chief work in this)" (6:126). It is, consequently, not "a religion at all" (6:125).

To many contemporary readers, this may seem outright ludicrous and reek of anti-Semitism, for Kant is clearly accepting the classic Christian polemic against Judaism as a cult of empty legalism. This polemic has its foundations in the various challenges raised by Jesus against the absolutism of Judaic law (such as his decision to "work" on the Sabbath by healing the sick (Mark 3:1–5)); and it is amplified through Paul's many castigations of Jewish law throughout the Epistles. Judaism thus came to be viewed right from the dawnings of Christianity as unrelated to morality and as superseded by the New Covenant.

The Catholic Church perpetuated this view of Judaism, and though Luther at first opposed anti-Semitism, when his attempts at converting Jews failed, he became among the most caustic anti-Semites prior to the twentieth century. In his *On the Jews and Their Lies*, he wrote that the Jews are a "base, whoring people, that is, no people of God, and their boast of lineage, circumcision, and law must be accounted as filth" (Luther 1883: 1.53.442). He further asserts that they should be denied civil protections, enslaved, expelled, or killed.[10]

Sadly, Kant could not see past these entrenched attitudes, and though he had Jewish students and acquaintances, most notably Marcus Herz and Moses Mendelssohn, they did not disabuse him of the long-standing Christian conception of Judaism. In fact, we know from their correspondence that Herz inadvertently reinforced them. Although Kant thought very highly of Herz, and when we consider Kant's Christology, one may even wonder about the extent to which the Jewish denial of Jesus' divinity had an impact on his soteriology (see Shell 2007), nevertheless, his exposure to Jewish intellectuals may have actually reinforced his negative views about the religion. The reason for this is that many of his Jewish students, including Herz (the son of a Torah scribe), were of the first generation in their families to reject their heritage (or at least its more insular and demanding aspects), and so they themselves looked upon Judaism quite harshly. We can see this in various correspondences between Kant and his Jewish students, including the following from Herz: "without you I would still be like so many of my kinsmen, pursuing a life chained to the wagon of prejudices, a life no better than that of an animal. I would have a soul without powers, an understanding without efficacy, in short, without you I would be that which I was four years ago, in other words I would be nothing" (10:101, dated September 11, 1770).

Kant's conception of Judaism was surely influenced by the common attitudes of his day as well as the remarks of young Jews dealing with their decisions to separate themselves from family and tradition. But he also offers three arguments in defense of his position that Judaism is not a genuine religion.

His first accusation is that Judaism is concerned "simply and solely [with] external observance" (6:126), whereas religion's proper concern is moral improvement. He notes that even the

Ten Commandments make "no claim at all on the *moral disposition* in following them" (6:126). However, this is not quite accurate. The Commandments may focus primarily upon conduct rather than intent, but the final Commandment at least does concern our inner states. It is not a prohibition against a type of action, but rather against coveting (Ex 20:17; Deu 5:21). Moreover, Kant's characterization of Jewish law is that of an outsider. He seems unfamiliar with the oral law which, according to Jewish tradition, also comes from Mount Sinai, not written down until the second and third centuries.

According to traditional Judaism, from Sinai there also came an oral law that was then handed down through the centuries, until finally written down in the third century CE. In it we can find numerous discussions of the importance of one's attitudes and motivations, such as the following, all taken from the Mishna's Pirkei Avot (Ethics of the Fathers): "Be not like servants who minister unto their master for the sake of receiving a reward, instead be like servants who serve their master NOT for the sake of receiving a reward"(1:3); "There are four types of charity-givers: He who wants to give but does not wish that others should give – he begrudges what belongs to others. He who wants that others should give but not that he should give – he begrudges what belongs to himself. He who wants to give and also that others should give – he is a saintly man. He who does not want to give himself and does not wish that others should give – he is a wicked man" (5:16); "Whosoever possesses these three qualities belongs to the disciples of Abraham our father: a generous eye, a humble spirit, and a meek soul. But he who possesses the three opposite qualities – an evil eye, a proud spirit, and a haughty soul – is of the disciples of Balaam the wicked" (5:22).

Kant's second accusation against Judaism is that it has no doctrine of the afterlife: "no religion can be conceived without faith in a future life, Judaism as such, taken in its purity, entails absolutely no religious faith" (6:126). As we have discussed, the afterlife is vital to his understanding of religion because of its relevance to the Highest Good. His claim that "morality ... inevitably leads to religion" (6:6) is based upon the necessary role that the Highest Good must play in our practical lives. It functions as the "special point of reference" (6:5) that allows us to order our fundamental incentives, and in turn, we need to commit to the conditions that make its realization possible: God and immortality. The Pure Rational System of Religion thus emerges out of our practical needs, and a religion that does not include the conditions necessary for the Highest Good is a religion lacking a proper rational foundation. It is a mere cult, composed of doctrines that cannot be affirmed through a free, authentic faith. So, if Judaism lacks the Postulate of Immortality, we cannot (as we presumably can with Christianity) see through its historical clothing to its true inner core of rational faith.[11]

Kant is partially correct about Judaism's views concerning the afterlife. By contrast to Christianity (and Islam), it places less emphasis on the hereafter. Yet it is an overstatement to claim that it has no role. In fact, just as Kant on various occasions emphasizes the importance of not taking up any specific conception of the afterlife as an official dogma (6:71n; ET: 8:329), so too does Judaism discourage such speculations. Its focus is on this life and if Kant were to accept that Judaism is not merely a cult of morally irrelevant statutes, but a religion devoted to morality, then that focus could be seen as praiseworthy.

Kant's third objection is that Judaism understands its people as a unique group chosen by God to follow laws to which the rest of humanity are not subject. Consequently, their "cult" is fundamentally opposed to the Universal Church. But the latter does not follow. Gentiles may not be seen as obligated to follow Halakha and there is little interest among Jews in evangelism. Nevertheless, they maintain that everyone is still subject to a common moral code, the core of which is known as the Seven Laws of Noah. These laws are alluded to in Genesis 9, are mentioned in various pre–Common Era works (such as the Book of Jubilees), and are more amply discussed in the Talmud and post-Talmudic Rabbinic literature. Classically, they include, as one would expect, prohibitions against murder, theft, and sexual immorality. They also prohibit idolatry, blasphemy, and the eating of the flesh of animals while still alive; they also contain a positive command that no civil law should ever pass that is unjust.

However limited, these Seven Laws illustrate that traditional Judaism does see all of humanity as standing in moral relation to one universal God. It is just that Jews are also subject to additional commands beyond these. Again, this is something that Christians generally do not understand and, sadly, despite Kant's various affiliations with Jewish students and scholars, he remained within the all too pervasive Christian distortions of Judaism. So, despite his accusations, Judaism can be understood as standing in "essential connection" (6:125) with Christianity. Given its monotheism as well as the Noahic Covenant, it can be seen not only as another vehicle for the Universal Church, but, ironically, should be recognized as the original historical source for much of what Kant regards as most important in Christianity.

A BRIEF HISTORY OF THE UNIVERSAL CHURCH (6:128–33)

Given Kant's views on Judaism, he sees the actual history of the Universal Church beginning with the life of Jesus, who introduced "a pure moral religion in place of an old cult" (6:127). The veracity of what is recorded in the Gospels is, however, of little consequence to Kant. As with the rest of the Bible (and any other documents of Historical Faith), what really matters for our salvation is what within them may inspire us to more ardently pursue our moral vocation (see 7:66–69). The rest can be set aside, for the truth of Pure Rational Faith "does not need any such documentation but is its own proof" (6:129). Kant even adds a dollop of skepticism regarding its reports of miracles since in all other writings of the time there is "no mention, neither of the miracles nor of the equally public revolution which these caused (with respect to religion) among that people subjected to them, although they were contemporary witnesses" (6:130).

He then offers a very brief schematic of what transpired in Christendom until his own era, listing the various ways in which the fledgling Universal Church has been weighted down by superstition, enthusiasm, secular politics, and feuds, assigning as their common cause "the bad propensity in human nature" (6:131). Given that it actively opposes our moral efforts, it should be no surprise that it also targets the institution whose essential function is to fight against it and morally uplift humanity. It has infected the entire history of the Church, but as a consequence of the Reformation, Kant sees his own day as an opportunity for the original seed of Pure Rational Faith to again be sown (6:131). Likewise, he hopes that a shared Scripture, which contains a "vivid presentation of its true object" (6:132), now freed from the despotic powers that have controlled it, can be used "in the interest of morality" (6:132).

Lastly, Kant takes a moment to consider what is yet to come, expressing hope that after "an approach long delayed" (6:134) the Kingdom of Heaven finally comes nearer. This eschatological hope is first presented "as a symbolic representation aimed merely at stimulating greater hope and courage and effort in achieving it" (6:134); he then later adds that its imagery has a "proper symbolic meaning before reason" (6:136). That meaning pertains to "a beautiful idea of the moral world-epoch brought about by the introduction of the true universal religion" (6:136). Its symbolism includes "the Antichrist, the millennium, the announcement of the proximity of the end of the world." But these refer to our inward struggle against the evil Propensity. Even the Apocalypse may be understood in this way, as a symbolic representation of the culmination of our inward struggle – from the perspective of the old self, it feels as if all that was held dear would be destroyed with the emergence of the new man.

In this brief discussion of where Providence will bring us, Kant also returns us to the doctrine of the Highest Good and the Ethical Community, for in the Kingdom that is to come, we gain our citizenship through our moral merit as well as happiness, "the other part of the human being's unavoidable desire" (6:134). However, as Kant so often asserts, it (or at least its distribution in accordance with moral worth) is not something anyone can "count on during ... life on earth" (6:135) but awaits a future life.

This section may seem confusing to many since Kant both states that this happiness cannot be expected during "life on earth" yet is "crowned with happiness here on earth" (6:135), with "the establishment of the divine state" where all "earthly life comes to an end" and "immortality commences on both sides [for those damned and elected]" (6:135). To most contemporary readers, the idea of immortality will suggest some state of being whose imagery has its roots in the Hellenic Elysian Fields – or more fully, the Hellenic Elysian Fields and Tartarus. Such imagery is used in popular culture, including the lay depictions of the Christian afterlife. But, as discussed in Chapters 1 and 4, this is not what Kant intends. His model of the afterlife actually conforms more with Judaism's conception of the World to Come, the *Olam Ha-Ba*, which can also be found in the New Testament and was quite prevalent in early Lutheran thought, including its Pietistic offshoot.

According to this model, the afterlife is not a different plane of reality where the dead float around with harps and halos or suffer under some demon's whip. Rather, the World to Come that is articulated in Judaism and some sects of Christianity involves the coming (or second coming as the case may be) of the messiah, a transformation of the world both socially and materially, as well as the resurrection of the (righteous) dead. It is this world "glorified" or "purified" – though Kant is far from clear as to exactly what this means.

For instance, he seems quite ambivalent as to whether the afterlife is corporeal or not. The former was a popular view among Pietists, including Franz Albert Schulz, who had considerable influence in Königsberg and was an important figure in the religious life of Kant's family. For philosophical reasons as well, there is something to be said in favor of corporeal afterlife. Since Kant's understanding of happiness is so intimately tied to the physical, one might see a body as necessary for happiness to remain possible. However, elsewhere Kant writes that "pleasure and pain (since they belong to the senses) are both included in the temporal series, and disappear with it" (6:70n). Moreover, he repeatedly expresses distaste for the idea of "dragging along, through eternity, a body" (6:129n), even if it is in some "purified" form (6:129n). Thus, even though Kant seems to prefer a Judaic rather than Hellenistic conception of the afterlife, the details remain unclear.[12]

But this is, presumably, what Kant intends, for as we have discussed, he repudiates any attempt to establish dogmas about what the afterlife is like. Aside from what is dictated by the needs of pure practical reason, and what may quite accidentally be useful in motivating individuals to morally improve themselves, we should not put much weight on any further claims about the hereafter. So if, as I suggested, he nevertheless does prefer the Judaic conception over the Hellenistic, we still have no way of understanding what our "glorified" or "purified" state would be like. It is something that we simply cannot resolve and for "practical purposes we can be quite indifferent as to whether we shall live merely as souls after death or whether our personal identity in the next world requires the same matter that now forms our body" (CF: 7:40).

GENERAL REMARK: ON HOLY MYSTERIES (6:137–47)

Part Three ends with a discussion of the Holy Mysteries. In Lutheran Theology, these are also called "pure" as opposed to "mixed" articles of faith (see Schmid 1889: 55, 115). The latter have to do with doctrines that are intelligible to us and can be defended rationally. Pure articles, on the other hand, are taken as not merely beyond rational demonstration, but also beyond human understanding. Depending upon the religious tradition, the mysteries may include the Divine essence, the incarnation, and the Trinity. Lutheran theologians tend to take the last of these in particular as a pure article of faith. How three persons can be one person is, at least on the face of it, incoherent; yet many traditions that affirm this or other Holy Mysteries will accept their truth while also accepting that they cannot be rendered comprehensible to us – for such rendering would take away the mystery.

What is particularly extraordinary about this General Remark is that there is an inherent tension between its subject matter and the Pure Rational System of Religion. Although all four General Remarks are *"parerga* to religion" – that is, they concern principles that "do not belong within it [Pure Rational Faith] yet border on it" (6:52), this one in particular seems patently incompatible with the System. As the Holy Mysteries are supposed to be unintelligible, it is hard to imagine how Kant could preserve this quality while at the same time finding a place for them within, or even on the border of, the System.

He does, however, acknowledge the tension here. For reasons we have discussed, all soteriologically necessary doctrines of the True and Universal Church require that they are capable of being "convincingly communicated to everyone" (6:103) or capable of "transmission that commands conviction universally" (6:109). Yet the Holy Mysteries, Kant acknowledges, do not meet this standard. They "cannot be *professed* publicly, i.e. cannot be communicated universally" (6:137). Again, one might therefore expect him to reject the Mysteries, treating them as part of the detritus of the outer sphere of religion. Instead, Kant seeks a way to bring the Mysteries into the fold of Pure Rational Faith. But in order to make this possible, he must deviate from the tradition, or, one might say, from the more radical thread of tradition, which declares that the Mysteries cannot even be made intelligible to us.[13]

So, even though Kant accepts that they "cannot be communicated universally" (6:137), he still claims that they can "indeed be *cognized* by every individual" (6:137). That is, in the Holy Mysteries we find religious principles that cannot be communicated or transmitted to others, but still can, despite the tradition, be cognized by us. As we see in this section, Kant clearly wants to find a place for the Mysteries within the System, and thus they must somehow be rendered in a way consonant with practical reason. We can see this even in his account of what it is to be a "Holy Mystery": "As something *holy* it must be a moral object, hence an object of reason and one capable of being sufficiently recognized for practical use; yet as something *mysterious*, not for theoretical use, for then it would have to be communicable to everyone and hence also capable of being externally and publicly professed" (6:137).[14]

One might naturally assume that anything that can be cognized can also be communicated, but this is not necessarily so, for "communication" here does not merely mean uttering a lexically intelligible and grammatically correct sentence. After all, even "Three are one" follows normal English grammar and is composed of words found in standard dictionaries. The force of "communication" here is rather, as seen in the quotations of the previous paragraph, in its capacity to convince others.

As we have previously discussed, Kant draws a distinction between conviction (*Überzeugung*) and persuasion (*Überredung*). The latter concerns modes of assent that arise out of idiosyncratic, subjective grounds such as wishful thinking, peer pressure, or other affective drives without a tether to truth, while the former refers to instances of assent with grounds that are intersubjectively valid and, insofar as they can be communicated, would lead others to assent as well. Matters of faith, however, sometimes agitate against this distinction. Although Kant uses communicability and conviction as a general standard for what can be included within the Pure Rational System of Religion, a modest emendation is employed in order to allow the Holy Mysteries to find a place within the System.

To achieve this, Kant shifts away from the standard of communicability to a cognition that is available to *everyone* but cannot be articulated in such a way that others can be convinced: "each individual will have to look for it (if there is such a thing) in his own reason ... we shall have to look directly into the inner, the subjective, part of our moral predisposition in order to see whether any can be found in us" (6:138). This shift may seem utterly ad hoc, but there is an important precedent in Kant's practical philosophy: the Fact of Reason in the *Critique of Practical Reason*.

This Fact refers to the bindingness of the moral law upon us. It "is given, as it were, as a fact of pure reason of which we are a priori conscious and which is apodictically certain" (CPrR: 5:47). Yet it "cannot be proved by any deduction, by any efforts of theoretical reason, speculative or empirically supported" (CPrR: 5:47). So as we look into "the inner, the subjective, part of our moral predisposition" (6:138) what we can find is the moral law's call upon us: "one need only analyze the judgment that people pass on the lawfulness of their actions in order to find that, whatever inclination may say to the contrary, their reason, incorruptible and self-constrained, always holds the maxim of the will in an action up to the pure will" (CPrR: 5:32).

The Fact of Reason is for each of us "apodictically certain." However, this certainty arises from a cognition that has a privileged first-person character analogous to Descartes' *Cogito*. The certainty we have about the moral law for ourselves is not of the sort that can be shared with others. It is likewise with the Holy Mystery of the call. Each individual can be certain that he is bound by the moral law, but the consciousness through which this certainty is gained cannot be used to prove the same of another. We each encounter the moral law's force in our own practical consciousness and can thereby be certain only of its bindingness upon ourselves. It is thus something that can be universally recognized by every individual, but not in such a way that can be convincingly communicated to everyone.

With the stage now set, let us turn to Kant's presentation of the Holy Mysteries themselves. Following his Lutheran contemporaries, Kant too focuses on the doctrine of the Trinity, but rather than treating it in its literal form as the unity of the Father, Son, and Holy Spirit, he correlates the three with "the mystery of the *call*," "the mystery of *satisfaction*," and "the mystery of *election*."

As discussed above, we can understand the Holy Mysteries as finding their way into the Pure Rational System of Religion through a distinction between that which can be communicated to everyone and that which may not be communicable, but is available to "each individual ... in his own reason" (6:138). The Fact of Reason exemplifies the latter and can also be correlated with the first Mystery. As Kant describes it in the Second *Critique*, it cannot be proven through any "exertion of the theoretical, speculative, or empirically supported reason" (CPrR: 5:47). Yet it is "apodictically certain" and "firmly established of itself" (CPrR: 5:47). As soon as one begins to practically deliberate: "one need only analyze the judgment that people pass on the lawfulness of their actions in order to find that, whatever inclination may say to the contrary, their reason, incorruptible and self-constrained, always holds the maxim of the will in an action up to the pure will" (CPrR: 5:32). In this we have "the call," the demand of morality upon us. It is not something that can be proven about another person, for there is no third-person argument available to demonstrate that one is bound by the moral law. It must, rather, be recognized in the performance of one's practical life. Thus, each person finds it "in his own reason," in "the inner, the subjective, part of our moral predisposition" (6:138).[15]

The second Holy Mystery is that of "satisfaction." While the former Mystery is at best loosely related to the Father (as source or creator of morality), the second Mystery more obviously relates to the Son. Kant quickly reviews the problem of Justification and reiterates his opposition to the doctrine of Vicarious Atonement: "Inasmuch as reason can see ... no one can stand in for another" (6:143). Yet he then adds, "if we must *assume* any such thing, this can be only for moral purposes, since for ratiocination it is an unfathomable mystery" (6:143). This could be read as some concession to the tradition. But it need not. On the one hand, Kant states that this is not something we can comprehend rationally, but "if we must *assume* any such thing, this can be only for moral purposes" (6:143). Still, this might be understood as an acknowledgment that Vicarious Atonement falls short of "ratiocination" but for moral purposes, it *may* be something we need to assume. On the other hand, we should not forget that the Pure Rational System of Religion is shaped by what is necessary for our salvation. If the doctrine of Vicarious Atonement were necessary, it would have to be part of the System (or the System would fail). But hardly is the above sentence affirming this. First, the sentence begins with a conditional "if": "*if* we must assume any such thing." So if the System is lacking, we may need to make such a concession. However, we have through much of Part Two, and through the solution to the Remarkable Antinomy in Part Three, already seen why Kant rejects the doctrine of Vicarious Atonement and have examined the alternate solution he proffers for the problem of Justification.

The third Mystery concerns the notion that only some people while not others will receive Sanctifying Grace through which they are aided in their moral transformation to become well-pleasing to God. Kant recognizes that this "does not yield the concept of a divine justice" (6:143) and as a Holy Mystery "must at best be deferred to a wisdom whose rule is an absolute mystery to us" (6:143). So, once again, we see what appears to be a claim that is inconsistent with the soteriology developed through most of *Religion*. As we have discussed, Kant has given us three different reasons for not affirming such aid (or at least that such aid is necessary): a) from the logic of *ought implies can*, it is something we should be able to achieve on our own; b) if we are to deserve happiness through this transformation, we must be responsible for it; and c) if we add it to our religious principles, we risk becoming morally lazy.

Nevertheless, Kant does not in principle reject the possibility of Divine aid. He allows for its possibility so long as it does not compromise any of the above three conditions. This can be accomplished through aid that does not substitute for our own efforts, but rather supplements them though indirect means. For example, Divine aid may redirect one away from a temptation so that one does not even encounter it, or introduce suitable challenges through which the agent could through his own efforts make moral progress. Such assistance does not step in to the agent's own will and take it over. Rather, it merely adds or subtracts external trials, offering opportunities for moral improvement or guarding the agent from more extreme temptations. The Mystery here arises from the conjecture that such aid is not offered uniformly to all of humanity. But this we cannot really know. It could instead be that some are more successful than others in meeting the challenges put before them.

From the above, the reader may wonder whether in this General Remark, Kant made any concessions to more traditional views. I have suggested that that is not the case, though he is trying to find a way to bring the doctrine of the Trinity into the Pure Rational System. He does this by associating each "person" of the Trinity with specific aspects of our moral-religious journey. Although as we have seen, he still does want to preserve the "mysterious" in the Holy Mysteries, it should be apparent that he does not actually commit to the traditional doctrine. It is, rather, adjusted, taken symbolically, to reflect different elements within our moral lives.

This, however, is not Kant's final word on the Trinity. He revisits it in the *Conflict of the Faculties* and is there far less willing to find a role for it in the Pure Rational System: "The doctrine of the Trinity, taken literally, has *no practical relevance at all* … and it is even more clearly irrelevant if we realize that it transcends all our concepts" (CF: 7:38–39). In fact, he also comments on what was said in *Religion*, where he attempted to "read a moral meaning into this article of faith" (CF: 7:39). So it seems in this later text he admits that too little of the traditional doctrine was retained in this attempt, and accepts that there are some elements of Historical Faith that are best put to the side without trying to force into them some symbolism of use within our practical lives.[16]

NOTES

1 The reader may wonder whether Kant is somewhat naive here, as he does not seem to take into account the extent to which even the institutions of his day were able to inculcate various motives and beliefs. Through our families, peers, schools, and other organizations, there are mechanisms that can influence our inner states. Skilled manipulators can exploit our Predisposition to Humanity and lead us into changing much of who we are. Moreover, it often also happens that without any explicit intention, but rather through a sort of osmosis, we change ourselves in order to fit in.

Thus, it might seem that Kant failed to consider the extent to which our minds can be directed. But in his defense, we can still separate out from all that is subject to such influence and control the fact that there is no way to coerce moral commitment in particular. Despite all the mechanisms that exist which can alter many of our inner states, the commitment to morality seems beyond such manipulation since it "entails freedom from coercion in its very concept" (6:95). Although there are many tricks available that can help break through inner lies and draw one's attention to morality, to genuinely act from duty is something that by its very nature cannot come out of coercion or manipulation, for if it did, then we would not really be acting from duty but from some other motive, be it fear of punishment, the desire to fit in, etc.

2 Such an eschatology should not be considered a Kantian idiosyncrasy. Rather, it has a biblical origin, and the hope in Christ's final victory and the coming of a new kingdom was a vital element within

Lutheranism, especially among Pietists. Lutheran eschatology is this-worldly, a transformation of material reality into a "glorified" form, one which includes the bodily resurrection of the righteous into an eternal existence that is not of the sort derived from the Greek mythology of the Elysian Fields, or with wings and halos among the clouds, as it is popularly portrayed, but far more in line with the Judaic imagery of a "New Jerusalem." In fact, shortly after writing *Religion*, Kant composes his essay "The End of All Things," which even more explicitly dis-cusses an apocalyptic transformation of the world into a "new earth," one whose order is not natural but moral (ET: 8:328). "The End of All Things" cautions us against indulging in speculation about this order, though we can make some claims about it for practical purposes. He also cautions against its misuse, something he saw in the projects of the Prussian authorities under Frederick William II. The Ethical Com-munity promises rewards in accordance with our moral worth (6:99), but they should not be promoted as incentives for action: "one must not take that promise in this sense, as if the rewards are to be taken for the incentives of the actions" (ET: 8:339). These rewards only come to those who become worthy of them through unselfish motives (ET: 8:339).

3 As discussed in Chapter 1, PPD would technically be satisfied if every-one deserved and so received punishment. In a sense, this too would be a realization of the Highest Good, but only in an ersatz form since there is still something better. A state of affairs where PPD is satisfied, but also where some (or ideally all) deserve happiness, more fully reflects the *Highest* Good. It is in this way that we gain our duty to promote the Highest Good, for it is up to us to populate HG_i with agents who are worthy of happiness.

4 For further discussion of the relevance of the public use of reason, see Rawls 1997, O'Neill 2001, and Gelfert 2006.

Kant's commitment to communication is also illustrative of a his-torical shift from an earlier paradigm of inquiry. Consider Descartes' advocacy for the Geometrical Method and its putative epistemological guarantee if one merely conducts each step with clarity and distinct-ness. Likewise, Descartes puts aside all learning so *he* can start fresh. But Kant rejects the paradigm of the private thinker rationally dedu-cing all knowledge and instead philosophically (though not personally) embraces the Enlightenment's public venues of inquiry: learned societies and salons. Königsberg may not have provided Kant with such forums, but we know that he had an indirect involvement in the Berlin salon run by Marcus Herz and his wife.

5 The conviction/persuasion distinction also seems to apply to aesthetic judgment. But in its case, we would not have objective validity, but subjective-universal validity. See Kant's discussion of the young poet at CJ: 5:282. As noted previously, Guyer/Matthews mistranslates *Überredung* as "conviction" in a crucial sentence within this discussion. That the poet is erroneously holding his work to be beautiful due to his personal bias should make it evident that the German *Überredung* is what Kant did intend and should have been translated as "persuasion."

6 One particularly illuminating passage on this issue, directed specifically to the distinction between Natural and Revealed Religion, appears at 6:155–56. We will discuss Kant's rendering of this distinction in Chapter 6.

7 Although Kant rejects the antithesis, and instead holds to how Pure Rational Faith would render the thesis (i.e., that moral improvement is a condition for grace), the antithesis points to an important problem. When self-interest is given priority over morality, how could one under its governance choose to depose it? I have been arguing that Kant's ultimate view is that this does happen through (either primarily or solely) our own effort, but Part One does nevertheless show that Kant did struggle with the issue: "How is it possible that a naturally evil human being should make himself into a good human being surpasses every concept of ours" (6:44). See also note 7 of Chapter 4.

8 This is, of course, also what is claimed in Part One: "the human being must nonetheless make himself antecedently worthy of receiving it [Divine aid]" (6:44).

9 I by no means intend here that these different representations of the telos are equivalent. Some are merely political/juridical whereas others are moral. The former may have a role in the latter, but the Highest Good, as I have argued, exceeds what we can on our own achieve and rather coordinates with the eschatological Ethical Community as the Kingdom of God on Earth. In addition to my eschatological rendering in this chapter, see also Chapter 7.

10 One can find these views strewn throughout his writings, and most notoriously in his 1543 *On the Jews and Their Lies* (Luther 1883: 1.53.417–552). See also Gritsch 2012.

11 As a minor side point, it is worth considering the above objection to Judaism in relation to some of the contemporary attempts to secularize Kant, or at least the tendency to remove the Postulate of Immortality from his positive philosophy of religion. That is, clearly Kant saw the Postulate of Immortality as an indispensable principle for his positive philosophy of religion.

12 The most careful textual work on this issue appears in Bunch 2010. In addition, Lara Denis has argued that Kant believes that happiness depends upon corporeality. She uses this to undercut the Postulate of Immortality, but as Bunch observes, Kant, like many of his contemporaries, thought of our afterlife as either corporeal or having something like a body – a "glorified" or "purified" form. See note 2 above.

13 It is in relation to the issue of communicability that we can understand Kant's rejection of the freedom of the will as a mystery. Although throughout the corpus, Kant claims that we have no grasp of how freedom itself is possible, that we are free, he claims, cannot be counted as a mystery. Freedom is "a property which is made manifest for the human being through the determination of his power of choice by the unconditioned moral law" (6:138). That is, through our consciousness of being bound by the moral law, we *infer* that we are free. It is a necessary condition for the moral law's bindingness, and this inference relation is something that can be communicated. Thus, Kant asserts, it cannot count among the mysteries because "cognition of it can be *communicated* to everyone" (6:138). Of course, this does not mean that we can make freedom empirically manifest or theoretically demonstrable, but we can present the conditional argument for freedom in such a way that can be universally communicated: *if* we are bound by the moral law, *then* we are free. Note as well how Kant distinguishes between the Postulate of Freedom and God and Immortality at CJ: 5:468–69. Whereas the former, along with the Highest Good, are highlighted as the sole matters of faith, "the only ones among all objects that can be so designated" (5:469), Kant characterizes the Postulate of Freedom as "*res facti*" (5:468). See Pasternack 2011 for a discussion of the relationship between faith, communication, and validity.

14 The astute reader may notice in this quote something peculiar – the association between theoretical reason and communicability. Although

it does follow from the judgments of theoretical reason (at least nearly all of them) that they can (or should) be convincingly communicable to everyone, Kant has repeatedly claimed that this also holds for practical reason (at least nearly all of its principles). What comes next in his discussion is an exception to his standard of communicability, one that Kant uses to satisfy the "mystery" of the Holy Mysteries.

15 In Pasternack 2011, I examine the relevance of the Fact of Reason for Kant's overall positive philosophy of religion. I suggest that we can distinguish between two types of moral belief (*Glaube*): direct moral belief versus derivative moral belief. My contention is that the Highest Good and the Practical Postulates are of the latter type for reasons similar to what Kant here says about freedom. They are products of inference, and that inferential relation is one that can be universally communicated. Hence, as inferences, they involve a cognition more suitably rendered in terms of knowledge than faith. By contrast, the Fact of Reason is, as Kant portrays it, something that is certain yet "cannot be proved by any deduction, by any efforts of theoretical reason, speculative or empirically supported" (CPrR: 5:47). Thus, I contend that the sole article of direct belief, the only one that is not something more like a hybrid assent, merging faith and inferential reasoning, is the Fact of Reason.

16 Towards the end of Part Two, Kant makes a similar point with regards to the Virgin Birth (see 6:80).

6

PART FOUR OF *RELIGION*
AUTHENTIC AND COUNTERFEIT
SERVICE TO GOD

This final chapter of commentary ventures into the least studied part of *Religion*. Part One's account of evil, Part Two's discussion of moral transformation, and even a few elements of Part Three, such as its introduction of the Ethical Community and its Remarkable Antinomy, have been amply discussed in the secondary literature. But there is no core theme or pivotal moment in Part Four that has drawn like attention. Its inner structure remains obscure to most and its relationship to the whole of *Religion* has not been adequately examined.

Given the last of these lacunae, let me repeat a few points regarding *Religion*'s literary structure before moving on to the philosophical issues in Part Four. As I suggested in the Introduction to this book, we may divide *Religion* into two halves: the first examines the moral trajectory of the individual through sin and salvation; then, in Parts Three and Four, Kant transitions to the level of the collective, as he turns to the Ethical Community and the Universal Church. *Religion*, thus, has an overall balance with two parts devoted to the individual's moral/religious journey and two parts devoted to the common institutions that can help or hinder that journey.

A second literary characteristic of *Religion* is that it has an overall chiastic structure. Chiasms are symmetries in presentation that can occur within sentences, paragraphs, or even a work's entire dramatic arc. They can be found throughout the Bible, Hellenistic literature, in Milton, Shakespeare, etc. In the case of *Religion*, we can see an ABBA chiasm with Parts Two and Three taking up the center, exploring the positive hope for moral transformation within the individual and society, respectively. Parts One and Four complete the symmetry, addressing the negative conditions that we individually and collectively must overcome. Thus, we move from: the moral corruption of the individual, the moral transformation of the individual, the moral transformation of society through the emergence of the Universal Church and the Ethical Community, and finally, the nature of ecclesiastical corruption.

There are further parallels that help fill out this chiasm, including similarities between the corruption of the individual and the corruption of the church, both through an inner perfidy. Just as the corrupt individual has inverted the proper order of incentives, giving priority to self-interest over morality, so likewise a church that advocates "counterfeit service" and "delusory faith" harbors "a hidden inclination to deceit" (6:170) and inverts its own order of principles. The root of the latter inversion is presumably still ultimately the sinfulness of its members, especially those who shape doctrine. But the specific inversion that

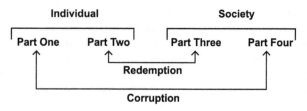

Figure 2 Religion's chiasmic structure

takes place within the church is between the outer form of faith, i.e., the rituals and practices, and the moral improvement and transformation that they are supposed to facilitate.

When "revealed faith is to come ahead of religion" the result is a *"counterfeit service* through which the moral order is totally reversed" (6:165). In counterfeit service, rituals themselves come to be treated as if they were what we are supposed to do to become well-pleasing to God. That is, what should be "mere means" are elevated "to the rank of saving faith" (6:165). Part Four thus exposes the source and structure of religious corruption. It returns us to Part One's inquiry into sin and builds a polemic against the "counterfeit service" that has historically dominated and continues to dominate ecclesiastical institutions.

DIVISION ONE: CONCERNING THE SERVICE OF GOD IN A RELIGION IN GENERAL (6:153–67)

Part Four begins by recalling why humanity needs a church. As argued at the opening of Part Three, Kant warns us that the Change of Heart is unstable and can be undone through our unsocial sociability. Even though we can restore morality to its rightful place in our supreme maxim, our Propensity to Evil will always remain with us. We will thus always remain morally vulnerable through our enduring need to establish and sustain a positive sense of self-worth, one that cannot be fully dislodged from the comparative self-love arising out of the Predisposition to Humanity.

The solution offered in Part Three is built around the idea of a society that shares the Highest Good as their common (and supreme) end. Its citizens will then be most fundamentally committed to the pursuit of this end rather than their own happiness and so will strive to both improve themselves morally as well as do what is within their power to facilitate the moral improvement of others. As we discussed in the previous chapter, despite what Kant writes in the *Metaphysics of Morals* regarding our responsibility for the moral perfection of others, the Highest Good is clearly presented as a corporate duty. This duty demands that we strive for our own moral improvement. But it also demands that we do what we can to promote the same in others.[1]

The visible church, or more precisely put *the true and universal visible church*, is the public organization that recruits, supports, and sustains potential citizens of God's Kingdom on Earth (the Ethical Community).[2] The origins of this church, as we saw in Part Three, are, according to Kant, within Christianity; and because of its specific history, it carries various ecclesiastical characteristics such as its organizational structure, rituals, symbols, doctrines, etc. But these characteristics, like the historical form of the Christian faith more generally, remain as the outer shell, the vehicle for the Pure Rational System of Religion.

Kant also reminds us that the True Church is by its own nature supposed to be temporary. It "contains within itself a principle of constantly coming closer to the pure faith of religion" (6:153) and when that goal is reached, i.e., when the Kingdom of God is established on Earth, it can be dissolved. As put in Part Three: "in the end religion will gradually be freed of all empirical grounds of determination. ... The leading strings of holy tradition, with its appendages, its statutes and observance, which in its time did good service, become bit by bit dispensable" (6:121); and so, as repeated here, the True Church should eventually "dispense with ecclesiastical faith (in its historical aspect)" (6:153).

By contrast false churches reify "the historical and statutory part of the church's faith as alone salvific" (6:153) and present rituals and dogmas as essential and ineliminable features of religion, held up as how we become well-pleasing to God. Such an attitude towards the historical and statutory aspects of the church Kant describes as "counterfeit service" to God. Its purveyors are ensnared within a delusion that is essentially due to their substituting for what God truly requires of us, what they instead would prefer God to be like and to command: "*we are making a God for ourselves*, we create him in the way we believe that we can most easily win him over to our advantage, and ourselves be dispensed from the arduous and uninterrupted effort of affecting the innermost part of our moral disposition" (6:168–69). In this, we can obviously see the inversion presented in Part One still playing itself out: for a false church is one that shapes its doctrines through the interests of the self rather than from the moral law.

CONCERNING THE SERVICE OF GOD IN A RELIGION IN GENERAL (6:153–57)

Before Kant moves more fully into how the True Church differs from the false, he offers a general taxonomy of religion. After defining religion as "(subjectively considered) the recognition of all our duties as divine commands" (6:153), he distinguishes two ways in which duty and Divine command can be associated with one another. The first is to have morality depend upon God's will, such that one must first know that a rule is commanded by God before it can be recognized as one's duty. This is the stance of *"revealed* religion (or a religion which requires a revelation)"* (6:154). The second, which Kant identifies with *"natural religion"* (6:154), is to begin with our duties, which are recognized through reason, and then to represent them as (also) what God wills.

Although the distinction between Natural and Revealed Religion concerns far more than the relationship between morality and Divine commands, Kant here uses their differing accounts of this relationship as his way of separating the two forms of religion. More generally, Natural Religion refers to those approaches to religion that stem from our natural epistemic capacities. For example, as we see so robustly examined in Hume's *Dialogues Concerning Natural Religion*, our observations of orderliness in nature have been used as the basis for arguing that there is an intelligent designer responsible for that order. Revealed Religion, by contrast, emphasizes, as its name clearly indicates, revelation as the source of our religious doctrines.

Beyond this basic division between Natural and Revealed Religion, Kant further distinguishes between Rationalism, Pure Rationalism, Naturalism, and Supernaturalism. To complicate matters even more, the taxonomy he presents does not use the original division between Natural and Revealed Religion as actual taxons, but rather they operate more like differentia. That is, the divisions between Rationalism, Pure Rationalism, Naturalism, and Supernaturalism are based upon their respective relationships to Natural versus Revealed Religion. More precisely, the taxons are distinguished in terms of whether or not Natural and Revealed Religion are each necessary, contingent, or impossible.

So Rationalism, the first taxon introduced, is defined as follows: "Anyone who declares natural religion as alone morally necessary, i.e., a duty, can also be called a *rationalist* (in matters of faith)" (6:154). However, this definition does not express what role should be granted to Revealed Religion. It may either be contingent or impossible. Hence, Kant moves on to depict these two options: "If he denies the reality of any supernatural divine revelation, he is called a *naturalist*; should he, however, allow this revelation, yet claim that to take cognizance of it and accept it as actual is not necessarily required for religion, then he can be named *pure rationalist*" (6:154–55). Naturalism and Pure Rationalism thus fall under Rationalism. The Naturalist follows the Rationalist's claim that Natural Religion is alone morally necessary, but also explicitly excludes Revealed Religion as having any possible role. By contrast, the Pure Rationalist likewise takes Natural Religion as alone morally necessary, but accepts Revealed Religion as a contingent adjunct. Lastly, there is also Supernaturalism, which should be understood as on the same taxonomic level as Rationalism, for these two reflect opposing positions regarding whether it is Revealed Religion or Natural Religion that is necessary: "if he holds that faith in divine revelation is necessary to universal religion, then he can be called pure *supernaturalist* in matters of faith" (6:155).

To restate the above: the genus of Rationalism takes reason as the source of our duties and our understanding of God; its Naturalist species subscribes to this view *and* rejects all other possible sources; the Pure Rationalist species accepts reason as the necessary source *but does not* exclude the possibility of revelation. Then, after presenting these two branches of Rationalism, Kant turns to Supernaturalism as the other genus, one which regards Revealed Religion as opposed to Natural Religion as necessary "in matters of faith."

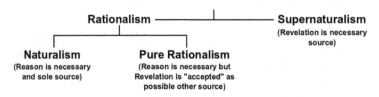

Figure 5 Kant's taxonomy of natural and revealed religion

Although some have found this array of religious categories confusing, the above taxonomic diagram should disambiguate the passage. To help justify it, let me add a few points. First, Kant obviously is not a Supernaturalist, for this view would not only stand in conflict with the epistemological constraints of Transcendental Idealism, but also opposes much of *Religion*. It would be, for instance, in violation of his claims regarding the communicability of the doctrines of the Universal Church and would allow some principle beyond the Pure Rational System of Religion to become soteriologically necessary.

Accordingly, Kant must be some form of Rationalist. But he cannot be a Naturalist, since they reject all possible sources of duty other than reason. Although this might sound like Kant in one way, the point here is not about the justificatory ground of our duties, but about the sources through which we come to be aware of them. Regarding the latter, Kant indicates that he is open to revelation as a possible source of our moral duties as well as even perhaps some further ecclesiastical non-moral duties. On the latter, Kant remarks: "it would be just as arrogant peremptorily to deny that the way a church is organized may perhaps also be a special divine dispensation" (6:105). So, although all moral duties must have their justificatory foundation in reason, Kant remains open to both reason and revelation as sources, so long as whatever is necessary for our salvation is still ultimately discoverable through reason alone.

This leaves us with Pure Rationalism, and that this is Kant's own view should be readily apparent by virtue of the term itself. After all, throughout *Religion*, Kant names the view he is advocating as Pure Rational Faith and defends his formula that Pure

Rational Faith = Saving Faith. The Rationalist maintains that Natural Religion is "alone morally necessary" (6:154); that is, all that is soteriologically necessary can be discovered through our own natural capacities. The Pure Rationalist, though, also allows for revelation, but maintains that it "is not necessarily required for religion" (6:155). It should also be apparent that this captures the essence of *Religion within the Boundaries of Mere Reason* and its experiment, inquiring into the scope of overlap between the record of revelation that shapes Christian doctrine and the Pure Rational System of Religion.[3]

It may be worth repeating that none of this denies the possibility of revelation (thus Kant's rejection of Naturalism). Rather, we see through the experiment of *Religion* that he accepts its possibility, but maintains that what of it is essential to our salvation can also be discovered through reason. Everything beyond what reason as well can discover is "intrinsically contingent" (6:105), accidental and arbitrary (6:158). However, from its contingency, it does not follow that we can outright dismiss the contents of Historical Faith. Kant is not simply agnostic about revelation, miracles, and the possibility of some "special divine dispensation" relevant to ecclesiology. He concedes that at least for most of human history the outer sphere of doctrine has been and continues to be important "because of the natural need of all human beings to demand for even the highest concepts and grounds of reason something that *the senses can hold on to*" (6:109). So, at least until the time that the Ethical Community is established, where perhaps the rituals and symbols of Historical Faith finally become "dispensable" and "religion will be ... freed of all empirical grounds of determination" (6:121), we must rely upon some of its features.

It may seem odd to call what might actually be a revelation from God "dispensable" or "arbitrary," but Kant's point is that even if God did provide us with some set of symbols and rituals, they remain just the instruments or vehicles for a truth that reason is still on its own able to discover. If God commanded the Jews to observe halakha, the Muslims to observe sharia, Christians to take communion, etc., such service is not in itself essential to our salvation – as these commands cannot be discovered through reason and so could not be "convincingly communicated to everyone" (6:103). These and other putative "special divine dispensations" facilitate our grasp of "the highest concepts and grounds of reason" and may in other ways be conducive towards a life that makes us well-pleasing to God. But they remain "arbitrary" accoutrements to our religious lives, whose observance is not necessary for our salvation.[4]

THE CHRISTIAN RELIGION AS NATURAL RELIGION (6:157–63)

This section is framed by the same point appearing at its beginning and its end: Natural Religion is composed of morality, the Highest Good, and its Postulates of God and Immortality. Near the end of this section, after Kant again lists these elements, he summarizes by stating that "[h]ere we have a complete religion" (6:162). That is, whether or not one wants to introduce any further principles, be they from revelation or elsewhere, Natural Religion is a "complete religion," i.e., one that contains all we need to do and to know in order to become well-pleasing to God.

Moreover, Kant also states at both the beginning and end of this section that Natural Religion can be "comprehensibly and convincingly communicated" (6:162). It can be uncovered by anyone using their own reason and thus "possess[es] the great prerequisite for the true church, namely the qualification for universality, inasmuch as by universality we mean validity for every human being ... , i.e. communality of insight" (6:157). However, for this complete religion to propagate itself in the form of a visible church, there must be added to it "certain statutory ordinances" (6:158) that nevertheless have "accidentality and arbitrariness" (6:158). As we have previously discussed, Kant recognizes that due to various shortcomings, humanity (at least for now) needs some set of rituals, symbols, etc. But we must ensure that these outer features are not confused with what is soteriologically necessary – a point that, according to Kant, Jesus well recognized: even "the founder of the first true *church*" maintained "that [it is] not the observance of external civil or statutory ecclesiastical duties but only the pure moral disposition of the heart can make a human being well-pleasing to God" (6:159). Thus, Kant moves on to catalog the moral teaching from the Gospel of Matthew: "to hate in one's heart is tantamount to killing" (6:159), "revenge must be transformed into tolerance" (6:160), etc. He then concludes this list with Jesus's statement that the "first and greatest command" that we should love God above all else and love one's neighbor as oneself. For Kant, this is equivalent to "[d]o your duty from no other incentive except the unmediated appreciation of duty itself" (6:160). With the addition of the Highest Good ("happiness ... will be proportionate to his moral conduct" (6:161)), the role of God in the distribution of happiness, and that this distribution will take place in a "future world" (6:161), "we then have a complete religion" (6:162).

We can clearly see in the above Kant's presentation of Jesus as a moral philosopher, whose aim was to articulate the Pure Rational System of Religion. Thus, the founder of Christianity was "the first to advocate a pure and compelling religion, one within the grasp of the whole world" (6:158). He was "free from every dogma" (6:159) and though miracles and other supernatural elements have been added to the Gospels, Kant looks past them to the actual teachings of Jesus whose legitimacy rests on reason alone. References to Old Testament prophecies, and the declaration ostensibly by Jesus that "he does intend to satisfy the Jewish law in full" (6:160), Kant takes to be rhetorical strategies intended for the "introduction among people who, without exception and blindly, clung to the old [law]" (6:162). He then concludes by generally discounting all but the moral teachings of the Gospels. The remainder comes from "the prejudices of the times" (6:163) and should have no bearing upon the True Universal Church (other than, perhaps, material available to shape its accidental and arbitrary statutes).

THE CHRISTIAN RELIGION AS A LEARNED RELIGION (6:163–67)

What makes Christianity stand out for Kant is that he sees it as carrying, far more completely than any other Historical Faith, the Pure Rational System of Religion. However, as it is still a

Historical Faith, it also has its "learned" side, i.e., a "sacred history," scriptures, rituals, and so forth. This side of Christianity is "built upon facts and not upon mere concepts of reason" (6:164). As we have discussed before, Kant both recognizes that due to our human limitations we rely upon the historical side of religion to help us with the "highest concepts and grounds of reason" (6:109) and hopes for a future time where we will no longer need "all statutes that rest on history" (6:121). In the meantime, though, we still need the historical, whose constituents should be "cherished and cultivated" and utilized as needed "for giving meaning, diffusion, and continuity to natural religion even among the ignorant" (6:165).

Kant then turns to the concern that dominates this part of *Religion*: that the historical can be (and often has been) distorted, treated as if it were "unconditionally commanded (as an end)" (6:165). When this happens, the church becomes despotic, and faith is no longer free. Rather than our assent arising from an inward recognition of the needs of practical reason, it is dictated by an outward authority. Authentic religion is thereby "robbed ... of its due dignity" (6:165). Scripture is turned into something that merely reinforces dogma, compels slavish obedience to ecclesiastical authority, and replaces the true service to God with "a counterfeit service through which the moral order [between means and ends] is totally reversed" (6:165).

DIVISION TWO: CONCERNING THE COUNTERFEIT SERVICE OF GOD (6:167–90)

Kant's critique of counterfeit service continues through the rest of Part Four, with its remaining sections devoted to four different issues: the subjective ground of counterfeit service, its relationship to authentic service, its manifestation as "priestcraft," and its violation of our moral conscience. As continuations of the polemic against counterfeit service and the religious delusions that have so dominated Historical Faiths, there is much in these sections that we have seen before. However, the last issue in particular offers some interesting considerations relevant to the nature of Pure Rational Faith not mentioned elsewhere in *Religion*.

THE UNIVERSAL SUBJECTIVE GROUND OF RELIGIOUS DELUSION (6:168–70)

Authentic religion is supposed to be the means through which we overcome our Propensity to Evil and undergo a Change of Heart. It offers us the answer to sin, but while in sin we will resist it, and through our "hidden inclination to deceit" (6:170), we will subvert the instrument that could have helped overthrow self-interest. Its outer form of ritual and symbol, which ought to serve as mere means to help us in our pursuit of moral ends, will instead be represented as what really matters. This inversion is especially insidious because of the close relationship through history between the inner truth of religion and its outer form.

The Eucharist, for instance, could be understood as a practice that helps one reflect on the moral Prototype. But in our state of sin, we may consider our receipt of this sacrament as itself what contributes to our becoming well-pleasing to God. The same holds true for fasting on Yom Kippur or during Ramadan, being baptized or bar mitzvahed. It is far easier to say a prayer, to attend a church service, to perform this or that ritual than it is for us to confront our inner corruption and take meaningful steps towards restoring morality to its rightful place within our will. In counterfeit service, we instead engage in ecclesiastical practices, as if they themselves were what God demands of us. We slip into this illusion very easily, not merely because our inner perfidy has become so adept at directing our attention away from morality's call, but also because religious ritual is ideally suited for this purpose. Of course, it is supposed to help us in our moral development, but it is precisely because the church and its rituals are supposed to have this function that they can be abused. We turn them against themselves when we go through the outward motions, using them to pretend as if we also put in the inward effort that really matters.

Such distortions pervade Historical Faith and are driven, according to Kant, by self-interest. An Atheist or Agnostic simply rejects religion, leaving it intact, in a sense. But Delusory Faith corrupts religion by reshaping what God demands of us to fit our own desires. This is why Kant claims that the universal ground of religious delusion is anthropomorphism. Self-interest finds in religion its greatest enemy and protects itself by reshaping the meaning and purpose of its rituals, while at the same time clothing this corruption in the lie that they are in themselves what God demands from us. We thus depict His commands in a way that better suits our desires, "*making a God for ourselves* ... that we can most easily win ... over to our advantage" (6:168).

Kant further adds that more often than not, Delusory Faith focuses on practices that have neither any practical nor moral worth. They may prohibit us from eating perfectly nutritious foods, require us to wear awkward or uncomfortable garments, or mandate that we frequently repeat various phrases or gestures. Such demands guard against authentic religion first, by simply filling up our lives with observances that presume to satisfy God's demands. But they also impose various hardships upon us that "have absolutely no use in the world" (6:169). This, ironically, is their source of power, for as Kant notes: "The less aimed at the universal moral improvement of the human being, the holier they seem to be. For, just because they have absolutely no use in the world, and yet cost effort, they seem to be aimed solely at attesting devotion to God" (6:169). That is, a Historical Faith can present various rituals as having supernatural effects by exploiting the assumption that all action has a purpose and selecting actions that will be seen as having no worldly purpose.

A third reason why such rituals are used is because their hardships mimic the efforts required of us in pursuit of a Change of Heart. As discussed in Part One, the call of morality threatens our sense of self-worth. It humiliates us and demands that we respect something higher than ourselves. This is, as Kant describes it, a powerful experience and if we want to block its influence, suitably powerful delusions are needed in order to take its place. Counterfeit service to God is, thus, ideal for this purpose. We impose hardships upon ourselves and use their burdens as substitutes for the hardships (what Kant claims to be even greater in degree) involved in becoming a morally better person. The best lies always have a grain of truth and so by taking on the external trappings of religion and treating them as if they were its core, we are more able to trick ourselves.

THE MORAL PRINCIPLE OF RELIGION OPPOSED TO THE DELUSION OF RELIGION (6:170–75)

Kant begins this section by restating one of *Religion*'s core claims: "Apart from a good life-conduct, anything which the human being supposes that he can do to become well-pleasing to God is mere religious delusion and counterfeit service to God" (6:170–71). He then concedes that there may be beyond our awareness something "which only God can do to make us human beings well-pleasing to him" (6:171), but whatever this is (if anything), it must not be brought into religion in such a way that it substitutes for good life-conduct.

What, in particular, Kant has in mind is, once again, the Crucifixion. He has already discussed it in Parts Two and Three, but once more he turns to it and again challenges the traditional view that we can through some "inner profession" receive redemption through Christ. To compound all the objections we have already examined, Kant now adds that the doctrine of Vicarious Atonement has become a "dangerous religious delusion" (6:171). In Part Two, he opposed it because the debt of sin "is not a *transmissible* liability" (6:72). In Part Three, he opposed it because no event in time can be soteriologically essential. Here, his objection is that the "inner profession" through which it supposedly becomes possible for us to partake in it is *necessarily* contrary to conscience.

He makes this claim because the demand that one makes an "inner profession" in order to receive salvation is "patently extracted through fear" (6:171). Unlike the performance of a superfluous ritual, which can be accomplished without real inward commitment, the demand of this "inner profession" is a demand that would go against conscience. It would be without any legitimate ground (either theoretically, or through practical reason); and even if one were concerned that some Divine aid were necessary beyond what we can accomplish on our own, it is an act of self-corruption to profess something that cannot be an object of authentic conviction (*Überzeugung*). That is, even if "*in some way or other*" (6:171) something beyond our moral efforts were necessary for our salvation, we cannot know what that something is. Hence to ignore all these doxic principles and make such an "inner profession" is to fall into persuasion (*Überredung*), allowing assent to arise out of an irrational need rather than one that has an intersubjectively valid ground.

Once we step away from the claim that opens this subsection, that nothing other than our moral efforts can make us well-pleasing to God (6:170), "there are *no bounds* for the counterfeit service of God (superstition), for everything is arbitrary past that maxim" (6:172). There is "no essential difference among the ways of serving him" (6:172), be it an inner profession, a pilgrimage, the spinning of a Tibetan prayer wheel, "or whatever the surrogate for the moral service of God might be, it is all the same and of equal worth" (6:173). To nothing else but the Change of Heart can we legitimately commit ourselves in hope of becoming well-pleasing to God. To think otherwise, to presume that we know how to influence the supersensible through one ritual or another is to think we can see beyond the Kingdom of Nature and into the Kingdom of Grace, and that "is a kind of madness" (6:174).

CONCERNING PRIESTCRAFT (6:175–85)

Kant defines "priestcraft" as "the constitution of a church to the extent that a *fetish-service* is the rule" (6:179). By "fetish-service" he means "the observance of statutory laws, requiring a revelation as necessary to religion, not indeed merely as a means to the moral disposition but as the objective condition for becoming well-pleasing to God directly" (6:178). This is, of course, an illustration of what he called Supernaturalism earlier (6:155). Kant also quite dramatically characterizes such observance as "sorcery" (6:177) since natural processes and objects (incantations, rituals, symbols, relics, etc.) are used as if they could influence the supernatural, to "*conjure up* as it were God's support" (6:178).

Sorcery is actually quite common in the lives of most religious people. It is employed when they use prayer in order to solicit God's assistance, when they make the sign of the cross to shield them from danger, or carry various pendants or talismans to help bring them luck. Similarly, baptism, communion, and so many other traditional practices that shape the outer form of the church are commonly viewed as infused with magical powers, as if they themselves can draw forth supernatural aid. Although the priesthood that administers these rites may be blamed for their corrupting influence, it may be better to see this as an unspoken collusion between the priesthood whose self-interest is being fulfilled by their power over others and the laity who accept their authority in order to simplify their path to salvation.

So, quite reminiscent of Luther's condemnation of the Catholic Church, Kant criticizes Christendom for its continued reification of the superficial trappings of tradition. The prioritization of ecclesiastical rituals and dogma serves the priesthood, giving them a reason to remain in authority, and helps the laity forsake their freedom by giving in to this authority and accepting heteronymous rule. We may say that there is therefore an unspoken collusion between the two bodies, together turning the church into an institution of despotic rule and servile faith. Priestcraft is the bait and switch whereby the true moral purpose of the church is replaced with a counterfeit service that "drive[s] out nearly all of morality" (6:180) from religion.

CONCERNING CONSCIENCE (6:185–90)

In the final section of the main body of Part Four, Kant finally moves forward from its polemic against Delusory Faith to how one might overcome its many layers. The unstated problem that Kant is here concerned with is whether or not an agent's ability to distinguish legitimate from illegitimate religion may become so corrupted that he could no longer, on his own, liberate himself from the delusions and despotism of the false church.

This is actually an extension of a broader epistemological problem that Kant discusses elsewhere. In the Canon of the *Critique of Pure Reason*, through his logic lectures and related *Reflexionen*, Kant claims that (a) we are highly prone to prejudices/cognitive biases through which we delude ourselves into affirming what we would like to be true; and (b) this tendency, which is intimately tied to the inner perfidy of the Propensity to Evil, results in our lacking the inner clarity through which we can discern when our own assent is an illicit "persuasion" (*Überredung*) or a legitimate "conviction" (*Überzeugung*).

In the First *Critique*, for instance, Kant claims that "persuasion cannot be distinguished from conviction subjectively, when the subject has taken something to be true merely as an appearance of his own mind" (A821/B849). This view underlies the call in "What Is Enlightenment?" for the "*public use* of one's reason" (WE: 8:36); and similarly in "What Does It Mean to Orient Oneself in Thinking?" Kant expresses considerable cynicism about the powers of the solitary thinker: "how much and how correctly would we *think* if we did not think as it were in community with others to which we *communicate* our thoughts, and who communicate theirs with us!" (WO: 8:145). Thus, we are already in a sorry state with regards to our capacity to differentiate between conviction and persuasion in ourselves. Despotic churches exploit this and abuse our natural recourse to communication. It is supposed to be the "touchstone [*Probierstein*] of whether taking something to be true is conviction or mere persuasion" (A820/B847). But if brought into the fold of a like-biased community, the technique we are supposed to use to uncover persuasion is subverted, used instead to help secure a shared delusion.

To make matters even worse, the despotic church compels assent *with certainty* where no such certainty is possible. The priesthood has traditionally sought to inculcate and police belief in matters that no one could authentically affirm as certain, or even comprehend, demanding "firm belief in a mystery which they do not even understand" (6:187). This is a "*violation of conscience* in proclaiming as certain, even before God, something of which ... cannot be asserted with unconditional confidence" (6:188–89). We saw this point also used two subsections past, where Kant challenged the doctrine of Vicarious Atonement as something that we are expected to profess, yet cannot be taken as a matter of conviction and so assent would be "something contrary to ... conscience" (6:171).

Religions often push us towards professing doctrines, professing them as if they were certain, even if they are not even intelligible. In doing so, it compels us to violate our conscience, ignoring epistemic norms and debasing our rationality. But these are all "artificially induced self-deceptions" (6:200) and they share as their common ground a desire to flee from "good life-conduct" (6:170). Ironically, Kant claims that in such a flight one's true lack of faith is revealed (6:172). Faith does not come from irrational assent, delusions about matters that are beyond our comprehension, but in one's commitment that nothing other than "good life-conduct" (6:170) will make us well-pleasing to God. We should not stray "even slightly from the above maxim" (6:172) regarding the proper object of faith, and rather than conceiving of it as granting us doxic latitude, we should ask ourselves: "Do you really dare to avow the truth of these propositions in the sight of him who scrutinizes the heart, and at the risk of relinquishing all that is valuable and holy to you?" (6:189). To expect assent in violation of one's conscience is to trample upon our God-given freedom and rationality (6:190).[5]

GENERAL REMARK (6:190–202)

The General Remark of Part Four is devoted to the "means of grace" or, more specifically, to the delusions related to such means. As we have discussed, Kant is agnostic as to whether or not we receive any Divine assistance in our efforts to morally improve ourselves, and here he states that "whether, if and when, or how much *grace* has effect on us – this remains totally hidden to us" (6:191). "Supernatural intervention" is "an idea of whose reality no experience can assure us" (6:191) and "even to accept it as idea for a purely practical intent is very risky and hard to reconcile with reason" (6:191). It is thus "salutary to keep ourselves at a respectful distance from it" (6:191).

Kant then enumerates four ecclesiastical practices that provide "sensible intermediaries" or "schemata" that can help awaken and sustain "our attention to the true service to God" (6:193). They are prayer, churchgoing, baptism, and communion. The first is meant to "awaken in our hearts the disposition for it [morality]" (6:193). The second serves as the means for fellowship among those who are on the same moral path; the third concerns the instruction of new members; and the fourth likewise serves to maintain fellowship "through repeated public formalities which stabilize the union of its members into an ethical body" as well as recognize "the mutual equality of the members' rights and their sharing in all fruits of moral goodness" (6:193).[6]

All four, however, can also be (and have often been) distorted into *"fetish-faith"* (6:193) – that is, treated as "a means *in itself* capable of propitiating God" (6:193). Prayer often employs various traditional "words and formulas" (6:195) that could, on the one hand, help enliven our moral disposition, but, on the other, serve as instruments of "courtly service" (6:198) whereby the supplicant seeks to gain favor and have his wishes fulfilled. Likewise, churchgoing can, on the one hand, help foster a community of those who share a commitment to pursue the Highest Good, but, when distorted, becomes a device of "external propriety" that may benefit the political community but "contributes nothing to the quality of the citizens as *citizens in the Kingdom of God.*" In the case of baptism, it can carry a solemnity rich in meaning, expressing one's initiation into "grave obligations" (6:199), but has been distorted into a sorcerer's ritual, using magical incantations to wash away all our sins at once. Lastly, communion and other ecclesiastical formalities may serve as shared rituals, expanding "people's narrow, selfish and intolerant cast of mind" (6:199) and enlivening "a community to the moral disposition of brotherly love" (6:200), but they have typically been degraded into priestcraft through which the clergy "has usurped over minds by pretending to have exclusive possession of the means of grace" (6:200).

Kant then ends *Religion* with a statement regarding the common ground of religious delusion. As he has explained previously, when self-interest responds to religion, it must conquer it or be conquered. To succeed in the former, it subverts the proper role that religious ritual is supposed to have, using "solemn rituals surrounding the use of certain means for enlivening truly practical dispositions as though they were means of grace in themselves" (6:201). Those who live within a Delusory Faith presume that they will become a "favorite" of the Divine through such external observances and so receive through grace all that they desire. But this conception of grace is one that Kant persistently attacks. It is traditionally understood as God's merciful assistance through which our path to His rewards are eased. But it should rather be the outcome of our own efforts at becoming worthy. When virtue is understood as "the deployment of one's forces in the observance of the duty [out of respect for it]" (6:201), through it we become worthy of a Divine grace that judges our *Gesinnung* and finds it worthy and well-pleasing. Sadly, the delusory conception of grace inverts this relationship and presumes that grace substitutes for our own efforts. Thus, Kant concludes with the dictum: "the right way to advance is not from grace to virtue but rather from virtue to grace" (6:202).

NOTES

1 Hence, in my opinion, we should disregard the claim in the *Metaphysics of Morals* where Kant denies that we have any duty to the moral improvement of others. The species-wide duty towards the Highest Good in *Religion* expresses a corporate obligation where we are mutually responsible for one another's moral improvement. As such, we have in this a duty to others – though it is *also* a duty to ourselves insofar as we address the risk of recidivism in ourselves through the collective pursuit of the Highest Good.

2 Kant continues to assert that "God must himself be the author of his Kingdom" (6:152); yet, as in Part Three, it is up to us to populate it – to become morally worthy of citizenship.

3 As discussed in note 6 of the Introduction, Allen Wood does not think that Kant is a Pure Rationalist, asserting that "it is hard to imagine anyone who would want to hold ... [that] God has given us certain commands supernaturally while denying that we are morally bound to carry them out" (Wood 1991: 11). But to repeat my earlier rejoinder, Kant writes that while we have "no reason" to assert that an ecclesiastical statute is Divine in origin, it would be "arrogant peremptorily to deny that the way a church is organized may perhaps also be a special divine dispensation" (6:105). Kant also accepts as possible that "the historical introduction of the latter [a new religion] be accompanied as it were adorned by miracles" (6:84). Hence, quite in

conformity with Pure Rationalism, these miracles could serve as the basis for celebratory festivals and other practices which are "intrinsically contingent" in that their observance is without moral value in itself, but nevertheless can be of instrumental value as means that help worshipers with "the highest concepts and grounds of reason" (6:109) or in other ways is conducive to the visible church. So, even though Wood dismisses Pure Rationalism, Kant quite clearly accepts the possibility of "divine dispensations" that pertain just to religion's outer form. Moreover, as has just been discussed, should not "Pure Rationalism" be the position held by an advocate of "Pure Rational Faith" and the "Pure Rational System of Religion"? Once one allows for the possibility of revelation (which Wood acknowledges Kant does) as well as a distinction between the inner and outer spheres of religion (as he also acknowledges), room is made for the possibility of revelation related to the outer sphere – and that room is positively affirmed in the passages I quote above.

4 A drab but helpful analogy is as follows. It is of no consequence to the proper functioning of one's vehicle that one has its oil changed on Tuesdays rather than Fridays. But oil changes are still important. So what symbols, rituals, and other ecclesiastical practices one adopts are themselves without intrinsic significance to our salvation. We may need *some* such practices as means that facilitate our moral improvement, but "statutory legislation (which presupposes a revelation) can be regarded only as contingent, as something that cannot have reached, nor can reach, every human being, hence does not bind human beings universally" (6:104). But nothing more than "good life-conduct" (6:105) is what God requires of us and what we must do in order to become well-pleasing to Him.

5 It should not be assumed here that Kant is following the Cartesian principle that we should always withhold our assent unless we are certain. Although matters of faith and knowledge do require certainty according to Kant, he also allows for opinion as a legitimate mode of assent. Unlike persuasion, the grounds of opinion can be convincingly communicated to others, but rather than these grounds leading to a firm conviction that carries certainty, they should rather lead to a more modest sort of assent, one whose degree may be weak if the grounds only modestly favor the proposition in question or stronger if the grounds, correspondingly, warrant greater confidence. See my

forthcoming "Kant on Opinion: Assent, Hypothesis and the Norms of General Applied Logic" (Pasternack 2014).

6 Kant also briefly associates these means with corresponding practices in Islam: "washing, praying, fasting, almsgiving, and the pilgrimage to Mecca" (6:194).

7

CONCLUSION

It has been my aim through this book to provide a holistic interpretation of *Religion*, one that is governed by a unifying principle, that is able to give due consideration to the role of each part to the whole, and is able to defend the philosophical theology developed throughout. As we progressed through the text, we had occasion to discuss a few of the more prominent objections that appear in the secondary literature. Many of these objections target specific issues: how the Propensity to Evil can be both innate and chosen, how Kant's conception of grace is compatible with Divine justice, and so forth. Various more general criticisms were also mentioned: John Hare's declaration that *Religion* is a "Failure"; Gordon Michalson's contention that the text "wobbles" back and forth between conflicting Christian and Enlightenment commitments; and also the contemporary trend that deflates Kant's positive philosophy of religion, treating it as if it were a sort of Error Theory.

In my view, these readings are the products of either the interpreter's prior philosophical or religious commitments, which make *Religion*'s actual views unpalatable, or confusions on the part of the interpreter, which are then, regretfully, imposed upon

Kant. The former, for instance, may very well underlie John Hare's reading, while the latter, I suspect, is the source of Michalson's. As we have seen, Kant's philosophical theology in many ways does not follow traditional Christianity, and thus, given some readers' particular presuppositions, it is hardly surprising that they would judge it to be a "failure." Secondly, although it is quite apparent that *Religion* does employ both Christian and Enlightenment theses, it does not follow from this that Kant failed to reconcile them, leaving the text as just an amalgam of unresolved "wobbles." In contrast to these and other readings, I have argued that *Religion* contains a philosophical theology that is both consistent and highly sophisticated. To read it as just a litany of "wobbles" is a failure on the part of the interpretation and not the text.

Guided by its Enlightenment commitment to a soteriology that "can be convincingly communicated to everyone" (6:103), Kant separates out the Christian doctrines that uphold this standard for a truly universal church from those that "extend its influence no further than the tidings relevant to a judgment on its credibility can reach" (6:103). In so doing, he has given us a philosophical theology which demands a faith that does not violate conscience and can be honestly accepted even "in the sight of him who scrutinizes the heart" (6:189). He has done this, moreover, while at the same time acknowledging a legitimate although ancillary role for Historical Faith. Because its doctrines, statutes, and rituals can *not* be convincingly communicated to everyone, they ought not to be taken as essential for our salvation. Yet it does not follow from this that they are false or should be purged from religious life. In fact, he even accepts the possibility that some of them are given to us through "a special divine dispensation" (6:105) – although whether or not this is actually their source is something we can never know (cf. 6:86; CF: 7:63).

Hence, I contend, *Religion* offers us a coherent, consistent, unified, and intellectually mature way of thinking about sin, faith, salvation, and worship. That is not to say that everyone should accept it, but hardly is it a series of unresolved wobbles. By contrast, John Hare's judgment, although drawn from a misunderstanding of Kant's soteriology, nevertheless points to a challenge that deserves to be taken more seriously. In its First Preface, and again in his response to the royal rescript, Kant seems very deferential to traditional Christianity, claiming that the biblical theologian has "privilege" "with respect to certain doctrines" (6:9), granting them the "prerogative" to censor philosophers if they "trespass" or "encroach" into biblical theology (6:9), declaring that he "make[s] no *appraisal* of Christianity" (7:8), and recommending that we "keep a respectful distance" (6:191) from claims about Divine agency (miracles, revelation, etc.). Yet it is difficult to see all this as sincere, for what we discover in the body of the text (and again in the *Conflict of the Faculties*) is a philosophical theology that has far less in common with traditional Christianity than Kant initially insinuates.

Given his historical circumstances, some of these claims may simply be taken as a strategic feint, perhaps offered in justification for the actual path he chose for *Religion*'s publication and/or to help protect him from possible legal repercussions.[1] However, behind their thin veil is a far more controversial treatment of many doctrines usually seen as essential to the Christian faith. We have discussed many of these doctrines throughout this work, but in this concluding chapter my aim is to reflect on some more general issues germane to the tension between Kant's philosophical theology and traditional Christianity. As many have claimed, Kant's philosophy of religion imposes various barriers to theology, ranging from his dismantling of the traditional proofs to God's existence to the many specific soteriological doctrines we have discussed. Of course, one solitary chapter cannot do justice to all points of conflict between Kant's philosophy of religion and traditional doctrine, but it can target some of the most abiding of them. Hence, we will consider three particular questions or concerns that have played a central role in the secondary literature.

The first and most general issue comes from Nicholas Wolterstorff's query: "Is it Possible and Desirable for Theologians to Recover from Kant?" (Wolterstorff 1998). We shall consider what exactly is the difficulty for which a recovery is allegedly needed. From this, we will move on to a second and more specific question, one that remains pivotal for all readers of *Religion*. The question, as expressed by Stephen Palmquist, is: "Does Kant

Reduce Religion to Morality?" (Palmquist 1992). We will need to understand what "reduce" here means – in what sense might there be such a reduction? Then, through a disambiguation of the term, we will move on to our final question, one first explicitly asked by Karl Barth: "Is Kant a Pelagian?" (Barth 1952). This third question I take to be decisive for many Christians. If, in the end, he is a Pelagian, then I presume that most Christian readers would want him expelled from the college of Christian theologians or, perhaps put more aptly, would want him finally denied admission after remaining on the waiting list for over two centuries. Such a judgment, however, is not against the philosophical merits of Kant's position, but merely against its Christian orthodoxy.

Through this concluding chapter, we will make our way to this final question. Attentive readers might have already surmised what view I take on it, but I will here move beyond what has already been discussed and introduce a new consideration. This still may not be enough to liberate Kant fully from the charge of Pelagianism, but it will help show that many of his accusers may themselves be no farther from the same Heresy.

IS IT POSSIBLE AND DESIRABLE FOR THEOLOGIANS TO RECOVER FROM KANT?

Of the three questions selected for this concluding chapter, it may seem that the above should be the last rather than the first, since if there is a "recovery" to be had, the next logical step is to ask "what next?" or "to what should we return?" But there is also implied in the question the assumption that Kant is responsible for some condition that calls for a recovery. We thus begin by asking what is this condition? or what is it thought to be?

According to Nicholas Wolterstorff, and he is far from alone in this charge, Transcendental Idealism does not merely reject the traditional arguments for God's existence, but more radically it outright blocks the meaningfulness of theological language, i.e., "God-talk." Despite the famous claim in the Second Preface to the *Critique of Pure Reason* as well as the many other affirmative gestures favoring the "room for faith," Kant's accusers contend that his distinction between the phenomenal and noumenal bars us from having any coherent thoughts about the latter. As understood by Wolterstorff, Kant holds that pure concepts can only have meaning in relation to possible experience, with no extension to anything noumenal, including to God. Thus, "predicating anything of God must always reflect deep confusion on the predicator's part" (Wolterstorff 1998: 13). In other words, since God is beyond all possible experience, not only can we have no knowledge of Him, but we even lack the resources through which we can coherently frame any theological concepts or make meaningful any language that refers to the Divine.

Similar views abound, from Jacobi's "On the Undertaking of Critique to Reduce Reason to Understanding" to Heine's "On the History of Religion and Philosophy in Germany," to Barth, Höffe, Byrne, and onwards. Kant is seen as a "stumbling-block" such that "even among those who wanted to go forward with him had first to re-interpret before they could do anything with him" (Barth 1952: 150). Although issues pertaining to theological semantics and epistemology have been with us far before Kant, the abiding impression is that Kant did not merely challenge the traditional proofs of God's existence, but set forth the barrier that "theoretical reason cannot even legitimately *ask* whether or not God exists" (Höffe 1994: 123).

But this is not how Kant saw his own approach to theology. Firstly, despite the view (which may finally be waning) that Kant was a proto-positivist, he does not so tightly restrict the meaning of concepts to the scope of possible experience. Our theoretical knowledge is certainly so restricted, but it should not be forgotten that Kant does not deny the thinkability of things-in-themselves. It is just that they can only be thought through unschematized categories (cf. Pasternack 2003 and Ameriks 2006). We see this point most fully discussed in the First *Critique*'s Phenomena/Noumena section. Causality, substance, magnitude, etc., all retain some meaning, though they are pared down in the absence of the further conditions for knowledge. For instance, of causality, Kant writes, "(if I leave out the time in which something follows something else in accordance with a rule), I will not find out anything more than that it is something that allows an inference to the existence of something else" (A243/B301).

Thus, the more rarefied notion of a ground-consequent relation can still be used in relation to things-in-themselves. Along with the other unschematized categories, we can muse about the noumenal, generate many hypotheses about it, but lacking both intuitions and the schema through which intuitions and concepts meet, speculation necessarily falls short of knowledge. In brief, Kant's semantic views are neither those of the Logical Positivist nor those of the Empiricist. One might recall that most of Berkeley's arguments for his idealism are semantic in nature. He claims that the language we use for the physical world – "matter," "exists," etc. – have, like all other terms, an origin in experience; and since our experience is only of sense data and not of matter as such, their meaning coordinates only with the feelings of solidity, heaviness, pressure, etc. In the absence of an actual experience of the physical, its language can have no meaning other than the sensory states we associate with the term.

Despite the many theologians who have, like Wolterstorff, attributed to Kant such semantic strictures, they do not accurately reflect Kant's own views. Yet this does not mean that Transcendental Idealism poses no stumbling blocks to theology or to theological language. As explained in the First *Critique*'s Ideal of Pure Reason, we can produce the idea of God, or more precisely the Ideal of God, through an abstract synthesis of all possible predicates. That is, all things can be thought as an assemblage of predicates and we can produce the idea of a being that "of every pair of *possible* predicates, one of them must always apply to it" (A573/B601). Kant calls this the *ens realissimum* and it serves as the formal template, or perhaps placeholder, for the traditional concept of God. Nevertheless, on its own, it still falls short of how we use "God."

Although we can through theoretical reason produce the idea of an entity that contains one of every pair of possible predicates, we cannot thereby also determine which one of each pair is to be assigned or whether the *ens realissimum* exists. Moreover, Kant also argues that theoretical reason cannot "on objective grounds give us even a hint, let alone convince us" of God's moral attributes

(A814/B842). As seen, for example, in his treatment of the Physico-Theological argument, what can be demonstrated is at best the idea of a "highest architect of the world." But in this we neither have moral attributes nor even the idea of a creator (A627/B655; LR: 28:1072). The Wise Author may, rather, be identified with the Greek Demiurge. But to further determine the idea of God as omnipotent, omniscient, and omnibenevolent, we must turn to morality. It is, first, through our cognizance of the moral law that we understand what it would be for a being to be moral, and thus our cognition of God as omnibenevolent depends upon our cognition of the moral law. Second, the doctrine of the Highest Good leads us to postulate a being who has the power to ensure that there is a proportionate distribution of happiness in accordance with moral worth and that our degrees of worthiness can be correctly judged. Although one might argue that a lesser being could still fulfill these demands, Kant claims that God's "will must be omnipotent, so that all of nature and its relation to morality in the world are subject to it; omniscient, so that it cognizes the inmost dispositions and their moral worth" (A815/B843).

Thus, we can see that Kant does not deny the intelligibility of theistic language. Although he clearly wants to take it out of the hands of metaphysics, he does this not to cut off its only source, but rather, as we discussed in the Introduction and Chapter 1, to protect it. If metaphysics were the proper place for theology, then Kant's critique of the former would undermine the latter as well. Instead, he maintains that its proper place is within our practical lives – and it is also through this domain that our conception of God gains its full determinacy. Although his critique of metaphysics demonstrates that it is not a possible source of knowledge, this critique does not in turn deny either our capacity to form metaphysical concepts or the possibility of a legitimate form of assent, rooted in the needs of pure practical reason for at least some propositions about the supersensible.

In sum, the constraints that Kant imposes upon theology do not, as Wolterstorff and others have claimed, block the meaningfulness of its language. That, as noted above, may be more suitably assigned to Empiricist and Positivist philosophers. Kant's semantics are not so narrow as to not allow us to produce ideas about things-in-themselves. His declaration that he has sought out the limits to knowledge in order to make room for faith is not a platitude. All three *Critique*s take this very seriously, as does *Religion*, "The End of All Things," "What Real Progress Has Metaphysics Made in Germany since the Time of Leibniz and Wolff?," "On a Recently Prominent Tone in Philosophy," and many of his other writings. It is a concern that does not merely appear periodically through the Critical Period, but is one of its essential characteristics.

DOES KANT REDUCE RELIGION TO MORALITY?

As I have argued, Kant does not impose the barrier to theology that Nicholas Wolterstorff and others have claimed. But he does, nevertheless, place it under the aegis of practical philosophy rather than theoretical. Some might see this as an immediate advantage, for religion's importance is supposed to be practical. It is supposed to concern how we live, who we are, and how we find meaning. Yet this placement may not be so innocuous, since it may have reductive consequences. It may limit what is legitimate in religion to our practical need or, as some have argued, it may turn religion into something like an Error Theory (cf. Davidovich 1993 and DiCenso 2012) where we deem it morally beneficial to inure a viewpoint that includes a wise and just God, without the sort of authentic commitment that is usually associated with faith. This is a vision that, as previously mentioned, parallels much of what Kant writes regarding purposiveness in the sciences, but it also ignores the surfeit of passages where he discusses the nature of faith itself, presenting it in a way that is not at all consistent with Error Theory.[2]

In his "Does Kant Reduce Religion to Morality?" Stephen Palmquist addresses this question, asking first what sort of "reduction" is presumably taking place. He first considers whether or not the alleged reduction is "eliminative" – that is, as the term suggests, this would be a reduction of religion to morality by the elimination of the entities that comprise the former. Such reduction is used when the domain to be eliminated is taken to have no positive ontological status, its elements not picking out anything that really exists. For example, in the philosophy of mind, some philosophers reduce mental states (feelings, sensations, etc.) to brain states and consider the former to be simply artifacts of an epiphenomenal folk psychology. In truth, so they contend, there are no feelings or sensory qualia. There are just brain states which in pre-scientific times were incorrectly thought to be modes of a mental substance.

When we apply this to the putative reduction of religion to morality in Kant, we have a denial of God's existence, of the soul, miracles, revelation, and so forth. They would all be products of a false theory without correlation to any real entities. Such reductionism is employed by some contemporary interpreters, at least with regard to certain aspects of Kant's philosophical theology. The two most obvious instances are the secularization of the Ethical Community, where its eschatological status is rejected, along with the related reading of the Highest Good, treating it as a worldly social ideal rather than one that involves a "future life" and the distribution of Divine justice. As we have discussed, some merely prefer to "update" Kant by removing these religious vestiges, while others believe that Kant himself withdrew his commitment to them.

However, as I have argued, these views are not fair representations of the text. We considered them in Chapters 1 and 5 and reviewed the many passages (from both the 1780s and 1790s) where Kant does quite clearly support their reality. In *Religion*, for example, Kant is quite clear that the Ethical Community "is conceivable only as a people under divine commands" (6:99) and can be founded "only from God himself" (6:100). It may be granted that the Third *Critique* does suggest something more akin to an Error Theory, but this should be limited to the use of God, as a Wise Author, within the natural sciences. With regards to our practical needs, on the other hand, there is no evidence that Kant eliminated the Postulates or secularized the Highest Good. He may recommend agnosticism with regards to miracles, revelation, and any other putative Divine action, but this does not take them to be elements of a false theory without any correlation to reality. It rather suggests that they may actually obtain, but that we just lack both theoretical and practical grounds for affirming them.

The second sort of reductionism that Palmquist mentions does not directly reject the ontological status of the entities to be reduced, but rather considers them as lacking explanatory value. If applied to the philosophy of mind, one might not reject the reality of folk psychological entities, but instead just take them to be explanatorily weak. For example, a folk psychological explanation of how smell is related to memory would be considered deficient in comparison to a detailed account of how our olfactory bulb is connected to the hippocampus, the combined function of the latter and the neocortex in the formation, retention, and recall of memories, and so forth. Ample technical principles are used in the latter model, including many biochemical mechanisms involved in all stages of memory. By contrast, the folk psychologist (putatively) has very little to say other than that smell sometimes seems to stimulate recall.

What then can we say about an explanatory reduction of religion to morality? The question here is not whether or not the principles of the former are granted a positive ontological status, but rather whether or not they can offer any explanations that are not then replaced by Kant with explanations from the Pure Rational System of Religion. As we have discussed, he acknowledges that revelation may have been "at a given time and a given place ... wise and very advantageous to the human race" (6:155). He also accepts the possibility that the founding of Christianity was accompanied by various miracles (6:84), again because at this given time and place, they would have been advantageous to humanity. Revelation, as well, is accepted by the "Pure Rationalist" (6:155) as a possible source of what is essential to our salvation (although as essential, it must also be available through reason alone).

Thus, even though he holds to the principle that whatever is essential to our salvation must be available through reason as well, he neither denies the possibility of revelation and miracles, nor does he deny their utility. Even though it is "salutary to keep ourselves at a respectful distance" (6:191) from the question of their historical veracity, he admits that throughout human history, the symbols, rituals, and tales that accompany them meet various needs including the "demand for even the highest concepts and grounds of reason something that *the senses can hold on to*" (6:109). Real or not, alleged miracles and revelation offer this, at least.

Hence, Kant does not outright explanatorily reduce miracles and revelation, though their function is nevertheless limited. If we frame this issue in relation to his distinction between the inner and outer spheres of religion, it is not as if all the functions assigned to the outer are reduced to the inner. The symbols and tales from the outer still can help explain and come to affirm "the highest concepts and grounds of reason." Its rituals help maintain fellowship in the church, help encourage churchgoing, and bring greater vibrancy to our religious lives (see 6:193). As he describes them at one point, they can "serve as schemata for the duties" (6:193) whose performance can make us well-pleasing to God. They may not be necessary in these regards, but they remain explanatorily and practically valuable. Kant's caution is just that we need to remain clear that they are of instrumental value and that our salvation cannot depend upon their observance.

Still, one might contend that the above analysis obfuscates the significance of this limitation to the role of miracles, revelation, and their consequent doctrines and rituals. Since Kant's philosophical theology contends that whatever is necessary for our salvation must be available through reason alone, various traditional doctrines are treated in a way that many Christians would find unacceptable. We see this in his interpretation of the Fall, where he claims that Original Sin cannot be explained in terms of an actual inheritance from Adam and Eve. That, he claims, would be "most inappropriate" (6:40). We see it in his challenge to the divinity of Jesus (6:64), in his rejection of Vicarious Atonement (6:72, 6:118), his rejection of an inward profession through which we become eligible for Divine aid (6:171, 6:174), and so forth.

In all these instances, he is guided by his practical philosophy, his commitment to *ought implies can*, and the related principles of universality (cf. 6:103 and 6:109). He may not be reducing religion *überhaupt* to morality, but the latter certainly does impose itself on the former, determining what biblical passages should be taken literally (such as the moral teachings of the Gospels) versus figuratively (as we see in Kant's treatment of the Fall), and what passages ought to be rejected (as Kant does with the story of Abraham's sacrifice of Isaac). He likewise shapes his soteriology according to his philosophical principles and so rejects any explanation of how we become Sanctified and Justified before God that depends, by necessity, upon supernatural aid – be it through a Vicarious Atonement in the Crucifixion or through a form of grace that violates his conception of Divine justice.

Hence, even if Kant does not fully reduce religion to morality, since he evaluates the doctrines of Historical Faith according to standards set by the latter, the result is that some of the most central doctrines of the Christian faith are rejected. In particular, one doctrine that is often used as a litmus test for a thinker's Christian credentials is whether or not their soteriology includes a *necessary* role for Divine assistance and, more precisely, a necessary role that arises because of our innate depravity. This is generally identified with the Pelagian Heresy, but as we will see its relationship is not as simple as some have assumed. Not only is there more to the Heresy than the above soteriological issue, but also we may find that Kant's stance on Divine aid has enough facets that some may still be willing to include him in the college of Christian theologians.

IS KANT A PELAGIAN?

I have argued in the above section that Kant does not so reduce religion to morality that all its doctrines and practices are merely in the service of morality. There is still much to religion that stands beyond the inner sphere of Pure Rational Faith, and it would be an error to interpret the doctrines of the outer sphere as unacceptable or false. Although their presence in the outer rather than inner sphere entails, according to Kant, that they are inessential to our salvation, they can still have relevance, albeit only instrumentally, to our religious life.

Nevertheless, it cannot be denied that Kant draws the line between the inner and outer sphere through reference to the needs of morality, and thus, it is those needs that shape the doctrines of the inner sphere, ranging from how to understand the immortality of the soul to the nature of sin and salvation. It is in this way that the accusation of reductionism carries, in my opinion, its greatest weight. For it is through Kant's conception of morality that he chooses between what aspects of religion are mere vehicles of symbolic or instrumental value versus what aspects are essential and should be affirmed as literal truths. It is also because of the role that morality plays in shaping the inner sphere that Kant's conception of salvation comes to have at least some similarities to Pelagianism.

The dominant Augustinian tradition maintains that as a result of Original Sin, it is not within our own power to become well-pleasing to God. Hence, the classical analogues to the Change of Heart depend upon Divine assistance. Yet Kant states that "if the moral law commands that we *ought* to be better human beings now, it inescapably follows that we must be *capable* of being better human beings" (6:50); and "this is a change of heart which must be possible because it is a duty" (6:67). Accordingly, it does appear that our moral condition is such that we are not so direly corrupt that we cannot manage our own salvation. It is not that Kant denies the existence of Divine aid, but he does maintain that if it is given, we must first make ourselves worthy of it (6:44, 6:118) and, if offered, it cannot compromise our still bearing responsibility for our becoming well-pleasing to God.[3]

Yet, insofar as Kant does limit the role of Divine aid and holds that we are not so corrupt that it is necessary, he does deviate from the Augustinian conception of sin and salvation, and instead follows the same trajectory as Pelagius and his followers. At its core, the Pelagian Heresy considers humanity as still capable of its own salvation, that Original Sin has not so profoundly corrupted us that this capacity is lost, and so (very much as Kant also claims at 6:64) the importance of Jesus Christ was not in his Atonement for our sins, but rather in his being the supreme moral example for us to emulate. More fully stated, the official charges brought against Pelagius and his followers are as follows:

1. that Adam would have died even if he did not sin;
2. that Adam's sin was borne by himself alone and not the whole human race;

3. that newborn infants are without sin;
4. that our death is not due to Adam's sin, and our resurrection is not due to Christ;
5. that Mosaic law as well as the moral teachings of the Gospels provide a path to Heaven;
6. that there were men before Christ who were wholly without sin.[4]

THE PELAGIAN HERESIES

Hopefully, it should now be clear that the allegation of Pelagianism is more complicated than a simple yes/no litmus test would indicate. Of course, it could be claimed that the true Christian would reject all of the above propositions and to affirm just one would be enough to be branded a heretic. But consider these propositions. If this Inquisitorial standard is used, it would condemn nearly all contemporary Christians. Anyone, for example, who did not read Genesis literally would likely not accept most of them. Anyone who believes that death is a biological inevitability for mammals, would commit Heresy 1 and the first part of Heresy 4. Even someone who believes in Original Sin, but considers it an innate feature of the species rather than a biological inheritance from our progenitors, would commit Heresy 2.

If we return to its rendering in the fifth century, the Pelagian Heresy would end up condemning nearly everyone outside of the most conservative quarters of Christianity. Given what is implied about the origin of our species, the inheritance of sin, the reason why we die, and so forth, anyone who subscribes to the theory of evolution would have to be branded a Heretic. Yet one might want to dismiss this rebuttal as simply a smokescreen. Although it may be granted that the Pelagian Heresy has historically involved all the above claims, none have retained the importance of the key issue: because of our innate depravity, salvation requires Divine aid. That is, regardless of what other claims were originally part of the Heresy, this has come to be viewed as its essential error. Hence, let us turn our attention back to it and reprise, once more, where Kant stands.

KANT ON SALVATION

As we have discussed, one of the more crucial passages relevant to Kant's soteriology is ambiguous: *"Gesetzt, zum Gut-oder Besserwerden sei noch eine übernatürliche Mitwirkung nöthig ... ."* George di Giovanni translates it as "[g]ranted that some supernatural cooperation is also needed in becoming good or better" and by translating *Gesetzt* as "granted" the natural reading suggests that our need for Divine aid is an unargued presupposition. Pluhar, however, reads *Gesetzt* differently and so translates the German into the subjunctive: "[s]upposing that, for him to become good or better, a supranatural cooperation were also needed" (6:44). The passage then continues by stating that "the human being must nonetheless make himself antecedently worthy of receiving it" (6:44).

In favor of Pluhar's reading is Kant's general commitment to our only deserving what we are responsible for. So, if we come to deserve a blessed afterlife, it must be because we have through our own efforts come to be worthy of it. Of course, Divine aid is still possible, but first we must commit ourselves to morality such that we become "antecedently worthy of receiving it," and then what aid, if any, we do receive serves more to inspire and protect our efforts than to substitute for them. In sum, our Sanctification remains our responsibility, and so as Kant sees humanity, however much we have corrupted ourselves by indulging our Propensity to Evil, we still are not as depraved as the Augustinian view proffers.

Despite the affinity between Pelagianism and Kant's treatment of our Sanctification, the same cannot be said of his views on Justification. Many Christians understand the purpose of the Crucifixion to be (at least in part) the repayment for our debt of sin. Following the traditional view, our state of sin incurs upon us an infinite debt, and as this is not something we are capable of repaying, Jesus Christ was made sacrifice on our behalf. Because he is of infinite worth, his death is adequate to this debt and so serves as the Vicarious Substitute for the penalty that we otherwise would deserve. As we discussed in Chapter 4, this interpretation is often associated with Saint Anselm, but it is also well entrenched in Luther and his followers up through Kant's time. Yet Kant directly opposes it, rejecting the transmissibility of the debt (see 6:72), and so offers a different treatment of it.

Unfortunately, his treatment has generally been misunderstood in the secondary literature, leading to many unnecessary and sweeping criticisms. John Hare, as noted earlier, deems *Religion* a "[f]ailure." He makes this claim on the grounds that its "stoic maxim" blocks Divine aid and forgiveness, thus chaining to us a debt that must, but cannot, be repaid (Hare 1996: 60). Hare actually draws this maxim from Nicholas Wolterstorff, who with Philip Quinn and Gordon Michalson, attribute to Kant a different error: that Kant ultimately concedes to a "Divine Supplement" which they claim stands in contradiction to his conception of Divine justice (cf. Wolterstorff 1991, Quinn 1986 and 1990, Michalson 1989 and 1990).

Hence, while Hare's critique of Kant accords with the accusation of Pelagianism, the "Divine Supplement" interpretation saves Kant from Pelagianism, but at the expense of accusing him of making an ad hoc concession incompatible with other aspects of his philosophical theology. My view, by contrast, maintains that Kant's soteriology is internally consistent, and though I agree that he does subscribe to this "stoic maxim," his account of our Justification is at least technically different from the Pelagian. The Pelagian would have our debt of sin repaid through our own efforts. Yet Kant actually accepts on the basis of its infinite magnitude that this is not something we can actually do on our own. Our moral efforts cannot rise to the level of an infinite payment nor, in fact, any payment at all since there is no "surplus over and above what … [we are already] under obligation to perform each time" (6:72).[5]

Thus, Kant does not follow the Pelagian Heresy on this count. Moreover, Kant does not trap himself with his "stoic maxim," making *Religion* into a "[f]ailure." Nor does he, as Wolterstorff, Quinn, and Michalson claim, concede to a "Divine Supplement" incompatible with the rest of his philosophical theology. The latter, I believe, was his view in the Second *Critique*, where our eternal striving towards moral perfection is accepted by God as equivalent to possession (CPrR: 5:123n). But it is not his view in

Religion. As discussed in Chapter 4 (and more fully in Pasternack 2012), Kant states that when judging our worthiness, God "penetrates to the intelligible ground of the heart" (6:48), sees whether we have given priority to self-interest or morality, and thereby passes judgment upon us. This is not a judgment we ourselves could make, for from our limited empirical viewpoint we can only measure worth through behavior. We would see ourselves as incapable of repaying the debt and so would be, just as Hare claims, forever shackled to it.

But this is merely our limited perspective, and Hare, it seems, has confused it with the solution Kant does offer once he brings in Transcendental Idealism's distinction between the phenomenal and noumenal. Kant writes that "we indeed have no rightful claim [to salvation] according to the empirical cognition we have of ourselves" (6:75) but, continuing further with his epistemological distinction, "God alone has cognition" (6:76) of us such that one who has undergone a Change of Heart can be deemed well-pleasing and so "punishment cannot be considered appropriate to his new quality" (6:73). This is because the new man no longer bears the debt of sin. It has not been forgiven. It has not been repaid. Rather, as Kant shifts from how the new man sees himself to how God sees him, he explains that the new man is "relieved [*entschlagen*] of all responsibility ... though fully in accord with divine justice" (6:76).

The solution here is not obvious, in part because the English "relieved" does not make it clear what has taken place. However, as discussed in Chapter 4 (and more fully in Pasternack 2012), it is not that the debt is forgiven (for that would violate Divine justice) or paid by another (for it is "not a transmissible liability"). Rather we are "relieved" of it because "of an improved disposition of which, however, God alone has cognition" (6:76). But to be "relieved" (*entschlagen*) of responsibility is different from being forgiven (*vergeben*). The German term here is crucial, for *entschlagen* is different from *vergeben*. The latter is used by Kant when discussing forgiveness in general contexts as well as when depicting more common soteriological views (cf. 6:71n; CF: 7:47; GR: 4:368, 10:279, 11:532). *Entschlagen*, by contrast, should be understood as a repeal or withdrawal of the debt in the same way that a legal judgment is dismissed or a statute struck down.

When a judgment is dismissed, or a statute struck down, it is not that the guilty are forgiven – rather, the change in evaluation occurs at a deeper level than with forgiveness. The forgiven are guilty, but treated mercifully. The "relieved" are no longer guilty. Accordingly, because the conditions upon which sin and its debt depend no longer obtain subsequent to the Change of Heart, the new man is "relieved" of responsibility.[6]

From this we can draw a distinction between the Pelagian and Kantian views regarding Justifying Grace. Pelagius denies it. He does so ultimately because he denies the doctrine of an inherited Original Sin that so corrupts us that we are left incapable of Justifying ourselves. Kant, on the other hand, denies the conception of Justifying Grace as, specifically, an act of *forgiveness*. Unlike Pelagius, Kant does accept that Justifying Grace involves God's judgment. He does not claim that we Justify ourselves, in the sense of doing something to repay our debt of sin. This debt, Kant agrees, is of infinite magnitude, and so it is not in our power to repay it. Instead, he turns to God at the heart of his solution and explains that from the *standpoint* of grace, the debt is *entschlagen*. Granted, this means that the new man is then not deserving of punishment because the debt has been *entschlagen*, but as the party to whom the debt is owed, God must accept the new man and pass judgment on his fate.

DIVINE AID AND THE ETHICAL COMMUNITY

As we have seen, there are many more facets to the Pelagian Heresy than is often assumed. In addition to the six historical charges discussed earlier, many of which most contemporary Christians would be as guilty of as Kant would be, a distinction may also be drawn between our role with regards to our Sanctification and our Justification. Given what we have discussed, I believe that we should grant that Kant does follow the Pelagian view with regards to the former, but the same does not hold for the latter. Although we are responsible for the Change of Heart through which God may then judge us to no longer bear the debt of sin, it is not as if we have also repaid it. In that respect, at least, Kant does not fall into Pelagianism.

This, however, may be considered too meager of a difference, since despite the relevance that Kant does assign to God, he nevertheless still follows the Pelagian versus Augustinian understanding of the depth of our human depravity and its consequences for our salvation. Hence, with regard to our individual salvation, we are not so depraved as to be unable, through our own efforts, to be both Sanctified through the Change of Heart and also thereby to be Justified (in God's judgment), since this transformation further *entschlägt* us from the debt of sin.

Yet we have thus far in the chapter only discussed our individual pursuit of salvation. It should not be forgotten that Kant also recognizes a corporate duty "a duty *sui generis*, not of human beings toward human beings but of the human race toward itself" (6:97). This corporate duty, or more fully the collective struggle of humanity towards salvation, is also crucial to Kant's soteriology (and to each of us as individuals) since it is the social Predisposition to Humanity that is instrumental in the rousing of our Propensity to Evil. This does not merely cease after the Change of Heart. Although through this change we make ourselves less susceptible, we nevertheless still remain subject to the corrupting influence of other human beings. Hence, the establishment of the Ethical Community is necessary for our salvation.[7] However, as Kant so clearly claims in Part Three of *Religion*, we cannot establish it through our own efforts. We need "a higher moral being through which universal organization the forces of single individuals, insufficient on their own, are united for a common effect" (6:98). That is, "a moral people of God is, therefore, a work whose execution cannot be hoped for from human beings but only from God himself" (6:100).

As we previously discussed with regards to the Highest Good, we neither have the powers over nature nor the insight into one another's worth that would make it possible for us to secure the distribution of happiness in accordance with moral worth. Moreover, Kant claims that the nature of law in the Ethical Community demands a non-human lawgiver. Although "the people, as a people" (6:98) can be responsible for the juridical laws that merely govern our outward behavior, Kant asserts that the laws of virtue that operate within the Ethical Community require Divine rule.

Hence, our duty to promote this end cannot extend to either its distribution of happiness or its internal mechanisms of governance. Rather, as discussed in Chapter 1, HG_d, our duty to promote the Highest Good, is a duty to populate HG_i with agents worthy of happiness. This is not a minor matter, and Kant is hardly exaggerating at all when he writes that "[e]ach must ... so conduct himself as if everything depended on him" (6:101). Despite the establishment and governance of the Ethical Community (and, as I have claimed, this is equal to HG_i) being placed in God's hands, unless we, through our own efforts, become worthy of membership in it, it would be left as a hollow shell, with no happiness distributed since there would be no one worthy to receive it.

Much of this has already been discussed in Chapter 5, but what I want to here emphasize is that unlike what we see in most of Kant's other discussions of Divine aid, where God's actions are considered unnecessary and His role (if any) uncertain, with regards to the Ethical Community in particular, *God's assistance is now taken as necessary*. Exactly what God will do to bring about the transformation of society remains an open question. As we see in "The End of All Things," Kant cautions us against giving too much importance to such speculations. But there is nevertheless a vital role here assigned to God, one that is necessary for "only in this way can we hope for a victory of the good principle over the evil one" (6:94). That is, without the establishment of the Ethical Community, there is no security or stability to the Change of Heart.

The Universal Church can help somewhat, as the shared moral commitment of its members helps counteract the corrupting influence of all human beings upon one another. But until the Ethical Community actually comes into being, there is still no final "victory of the good principle over the evil one" (6:94). So, in this way, we finally see in Kant a clear commitment to God having a *necessary* soteriological role. Moreover, our inability to achieve this victory is due to our innate limitations. It is, thus, because of our unsocial sociability that we ultimately need Divine aid in this battle. Just as I argued in Chapter 3 that our Predisposition to Humanity must be given greater consideration when interpreting the Propensity to Evil, so here we see it also having a crucial role in what we might call the end game of Kant's soteriology.

Of course, with regards to our individual efforts, God's role is left speculative, unclear, and seemingly unnecessary. But once we turn to the role of God in the establishment of the Ethical Community and the Highest Good, His aid does become necessary. And yet it is vital that we take great care when publicizing this point, for the idea that God's aid is necessary for our salvation could distract from what we in turn must also do. The belief that God's help is not merely available but necessary can easily corrupt the church, lead to counterfeit service, to "adoration and ingratiation" (6:185), beseeching God for His help and protection. So, to counteract this danger, Kant recommends that we rather conduct ourselves *as if* everything depended upon us. However much God is involved, we must not seek his aid through entreating Him, nor through ritual or sacrifice, but through the sort of moral effort that would be conducted *as if no aid were forthcoming*.

We thus should understand the True Church as shaped by a great irony: as the institution that works to aid humanity in their moral journey, it must operate as if no Divine aid will be offered. This is why Kant devotes the final part of *Religion* to a discussion of counterfeit service, for the historical tendency has been for the church to debase itself, requiring "the professions of statutory articles, the observance of ecclesiastical practice and discipline, etc." (6:174) under the "delusion that through religious acts of a cult" (6:174) we can secure God's graces. In fact, we may further deepen this irony, for in response to the longstanding tendency to religious delusion and counterfeit service, Kant recommends that the church operates as if it were Pelagian. Appeals to Divine aid are inherently dangerous, for they can lead to moral laziness. Hence, it is only through the condition that we put grace aside, and act as if everything depends upon us, that we may protect the validity of our "hope that a higher wisdom will provide the fulfillment of our well-intentioned effort" (6:101).

NOTES

1 See Kant to Carl Friderich Stäudlin, 11:430, dated May 4, 1793.

2 In addition to my discussion in the Introduction and Chapter 1, see Pasternack 2011. In the Canon of the First *Critique*, in the Dialectic of

the Second, in §91 of the Third, in *Religion*'s discussion of conscience, in §9 of the Jäsche Logic, and throughout the logic lectures and related *Reflexionen*, we find characterizations of the assent that take it as legitimate, intersubjectively valid, and *certain*. Unfortunately, those who tend to deflate Kant's positive philosophy of religion either ignore or are not familiar with the multitude of discussions of faith itself.

3 As I have suggested, it may be that we are presented with opportunities and challenges that can help us make moral progress and/or receive protection from various circumstances that could impair such progress or lead to backsliding.

4 These are the specific charges brought against Pelagius and Caelestius in 411. See Broaderick 1990.

5 Additionally, it cannot be that the "old man's death" compensates for the infinite debt (see Firestone and Jacobs 2008: 176). First, this "death" is figurative. It is neither a corporeal death nor the transfer of a soul from this world to the next. As such, why would this be compensatory for an infinite debt? Second, according to Kant, not even actual death is compensatory for the infinite debt. Since sin brings punishment (and the duty to progress morally) in the afterlife, clearly the debt must still abide after one's corporeal death. Nevertheless, despite these objections, I am in agreement with their interpretation of the moral status of the new man as without the debt of sin. See also Bojanowski (2011). But here too I am concerned that Bojanowski has used something of finite magnitude to pay back something that is infinite. He states: "The new man, as such, deserves no more punishment. By suffering/accepting the pain, he produces that 'excess' which compensates as atonement for the sins of the old man" (Bojanowski 2011: 107). I discuss this more fully in Pasternack 2012.

6 As discussed in Chapter 4, to be *entschlagen* likewise can be taken as to be "rid" of or "unbound" from the old man's debt of sin; or, based upon the root morpheme, the "strike" (*der Schlag*) upon him is "un-struck" (*ent-schlagen*).

7 There may in this be all the elements for something like a self-fulfilling prophecy since the risk of recidivism will put one on guard when dealing with others. That in turn will lead to suspicion or at least a weakening of the unity that is needed for the fulfillment of humanity's collective duty. Thus, the risk of recidivism itself sets off the conditions that can lead to recidivism.

BIBLIOGRAPHY

Abela, P. (2002) *Kant's Empirical Realism*, Oxford: Oxford University Press.

Adams, R. M. (1998) "Introduction" to *Religion within the Boundaries of Mere Reason and Other Writings*, Cambridge: Cambridge University Press.

Allison, H. E. (1990) *Kant's Theory of Freedom*, Cambridge: Cambridge University Press.

——(2002) "On the Very Idea of a Propensity to Evil," *The Journal of Value Inquiry*, 36: 337–48.

——(2004) *Kant's Transcendental Idealism: An Interpretation and Defense*, 2nd edition, New Haven, CT: Yale University Press.

Althaus, P. (1966) *The Theology of Martin Luther*, Philadelphia: Fortress Press.

Ameriks, K. (2006) *Kant and the Historical Turn: Philosophy as Critical Interpretation*, Oxford: Oxford University Press.

Anderson-Gold, S. (2001) *Unnecessary Evil: History and Moral Progress in the Philosophy of Immanuel Kant*, Albany: State University of New York Press.

Arnoldt, E. (1909) *Gesammelte Schriften*, Berlin: B. Cassirer.

Barth, K. (1952) *Protestant Theology in the Nineteenth Century*, London: SCM Press.

Bauch, B. (1904) *Luther und Kant*, Berlin: Verlag von Reuther & Reichard.

Baxley, A. M. (2010) *Kant's Theory of Virtue: The Value of Autocracy*, Cambridge: Cambridge University Press.

Bernstein, R. (2002) *Radical Evil: A Philosophical Interrogation*, Cambridge: Cambridge University Press.

Bojanowski, J. (2011) "Zweites Stück: Moralische Vollkommenheit." In Otfried Höffe (ed.), Immanuel Kant, *Die Religion innerhalb der Grenzen der Bloßen Vernunft*, Berlin: Akademie Verlag, 91–110.

Broaderick, R. (1990) *The Catholic Encyclopedia*, New York: Thomas Nelson.

Bunch, A. (2010) "The Resurrection of the Body as a 'Practical Postulate': Why Kant is Committed to Belief in an Embodied Afterlife," *Philosophia Christi* 12(1): 46–60.

Byrne, P. (2007) *Kant on God*, Aldershot: Ashgate.

Davidovich, A. (1993) "Kant's Theological Constructivism," *Harvard Theological Review* 86(3): 323–51.

——(1994) *Religion as a Province of Meaning: The Kantian Foundations of Modern Theology*, Minneapolis, MN: Fortress Press.

Denis, L. (2005) "Autonomy and the Highest Good," *Kantian Review* 10: 33–59.

DiCenso, J. (2011) *Kant, Religion, and Politics*, Cambridge: Cambridge University Press.

——(2012) *Kant's Religion within the Boundaries of Mere Reason: A Commentary*, Cambridge: Cambridge University Press.

di Giovanni, G. (1996) "Translator's Introduction" to Immanuel Kant, *Religion within the Boundaries of Mere Reason*, Cambridge: Cambridge University Press.

Dilthey, W. (1890) "Der Streit Kants mit der Zensur über das Recht freier Religionsforschung," *Archiv für Geschichte der Philosophie* 3: 418–50.

Feder, J. and C. Garve (1782) "*Critique of Pure Reason by Immanuel Kant. 1781. 856 pages in Octavo.*" Reprinted in B. Sassen, *Kant's Early Critics: The Empiricist Critique of the Theoretical Philosophy*, Cambridge: Cambridge University Press.

Firestone, C. L. and N. Jacobs (2008) *In Defense of Kant's Religion*, Bloomington: Indiana University Press.

Frierson, P. R. (2003) *Freedom and Anthropology in Kant's Moral Philosophy*, Cambridge: Cambridge University Press.

——(2010) "Kantian Moral Pessimism." In S. Anderson-Gold and P. Muchnik (eds.), *Kant's Anatomy of Evil*, Cambridge: Cambridge University Press, 33–56.

Gardner, S. (1999) *Routledge Philosophy Guidebook to Kant and the Critique of Pure Reason*, Abingdon: Routledge.

Garve, C. (1783) "*Critique of Pure Reason by Immanuel Kant. Riga, 1781. 856 pages in 8.*" Reprinted in B. Sassen, *Kant's Early Critics: The Empiricist Critique of the Theoretical Philosophy*, Cambridge: Cambridge University Press.

Gelfert, A. (2006) "Kant on Testimony," *British Journal for the History of Philosophy* 14 (4): 627–52.

Gerrish, B. (2006) "Natural and Revealed Religion," *The Cambridge History of Eighteenth-Century Philosophy*, Cambridge: Cambridge University Press, 641–65.

Griffin, E. and P. Erb (2006) *The Pietists*, New York: Harper.

Gritsch, E. (2012) *Martin Luther's Anti-Semitism: Against His Better Judgment*, Grand Rapids, MI: Eerdmans.

Guyer, P. (2000) *Kant on Freedom, Law, and Happiness*, Cambridge: Cambridge University Press.

——(2005) *Kant's System of Nature and Freedom*, Cambridge: Cambridge University Press.

Hare, J. E. (1996) *The Moral Gap: Kantian Ethics, Human Limits, and God's Assistance*, Oxford: Clarendon Press.

Hill, T. E. (1973) "The Hypothetical Imperative," *The Philosophical Review* 82(4): 429–50.

Höffe, O. (1994) *Immanuel Kant*, trans. M. Farrier, Albany: State University of New York Press.

Hunter, I. (2005) "Kant's *Religion* and Prussian Religious Policy," *Modern Intellectual History* 2(1): 1–27.

Insole, C. (2008) "The Irreducible Importance of Religious Hope in Kant's Conception of the Highest Good," *Philosophy* 83(3): 333–51.

Kain, P. (2005) "Interpreting Kant's Theory of Divine Commands," *Kantian Review* 9: 128–49.

Kuehn, M. (2001) *Kant: A Biography*, New York: Cambridge University Press.

Lestition, S. (1993) "Kant and the End of the Enlightenment in Prussia," *The Journal of Modern History* 65(1): 57–112.

Luther, M. (1883) *Martin Luthers Werke*, Weimar: Böhlaus.

Mariña, J. (1997) "Kant on Grace: A Reply to his Critics," *Religious Studies* 33: 379–400.

Meier, G. F. (1752) *Auszug aus der Vernunftlehre*, Halle: J. J.Gebauer.

Michalson, G. E. (1989) "Moral Regeneration and Divine Aid in Kant," *Religious Studies* 25(3): 259–70.

——(1990) *Fallen Freedom: Kant on Radical Evil and Moral Regeneration*, Cambridge: Cambridge University Press.

Moran, K. A. (2009) "Can Kant Have an Account of Moral Education?," *Journal of Philosophy of Education* 43(4): 471–84.

Morgan, S. (2005) "The Missing Formal Proof of Humanity's Radical Evil in Kant's *Religion*," *Philosophical Review* 114(1): 63–114.

Muchnik, P. (2009) *Kant's Theory of Evil: An Essay on the Dangers of Self-love and the Apriority of History*, Lanham, MD: Lexington Books.

O'Neill, O. (2001) "Kant's Conception of Public Reason." In V. Gerhardt, R. Horstmann, and R. Schumacher (eds.), *Kant und die Berliner Aufklärung: Akten des IX Internationalen Kant-Kongresses*, Berlin: Walter de Gruyter, vol. 1, 35–47.

Palmquist, S. (1992) "Does Kant Reduce Religion to Morality?," *Kant-Studien* 83(2): 129–48.

——(2000) *Kant's Critical Religion*, Aldershot: Ashgate.

——(2008) "Kant's Quasi-Transcendental Argument for a Necessary and Universal Evil Propensity in Human Nature," *The Southern Journal of Philosophy* 42(2): 261–97.

——(2010) "Kant's Ethics of Grace: Perspectival Solutions to the Moral Difficulties with Divine Assistance," *Journal of Religion* 90(4): 530–53.

Pasternack, L. (2003) "The Lawfulness of the Will and Timeless Agency," *Kant-Studien* 94(3): 352–61.

——(2011) "The Development and Scope of Kantian Belief: The Highest Good, the Practical Postulates, and the Fact of Reason," *Kant-Studien* 102(3): 290–315.

——(2012) "Kant on the Debt of Sin," *Faith and Philosophy* 29(1): 30–52.

——(2014) "Kant on Opinion: Assent, Hypothesis and the Norms of General Applied Logic," *Kant-Studien*, forthcoming.

——(2015) "Pure Rational Faith and Kant's Biblical Hermeneutics." In M. Cauchi and A. Kulak (eds.), *Biblical Philosophy: Exploratory Essays*, London: Continuum, forthcoming.

Quinn, P. L. (1986) "Christian Atonement and Kantian Justification," *Faith and Philosophy* 3(4): 440–62.

——(1990) "Saving Faith from Kant's Remarkable Antinomy," *Faith and Philosophy* 7 (4): 418–33.

Rawls, J. (1997) "The Idea of Public Reason Revisited," *The University of Chicago Law Review* 64(3): 765–807.

Reath, A. (1988) "Two Conceptions of the Highest Good in Kant," *Journal of the History of Philosophy* 26(4): 593–619.

——(1989) "Kant's Theory of Moral Sensibility: Respect for the Moral Law and the Influence of Inclination," *Kant-Studien* 80: 284–302.

Rescher, N. (1999) *Kant and the Reach of Reason*, Cambridge: Cambridge University Press.

Rossi, P. J. (2005) *The Social Authority of Reason: Kant's Critique, Radical Evil, and the Destiny of Humankind*, Albany: State University of New York Press.

Samet-Porat, I. (2007) "Satanic Motivations," *Journal of Value Inquiry* 41(1): 77–94.

Sassen, B. (2000) *Kant's Early Critics: The Empiricist Critique of the Theoretical Philosophy*, Cambridge: Cambridge University Press.

Schmid, H. (1889) *The Doctrinal Theology of the Evangelical Lutheran Church*, Philadelphia: Lutheran Publication Society.

Shade, P. (1995) "Does Kant's Ethics Imply Reincarnation?," *The Southern Journal of Philosophy* 33(3): 347–60.

Shell, S. M. (2007) "Kant and the Jewish Question," *Hebraic Political Studies* 2(1): 101–36.

Silber, J. R. (1959) "The Contents of Kant's Ethical Thought," *Philosophical Quarterly* 9: 193–207.

Strawson, P. F. (1966) *The Bounds of Sense: An Essay on Kant's* Critique of Pure Reason, New York: Routledge.

Stump, E. (1988) "Atonement According to Aquinas." In Thomas V. Morris (ed.), *Philosophy and the Christian Faith*, Notre Dame, IN: University of Notre Dame Press, 1988.

——(2003) *Aquinas*, New York: Routledge.

Surprenant, C. (2008) "Kant's Postulate of the Immortality of the Soul," *International Philosophical Quarterly* 48(1): 85–98.

Sussman, D. G. (2001) *The Idea of Humanity: Anthropology and Anthroponomy in Kant's Ethics*, New York: Routledge.

——(2009) "For Badness' Sake," *Journal of Philosophy* 106(11): 613–28.

Wand, B. (1971) "Religious Concepts and Moral Theory: Luther and Kant," *Journal of the History of Philosophy* 9:3 (1971): 329–48.

Wike, V. S. and R. L. Showler (2010) "Kant's Concept of the Highest Good and the Archetype-Ectype Distinction," *Journal of Value Inquiry* 44: 521–33.

Wolterstorff, N. (1991) "Conundrums in Kant's Rational Religion," in P. J. Rossi and M. J. Wreen (eds.), *Kant's Philosophy of Religion Reconsidered*, Bloomington: Indiana University Press, 40–53.

——(1998) "Is it Possible and Desirable for Theologians to Recover from Kant?," *Modern Theology* 14(1): 1–18.

Wood, A. W. (1970) *Kant's Moral Religion*, Ithaca, NY: Cornell University Press.

——(1978) *Kant's Rational Theology*, Ithaca, NY: Cornell University Press.

——(1991) "Kant's Deism." In P. J. Rossi and M. J. Wreen (eds.), *Kant's Philosophy of Religion Reconsidered*, Bloomington: Indiana University Press, 1–21.

——(1996) "General Introduction" to Immanuel Kant, *Religion and Rational Theology*, trans. and ed. Allen Wood and George di Giovanni, Cambridge: Cambridge University Press.

——(1999) *Kant's Ethical Thought*, Cambridge: Cambridge University Press.

——(2005) "Kant's History of Ethics," *Studies in the History of Ethics*. Retrieved from http://www.historyofethics.org/062005/062005\Wood.shtml.

Yovel, Y. (1989) *Kant and the Philosophy of History*, Princeton, NJ: Princeton University Press.

INDEX

Note: page numbers are grouped (e.g. 124–26) when the discussion of the term/concept spans across consecutive pages; pages are listed individually (e.g. 124, 125, 126) when the discussion of the term/concept is not ongoing or where there is a section break.

CPSIA information can be obtained
at www.ICGtesting.com
Printed in the USA
FFHW010306070319
50891761-56304FF